Max

and the

Revenge

of the

Polar Bears

A M Hankins

authorHOUSE®

AuthorHouse™ UK Ltd.
500 Avebury Boulevard
Central Milton Keynes, MK9 2BE
www.authorhouse.co.uk
Phone: 08001974150

First published by AuthorHouse 12/21/2010.

ISBN: 978-1-4567-0018-8 (sc)

This book is printed on acid-free paper.

DEDICATED TO TINA.

~~THURUGH~~ THOROUGH PROOF-READER
AND ENDLESS ~~SAUCE~~ SOURCE OF
INSPIRATION

FRONT COVER ILLUSTRATION FROM RON LEISHMAN'S TOONADAY
WEBSITE WWW.TOONADAY.COM

TWELVE MONTHS BEFORE THE POWER CRISIS:

TUESDAY 14:30HRS

"She's been gone far too long."

"Don't worry, she'll be back," his brother replied, trying to hide the fear in his voice. They were both well aware that their mother was long overdue.

The two brothers waited patiently for their mother's return huddled together for warmth in their snow den. Outside, a freezing Arctic wind had grown much stronger since their mother had left and gusts of over thirty miles an hour howled past the narrow entrance to their den. What had been gentle snowfall was now a gale-force blizzard of swirling snow and ice which whipped through the valley and along the hillside.

Over the deafening sound of the snowstorm they heard the snow creak. Then it creaked again.

"Here she is."

"Mum?"

"Move out of the way, I'll take a look," the bigger of the two brothers said.

He climbed up to their entrance hole and peered out into the near white-out conditions. His black nose and dark brown eyes contrasted against the total whiteness around him. As he squinted through the freezing icy snow he made out something on two legs that he had never seen before. Another one of these things on two legs appeared through the snowstorm and pointed in his direction. He looked back at them in amazement as they changed direction and came towards him.

Instinct told him this did not feel right and he quickly ducked back down into their snow den. Before he had a chance to tell his brother about the strange new two-legged things he had seen, the entrance to the den caved in around them and they were exposed to the harsh, freezing, gale-force wind. He barked at the intruders but they overpowered him using something that tightened around his neck. Mother could sometimes be rough but these things were worse, they cut in deep and stopped him breathing. More of these two-legs surrounded him and he felt himself being lifted up and placed in a new type of den with a solid door that slammed shut, one that was open to the wind but still surrounded him and separated him from his brother. Neither of the bears had any idea what a cage was.

He could hear his mother somewhere off in the distance, calling for them. He squinted through the blizzard's driving snow but he could not see her. Her cries begged them to run away but the new dens they were in stopped them from running anywhere.

Their mother's cries echoed through the valley, then she roared like they had never heard her roar before and they were afraid for the first time in their lives. For a fleeting moment, through the swirling powdery snow, he caught a glimpse of Mother. She was in one of these new dens and she was fighting to get free. He called out to her and she became more angry and more desperate, he watched helplessly as she launched herself time and time again into the door of her new den, calling out in pain and despair, frantically trying to reach him and reach his brother.

The freezing cold wind whipped through his cage blowing shards of ice into his eyes and he lost sight of Mother. He could still hear her calling for him over the sound of the storm, her cries travelled on the wind and echoed throughout the frozen valley, he called back but his cries went unanswered.

Around him, more two-legs appeared.

"We've got two cubs, about five or six months old. Not a

bad pair. Add them to the others and that pays for this trip, any more we get is profit."

"What about the mother?"

"She's worth nothing to us. Leave her."

"In the cage? But she'll die."

"Do *you* want to risk letting her out?"

Seven Weeks before the Power Crisis:

Monday 20:00Hrs

Channel Nine's celebrity reality show was in its fifth successful year of broadcast. *Star Struck* had become a TV phenomenon.

Twelve carefully chosen celebrities lived together in the close confines of a purpose-built, open-plan house. The house was decorated in bright primary colours on the interior walls, the furniture was designed to clash and there were pink sofas, purple beds and a garish orange kitchen with green worktops. The house was also full of mirrors which were not there just for the vanity of the housemates, they were also there for a purpose. Behind each one-way mirror was a cameraman that tracked and recorded their every word, look and gesture. Additional remote-control cameras and microphones were fitted throughout the house and all of these cameras were monitored and managed by a production team, located in a high-tech editing studio adjacent to the celebrity house.

Each week, the celebrities chose two housemates that would be put up for eviction, with the viewing public casting votes to evict their least favourite celebrity. Seven celebrities had already been evicted, it was now down to the final five. The winner received a cheque for £125,000 but the prize that they all really craved was popularity.

The production team, lead by long-term producer, Grant Blows, cleverly manipulated the celebrities' over-sized egos to create a volatile mix of clashing personalities. Every accusation, squabble and temper tantrum was caught on camera, edited and broadcast to an eager audience of tens of millions. As the weekly eviction approached, the production team cranked up the pressure between the celebrities, timing it perfectly to coincide with the peak voting period before eviction.

This season's celebrities were more spoilt, rude and outrageous than ever before. A whirlwind of media hype followed the show and every edited highlight made front page news. Everybody watched the show. Everybody talked about the show. The viewing figures multiplied to a record twenty five million, making *Star Struck* the most popular reality TV show in history.

Twenty five million people were addicted to the superficial lives of D-List celebrities in a manufactured-reality television show. Twenty five million people were so addicted, they were unaware of the all-too real reality that was about to enter *their* lives.

The headquarters of Fusion Energy were located near Canary Wharf in London's Docklands and from these modern purpose-built offices they managed Great Britain's electricity grid. Fusion Energy ensured that electricity generated from the country's powerstations was transmitted through the grid to regional substations which in turn provided this electricity, safely and efficiently, to tens of millions of homes.

A team of highly-skilled technicians, using a complex computer software system, constantly monitored electricity consumption so that they could synchronise the supply of electricity from powerstations into the grid to meet this demand.

Responsible for the South London region this evening was one of Fusion Energy's senior technicians, Dave Tanner and his assistant, Mike Bryant. They had been on the evening shift since six o'clock and were monitoring the power demand from the seven electrical substations they managed. On the corner of Mike's desk, a portable television was showing this evening's episode of *Star Struck.* They were both fans, like everybody else in the country, but while they were at work they were interested in the show for another reason.

"It's going to another advert break," Mike said, alerting his colleague.

Dave nodded and they both focused on the data updating on their computer terminals, anticipating a sudden surge in demand.

"Here we go again, South London is about to put the kettle on," Mike commented.

The trend-line of power consumption on their displays spiked rapidly upwards as several million people decided the advert break was a good opportunity to make a cup of tea.

"Judging by the size of that spike, it's not just the kettle, they've turned on computers, toasters, microwaves and everything else," Dave added.

"It's peaking higher than usual."

"Yeah, you best keep an eye on the substations, I'll check the grid."

While Mike monitored the seven substations in their region, Dave checked the grid's powerstation network on a large wall-mounted display that spread across the width of the control centre. Auxiliary power should have re-routed automatically and he was searching for any standby powerstations which could be brought on-grid manually. He looked back down at his monitor and watched with a growing sense of concern as the energy consumption across London spiked upwards again. He checked other areas and saw that the Midlands, South East and North West were also indicating a similar increase in power consumption.

"Dave, you'd better take a look at this," said Mike pointing to his PC monitor.

On the screen was a map which showed the locations of their region's electrical substations and what their current power status was. Two of their substations had flashing amber warning lights beside their names.

"That last spike," he said, "It's put Battersea and Blackfriars on alert."

Dave quickly checked the large wall-mounted display again, hoping to find auxiliary power in the central grid which could be rerouted, but there was none.

"Can we reroute from other subs?" asked Mike.

"Not in time, no," said Dave.

Elsewhere in the control centre, similar teams of technicians were experiencing the same as the South London Region. All of them were checking for auxiliary power and coming to the same conclusion as Dave Tanner had a few moments earlier. The grid was balanced on a knife edge.

After an agonising minute that seemed like two hours, the warning light at the Blackfriars substation went out. It took three minutes for the warning light at Battersea's substation to clear.

"Phew, that was a close one," said Mike.

"Way too close for comfort," replied his colleague.

Six Weeks before the Power Crisis:

Tuesday 16:00Hrs

"The demand for polar bears has dropped, they don't keep too well in captivity," the buyer said, "They get depressed then go mad. My private collectors don't want the hassle."

"I know that, but you pre-ordered them and we had a contract to supply two young polar bears."

"Markets change, people change and global climate has changed. That contract is terminated," the buyer replied, "You know as well as I do, polar bears are seen as the victims of climate change and none of my private collectors want them anymore, it's bad karma and bad for their image."

He leaned back in his chair and folded his arms. The buyer's body language said the bear deal was definitely off the agenda.

The animal dealer protested, "We barely broke even on the trip, we've had them in storage for the best part of a year and now you tell me you don't them?"

"I don't want them. They are yours now, do what you want with them. If they were panthers or tigers I'd be interested but polar bears you can keep."

The dealer got the message. The bears were now a lot larger than cute little cubs. They were nearly fully grown, weighed over two hundred and fifty kilos and were costing him a small fortune in food and storage. He would have to cut his losses and get rid of them but for now he had other animals to sell.

"The dolphins are en route and will be ready in a week," he offered.

The buyer moved slightly forward in his seat.

"I may still be interested in the dolphins. Tell me more."

"We have one adult male and one female, both are rare Snubfin Dolphins, caught off New Zealand two weeks ago and the price is $16,000 a piece or $30,000 the pair. Plus delivery costs, of course."

The buyer sucked air in over his teeth.

"Of course," he said, "I have an interested client but the deal is fifty percent on delivery with the remainder paid if they survive ninety days."

The dealer shook his head, "Seventy five, twenty five."

The buyer smiled, he knew he had the upper hand.

"It seems as if you don't have a great deal of confidence that they'll survive."

The dealer rubbed his chin and weighed up the risk of losing the dolphins if he kept them in storage for much longer.

"Sixty, forty," he offered.

Sixty percent recouped some of the losses he had accrued from keeping the bears in captivity, their voracious appetites were now quite literally eating into his profits.

The buyer took a moment to consider the offer.

"Sixty, forty it is then. Delivery will be to St Petersburg, is that a problem?"

"No problem," said the dealer.

The buyer reached inside his jacket pocket and took out an envelope. He passed it across the table to the animal dealer.

"Can you supply one of these?"

The dealer opened the envelope and took out a 6x4 photograph of an Oceanic White Tip, one of the most endangered species of open-ocean sharks.

"Turn it over, the price my client will pay is on the back."

The dealer flipped the photo over. $10,000. He shook his head because he knew the price was irrelevant.

"You know catching them is one thing, keeping them alive in a holding tank is a different matter."

They had tried and failed many times before. Each time the shark had stopped feeding and then rapidly declined in health. Something designed for the open seas was not hard-wired for a life in an aquarium.

"What about Sand Tiger Sharks, they do better in aquariums?"

"Sand Tigers I can get anywhere, I'd be willing to pay $500 a fish."

"$500 a fish? I could get more for just the fins."

And so the dealing went on. The two men were brokering deals on animals from the world's most endangered species list as if they were nothing more than white mice in a pet shop. The buyer had a list of wealthy clients who wanted rare animals for their private collections and the dealer efficiently, and ruthlessly, met this demand.

The meeting came to a mutually agreeable closure. Some of the world's most endangered species had been traded for cash in a low-cost hotel room, in a rundown industrial area on the south side of Aachen. The buyer and dealer leaned over the small wooden table and shook hands on the deal. The buyer stood up and left the room, leaving the dealer alone in the hotel room.

Not a bad day's work, the dealer thought to himself. He had made a profit on the deals but his mind refocused on the bears he had in storage which were now more of a nuisance than an asset. Time to cut my losses on them, he thought.

He waited for a good twenty minutes before he left the hotel room to avoid being associated with the buyer. He had paid for the hotel room using cash and had booked in under the name of Alain Remersdaal, using a fake driving licence and passport as I.D. This did not arouse any suspicion with the hotel staff as Aachen is located in Western Germany, very close to the borders with Holland and Belgium where travelling businessmen are commonplace.

He left the hotel without attracting any attention from the desk clerk. He walked across the road outside the hotel to a side road where he had inconspicuously parked a silver coloured Ford Mondeo. As he approached it, he pressed the key fob and the doors unlocked. It was the standard issue businessman's car, except this one had been stolen and was on fake Belgian number plates, cloned from an identical Ford Mondeo. He drove slowly out of the side road and onto Route 264, heading west. The Belgian border was only a few minutes away. He crossed over without incident and parked the car further along the 264 in the small town of Kelmis.

He reached into his pocket and took out a Nokia 6310 mobile phone and with one movement he flicked the rear cover off the phone and removed the battery. He reached into his pocket again and produced a new SIM card. He clicked the SIM into place and reassembled the phone. He switched it on and waited to get a signal. His regular mobile he had left behind in England, anyone tracking his whereabouts through that phone's signal would be clueless as to where he was and where he had been for the past 24 hours. He was effectively off the grid.

He dialled a number and a voice answered.

"How did it go?"

"All done, except our two unwanted guests. They are now a liability."

"I may have the answer. I have someone interested in them but we'll only get a thousand each."

"That's better than nothing. Do the deal."

"Plus we have some potential new trade in our close cousins."

The dealer smiled to himself. Close cousins was code for the Great Apes. Gorillas and orang-utans were far easier to handle than polar bears.

"I'll be on time as planned."

The dealer disassembled the phone and broke the SIM card into tiny pieces. He threw the pieces out of the window into the gutter and then drove westward, non-stop towards Ostend. There, he would ditch the car and cross as a foot passenger to Dover, leaving no trace of his whereabouts in Europe during the past twenty four hours.

Three Weeks before the Power Crisis:

Monday 16:00Hrs

A well-used, unwashed bus wound its way slowly through the Devon countryside heading towards its final stop in the small village of Witheridge.

Witheridge nestled amongst the green countryside and woodland of Mid Devon. To the north of the village was the spectacular open moorland of Exmoor and to the south, were the rolling hills of Dartmoor National Park. The countryside surrounding the village was a green quilt of fields and hedgerows that followed the natural meanderings of the Little Dart River as it flowed through unspoilt valleys and secluded copses. An ancient footpath, the Two Moors Way, linked both moors together and ran directly through the village making the two pubs in the centre of the village welcome rest stops for tired, foot-sore ramblers.

The bus gradually slowed to a stop opposite the village square and a handful of teenagers from Chulmleigh Community College stepped down to the pavement. Amongst them were three boys from the Sixth Form called Max Chambers, his friend Brian Marshall and Brian's older brother Peter.

"Hold up," said Brian, "I need to check the post office."

"Knock yourself out, Bruv," said Peter, "We'll wait here."

Brian disappeared across the village square towards the local village shop that doubled as a post office.

"What's he after?" asked Max.

"Some electronics he's ordered from EBay, you know what he's like."

15

Max smiled because he knew exactly what Brian was like. They had sat together on their first day at Witheridge Primary School and now in the first year of Sixth Form, they were still best friends. Most people at college labelled Brian as a weirdo and his overall appearance did nothing to suggest otherwise. Elbow patches on his jumper, thick rimmed, heavy-lensed glasses and natural bed-head hairstyle, (without the need for gel), gave Brian the overall appearance of someone who had been dragged backwards through the bargain bin at Oxfam and had come out fully clothed. If his disregard for fashion was not proof enough, then his selection of pens and micro-screwdrivers neatly organised in his top pocket identified Brian as a stereotypical, 100% certified geek.

Someone like Brian would have been singled out and regularly picked on but he had his older brother Peter in the upper Sixth Form, a year above, to look out for him. At six foot two and a muscular eighty five kilograms, Peter was far too strong to have ever been the focus of bullying and his size and protective nature guaranteed no bullies would risk picking on Brian or Max. Where Brian was naturally academic, Peter was gifted athletically. He may have struggled working out the hypotenuse in a right angle triangle but he could work out the correct angle required to intercept a fly-half on a rugby field at full speed, much to the delight of the college's sports master and his rugby coach at Tiverton RFC.

Peter placed a heavy hand on Max's shoulder and nodded towards a group of walkers that were sitting on a picnic bench outside the village pub.

"So, do you fancy doing the Ten Tors again next year?" Peter asked Max, "You know you loved it," he added.

"Yeah, right, I *really* loved it. I loved it so much I can't wait. In fact, why don't we do it again this weekend?"

Peter laughed out loud because he knew the Ten Tors was a sore subject with Max. Four weeks ago, they had been part of the college's Sixth Form team taking part in the annual challenge of reaching ten of the highest peaks on Dartmoor, following a forty five mile cross country route up and down the barren, weather-beaten hills. It was the changeable weather that often dictated the outcome of the challenge and this year's event was no different. It had started out dry and sunny but within a few hours and with only one tor completed, dark, ominous, heavy clouds rolled in from North Cornwall and deposited their contents across the moor. It had rained non-stop for 48 hours.

"Ok," said Peter barely suppressing his amusement, "Has your sleeping bag dried out yet?"

"Very funny, Big Lad," Max replied, "Next year I'm not bothering with a tent, I'll take a boat."

"Maybe I should let Thompson's gang flush your head down the bogs some more, as a way of training you up for wet weather conditions."

The two boys laughed at the thought. The last time Thompson's gang had tried that, Peter had intervened, effortlessly picking Thompson up by the back of his trousers with a fistful of underpants, forcing a wedgie of such magnitude and abrasion that Thompson was rendered immobile and defenceless. With his underpants hoisted high out of the back of his trousers, evidence of poor wiping skills became clearly visible due to the deep brown skid-marks on show. Embarrassed and clearly in pain, Thompson had been lifted up by Peter and suspended by his blazer collar from the hook on the back of the toilet door which swung open for all to see. Thompson, or Skidders, as he soon became known, had learned the hard way not to mess with Peter, his brother or any of his friends.

"I'd hate to be his mum 'cos no amount of soap powder would make washing those pants safe."

"If he tries it again, perhaps we can do his mum a favour and put him through my dad's sheep dip?" Peter laughed, "That'll clean him up, and get rid of any ticks as well."

Both boys were laughing so much that they did not notice

Brian was next to them opening the seal on a cardboard parcel.

"Guys, the pagers have arrived."

Brian took one of them out of its protective bubble wrap. Max and Peter examined it, not having a clue what it was.

It was a small plastic device, about 75mm wide by 50mm high with a small grey LCD screen across most of its width. Underneath the screen were four buttons, their markings had long been worn away, indicating that this device was quite a few years old.

Brian handed it to Peter, "Here, take a look."

"What's a pager?" asked Max.

"Well," explained Brian, "It's what people used before mobile phones. The pager would beep and a message would come up on the screen from the sender, then you'd have to find a phone and call the sender back, or do whatever it said on the message."

"No way, you're kidding me," said Peter, "You're telling me people used to carry these about?"

"Yeah, they were like the first mobile phones but you couldn't call the person back or even respond with a text reply, all it did was beep, alerting you with a very basic one or two line message."

"Yeah, right, if you say so."

"It's true," protested Brian, "When mobile phones came out with text messaging, these pagers became obsolete overnight."

"Does it still work?" asked Max.

"No, these are broken but I reckon I can get them working again."

Brian checked through the box and found another four pagers, just like the one Peter was playing with.

"Hospitals still use them instead of mobile phones to alert doctors. They work better inside buildings and have a good range, so messages are guaranteed to get through. Most hospitals operate their own network so they can broadcast messages to loads of doctors all at once, and they don't mess up the electronic equipment either."

"Pretty cool, but what are you going to use them for?" asked Peter.

"You'll see," Brian replied.

THREE WEEKS BEFORE THE POWER CRISIS:

MONDAY 16:20HRS

Located on the outskirts of Exeter International Airport, in a secluded corner of the airport's business centre stood a six story high, glass panelled building. The building occupied an area the size of a football field and was bordered by perfectly flat landscaped lawns. The lawns were bordered by four metre high conifers, which hid from view a three metre high, barbed-wire security fence. A single pathway led from an adjacent car park to the building's reception but unlike most of the business units at the airport, there was no business name or corporate logo anywhere on the building. The exterior was constructed totally from panels of toughened, mirrored glass. From ground level, anyone taking anything less than a direct look at the building saw only the reflections of adjacent buildings and the conifer tree border. This was not by accident or coincidence, the building had been specifically designed to be anonymous. Like the irregular shape of a stealth plane, the glass panels were not truly perpendicular, every panel was offset by tiny fractions of a degree to distort their reflected image and this effectively made the building blend in amongst its surroundings. At night, the building almost totally disappeared. If you didn't know it was there, you would never have noticed it.

Martin Purnell, Managing Director of Muller and Rathbone Media Associates, drove slowly along Airport Way for the second time. His Sat-Nav repeatedly and rather annoyingly, told him that he had already reached his destination. He brought his BMW to a stop in the road opposite a large freight handling depot. The Sat-Nav was now telling him to execute a U-Turn wherever it was safe to do so. He checked over his left shoulder to where the building he was looking for should have been and he could make out a glass building set back from the road that he hadn't noticed before. That must be it he thought and then wondered to himself how he had managed to miss the building the first time he had driven by.

He checked the traffic and when it was clear he made a U-turn and took the next right turn into the glass building's driveway. Halfway along, he had to stop at an unmanned security barrier. There was a button marked RECEPTION. He opened his window and waited.

After a few seconds a voice answered and Martin Purnell confirmed he had an appointment at 4:30pm with a Mr Bishop. The metal barrier lifted up and he continued along the driveway to the glass building's car park.

He parked his BMW in a vacant spot next to a line of twelve identical metallic black BMW 5 Series saloons. He noticed they were all M5 models from BMW's M Sport high performance division and his standard 530D diesel model appeared rather bland in comparison. He switched his mobile phone to silent and placed it inside his tan leather briefcase.

On a low wall at the far end of the car park he noticed a small sign which indicated the way to the building's reception and he followed the path around the corner of the building to a pair of glass doors which opened automatically as he approached. He stepped inside the building and found himself in a small glass-sided hallway with a second pair of glass doors at the opposite end. Above the doors was a small security camera and to his left an intercom panel with a button marked RECEPTION. As he took a few paces towards the intercom, he was aware that the first pair of glass doors had shut quietly behind him which made him feel more than a little claustrophobic. He did not like lifts, and this felt uncomfortably like being in a lift.

He pressed the intercom button.

"Good afternoon, Mr Purnell," a female voice said through the intercom.

"Good afternoon," he replied, looking up at the camera, "I have a meeting with Mr Bishop at four thirty."

"We have been expecting you. Please come through," the voice replied.

The glass doors leading into the building opened smoothly outwards and Martin Purnell took a few steps forward out of the small entrance hallway into a much larger open-plan reception area. The heavily tinted exterior glass filtered out most of the natural sunlight and the interior was illuminated by cool-white fluorescent lighting which produced a sharp, clinical ambience. It reminded him of the large expansive lobbies found at airport terminals and it certainly lacked the welcoming warmth of traditional office receptions. The interior walls were plain matt white which added to the overall feeling that this building had been designed to be functional and clinical, without any unnecessary added luxuries.

He was immediately greeted by a tall, smartly dressed woman in a navy blue business suit and plain white blouse. Her brown hair was tied back in a simple pony tail. No nonsense, business style glasses with the absolute minimum of makeup gave this young woman a look that matched the building. On the left lapel of her jacket was an ID card with the unmistakable corporate logo of MegaCorp. The ID card also contained a rather unflattering portrait photo with her employee number and her name, Ms J Wright.

"Welcome to MegaCorp's Research and Development Division, Mr Purnell," Ms Wright said, "I hope you found us without too much difficulty."

He was about to say that because the building was unmarked he had passed it twice when he realised Ms Wright was not really interested in idle chit chat and he decided it was best to keep his reply brief and to the point.

"Yes, thank you," he replied.

"You may find this building a little different to our London head office. We have much tighter security with this being our research facility, as I'm sure you will understand."

She handed him a lapel badge with the word ESCORTED VISITOR in red, which also contained a colour photograph of him looking slightly upwards.

"I took the liberty of using your photo from the reception camera," she explained.

Martin Purnell nodded and clipped the badge to his lapel.

"Unfortunately, Mr Bishop sends his apologies," Ms Wright said, "He has had to attend to some urgent business. His personal assistant Ms Glover will be meeting with you."

Before he had time to comment, Ms Wright added, "Please follow me, Mr Purnell."

He followed a few paces behind as she led the way through the reception area towards a pair of solid white doors which had a card swipe keypad on the left-hand side of the wall beside the door. As she approached the doors, she unbuttoned her suit jacket which revealed a second ID card attached to her trouser waistband by an extendable cord. The cord extended as she swiped the card through the keypad slot in one well practised movement. The keypad illuminated with a green glow. She let the card retract slowly back to her trouser waistband while she simultaneously typed in her access code into the keypad. The door unlocked with a solid click and she pulled the door open to reveal a long corridor, with floor-to-ceiling high tinted glass walls on either side. She indicated for him to follow her and they walked in silence along the corridor.

He assumed that on either side of the corridor there were offices but the tinted glass obscured his view. The corridor was illuminated by recessed ceiling lights which created soft pools of light which were focused on the corridor floor at regular intervals. Very hi-tech, he thought, this building could have been designed by NASA.

Ms Wright led the way, walking a few steps ahead of him.

The only sound was his leather-soled brogues that echoed on the tiled floor. Ms Wright wore black, low-heeled, sensible-style rubber-soled shoes that made no noise as she walked. Her quick pace slowed a little as they drew level with a glass door which was exactly the same as all the other doors along the corridor, except a small etched sign identified this door as MEETING ROOM 4.

"Here we are, Mr Purnell," she said as she gently knocked on the door.

A voice from within responded with a short and simple, "Enter."

Ms Wright opened the door for him and indicated he should enter first. The meeting room was rectangular in shape and about the size of half a tennis court. The walls were the same featureless matt white as the reception. At the far end of the room was a glass topped desk with a solid stainless steel base. Behind the desk sat a petite, dark-haired, middle-aged woman, in a similar navy blue suit to Ms Wright. He noticed she did not wear an identity card on her lapel, she was clearly important enough to not require security clearance.

As he approached the desk he noticed the glass surface was completely empty, except for a leather bound portfolio with a gold embossed MegaCorp logo. The middle-aged woman stood up and greeted him with an outstretched right hand.

"Good afternoon, Mr Purnell," she said as they shook hands, "Please take a seat."

She gestured for him to take the plain grey seat in front of the desk and he sat down, placing his briefcase on the floor beside his chair.

"I don't think we have met before, my name is Nina Glover, and I am Mr Bishop's personal assistant. Mr Bishop asked me to convey his sincere apologies for being called away on other business."

"I understand it was unavoidable and that these

things sometimes happen," he replied, concealing the disappointment he felt.

This meeting was to have been an addition to the lucrative advertising contract already in place with MegaCorp and he had hoped to return to Muller and Rathbone with confirmation of the new contract.

"Let me assure you that you have not had a wasted journey," she added as though she had read his mind, "Mr Bishop has briefed me on your past meetings and today's agenda."

Before he could reply, she leaned slightly forward and slid the leather portfolio case across the desk turning it around so that it was the right way up for him to read.

"The contract has been signed by Mr Bishop, with the Board of Directors' approval earlier this morning."

Martin Purnell opened the folder. It contained the proposed contract between their two companies that he had been working on for over ten hours a day, six days a week for the past two months. The contract included his detailed report of the marketing strategy for every one of MegaCorp's brands. MegaCorp already had a considerable proportion of the household market, spread across a wide range of products. In the average supermarket, MegaCorp accounted for 44.7% of all cosmetic products on the shelves. Likewise, MegaCorp brands accounted for 46.3% of all pet food, 52.4% of all cleaning products, 41.5% of all personal hygiene products and 38.3% of all medicinal products sold across the UK. In the average supermarket shopping trolley, MegaCorp would account for well over one third of its contents.

"Muller and Rathbone's management of MegaCorp's key brands has generated considerable growth and increased market share across all product sectors."

She didn't pause long enough for Martin to respond.

"The contract has been approved, Mr Purnell," she continued, "Mr Bishop wishes to express that he looks forward to continued success." She paused for effect before she added, "For both our companies."

It was no secret to Nina Glover what this contract was worth. She had just given him a signed contract worth two point five million pounds plus another million in performance bonuses.

Martin Purnell could not believe what he had just heard and her directness had taken the wind out his sails as he was not expecting the contract to be approved without further negotiations. He had spent a considerable amount of time preparing a convincing argument to close this deal and it felt as if he had been knocked off-balance by MegaCorp's relatively unchallenged acceptance.

"That is good news," he managed to say, "Muller and Rathbone look forward to continuing to work with MegaCorp."

"I expect our respective departments will be in contact with each other in due course to discuss the finer details of each marketing campaign. Unless you have any questions, I believe this brings our meeting to an agreeable conclusion." The faint hint of a smile broke out on her face. She stood up and offered her hand to Martin, to seal the deal.

Martin stood up and shook Nina's outstretched hand. He was conscious that he had said next to nothing in this very short, one-sided meeting and quickly thought of something coherent to say.

"Thank you," he said, "And please extend my regards to Mr Bishop. I am sure Muller and Rathbone will continue to be a successful business partner with MegaCorp."

"I am sure you will," she replied, "Ms Wright will escort you out."

"Please come with me, Mr Purnell," Ms Wright said as she opened the door leading out to the corridor.

He had been unaware that the silent Ms Wright had been standing by the door throughout the meeting. He picked up the leather portfolio and reached down for his briefcase, tucking the portfolio inside as he turned towards the door.

"Good bye, Mr Purnell," Nina said as the door closed behind them.

Martin Purnell followed Ms Wright as they walked in silence back along the glass walled corridor towards the reception. When they reached the doors at the end of the corridor, Martin Purnell instinctively reached for the handle and tried to open the door but it was locked.

"The door is locked," she said, "This building's security system works both ways, coming in and going out."

She swiped her access card through the keypad slot, the keys illuminated and she typed in her access code. The door unlocked and she led the way back into the reception. She walked with him through the reception area towards the lift style entrance hallway where it was again necessary for her to deactivate the door's lock mechanism before the doors automatically opened.

She turned to face him. "I'll take your visitor's badge, please Mr Purnell."

He unclipped the badge and placed it into her open hand. She smiled and gestured for him to head through the open doors into the entrance hallway. He stepped forward through the first pair of doors which again closed automatically behind him and he found himself back in the air-lock, lift-type hallway.

Ms Wright spoke through the intercom.

"The outer doors will now unlock, Mr Purnell."

When he stepped outside into the daylight, it took his eyes a moment or two to adjust to the bright daylight. He headed back to his car and thought to himself that it was one of the strangest meetings he had ever attended and it had not really sunk in yet that he had in his briefcase a contract worth over three million pounds.

Three Weeks before the Power Crisis:

Monday 17:00Hrs

Elsewhere in the MegaCorp building, in the fourth floor conference room, Bishop addressed MegaCorp's Board of Directors.

"Meeting Agenda Item Four," said Bishop, referring to the meeting notes in front of him on the conference table. He read aloud the agenda item:

"Settlement payments for product-related compensation claims. Implement alternative means of product testing."

The twelve members of the MegaCorp Board of Directors nodded in agreement. Bishop opened the debate on the agenda item with a formal statement.

"In the last three months, we have paid over thirteen point four million pounds in compensation claims. This is a 14% increase on the previous three months and a 27% overall increase on last year's figures. Payments to claimants are increasing month on month and continue to increase unchecked. This agenda item proposes we must implement alternative product testing methods to keep claims to a minimum."

"Here, here", said one of the board members, "Compensation is becoming a right pain in the back-side and…."

"Yes, indeed it is," interrupted Bishop, "And quite *literally* a pain in the backside when one considers our ongoing issues with *Steadi-Tum.*"

Steadi-Tum was a top-selling MegaCorp drug which was designed to stop chronic diarrhoea. It was initially a successful product but in certain instances the drug stayed in the human body a lot longer than first anticipated and the cumulative result of the drug's stool-solidifying properties continued to work long after the diarrhoea symptoms had ceased, resulting in chronic constipation of epic proportions.

Bishop continued, "The *Steadi-Tum* issue alone has cost us three point seven million so far."

"So far?" said one of the Board members.

"Yes. So far," Bishop answered.

He went on to explain to the Board that two *Steadi-Tum* compensation claimants had been admitted to hospital where x-rays had revealed backed-up poop so compacted that surgery had been required to remove it. Another claimant had strained so hard to pass a solidified poop the size of a grapefruit, that he had needed reconstructive surgery of his sphincter.   No one knew for certain how the video of the operation found its way onto YouTube, but it did attract over five hundred thousand online viewers.

"These payments and the resulting negative publicity towards *Steadi-Tum* have a forecasted cost of over six million pounds," Bishop tapped the table to get complete attention, "And this has to stop. I propose MegaCorp reverts to more traditional product testing immediately."

The Board of Directors knew exactly what *traditional* meant. It meant testing their products more thoroughly on animals but in the corporate world, profitability out-trumps morality and the Board of Directors would turn a blind-eye to what Bishop was proposing in his test labs if it meant there were no more high-value compensatory claims.

Bishop continued, "Once the product is proven 100% safe using traditional animal-testing methods we will then proceed to controlled human trials where the product will be guaranteed to have no risk of future damages claims."

One by one, they verbally agreed to Bishop's proposal, except one director who paused over passing his vote.

"Mr Bishop," he said, "I'm not happy to condone the use of

large numbers of animals being tested in our laboratories. What if it was leaked to the media, the consequences would be catastrophic and more damaging than the compensation claims. What guarantees can you give that this will not be the case?"

Bishop responded, "We plan to focus our testing upon small numbers of animals which are specifically matched to the product under test. Animals with, let's say, a certain disposition towards skin complaints would be part of our scientific research in skin products and we would not have to use much more than a handful of animals."

"Be specific, please Mr Bishop."

"For instance," continued Bishop, "Supposing we identified an animal with a tendency towards mental illness and depression when it is kept in captivity, this animal would become the focus for our anti-depression drug programme."

"And the animals would be *what* exactly?"

"I think the Board can leave the finer details to me, don't you?"

"And if this was leaked to the media?"

"Our test subjects will be disposed of humanely and in-house using existing MegaCorp facilities. I can assure you that the media will be none the wiser," assured Bishop.

The director nodded his agreement, "If you can guarantee no media exposure, then I approve your proposal, Mr Bishop."

"Then we are all agreed," said Bishop, "Thank you, gentlemen. I will report on progress in our next meeting."

The meeting continued to discuss other agenda items for another thirty minutes. When the meeting came to an end, Bishop returned to his office where Nina Glover had been waiting for him.

"Do we have approval from the Board?" she asked.

"Yes, full approval."

"Better late than never," Nina said with a wry smile.

She and Bishop had already implemented 'traditional' testing without the Board's approval many months earlier and the test laboratories had been in full operation for over a year.

"Progress is excellent with the Exotics," Nina said, "Although the mortality rate is a little higher than we first forecast."

Bishop remained emotionless, "And are we disposing of the bodies as planned?"

"Yes," Nina confirmed, "No trace."

"How are things progressing on Project X?"

"Progress is exactly as we anticipated. *'KwiknSlim'* and *Pro-Retanzin* have passed all X-Ingredient laboratory tests and we are also close to completing the final tests on the rest of our medicinal range."

"You appear to have things firmly under control," Bishop said, "But what about replacement subjects?"

"We have more due today and some are arriving as we speak," said Nina, "These ones were half the price of the last ones."

"Much cheaper than a human law-suit then," said Bishop, with a faint smile breaking out on his usually emotionless face.

Nina and Bishop walked over to his office window and they looked out towards the airport's freight handling depot where a procession of forklift trucks with large wooden crates made their way to the loading bay doors at the rear the MegaCorp building. The wooden sides of the crate were plain, with no shipping details or customs stamps. A row of tiny holes was all that could be seen on the unmarked crates.

Inside the crate, the tiny air-holes cast beams of light that did very little to brighten up the interior. The crate contained a three metre square, one and half metre high steel cage and in the corner of the cage the young polar bear sat hunched over cramped and uncomfortable. The crate jolted back and forth before coming to an abrupt stop. The bear lifted up his head and poked his nose through the bars until his nostrils were level with the crate's air holes. He sniffed. He could not see him, but he could smell his brother so he let out a low growl and his brother answered.

The forklift driver was met by a man with a clipboard that checked over the crate and directed the driver on the crate's final destination.

"These two crates are for the lower labs, level B3, laboratory 12."

"Okay," said the driver, "Down to B3."

After a short while, the crate was travelling again. The bear sniffed at the air-holes as a light breeze brought new smells into the crate which all smelled unfamiliar. Since they had left the Arctic, the bears had spent most of their lives in a three metre by three metre square cage. On the very rare occasions they were let out of the cage they were moved into an exercise enclosure where they were washed down, sedated and given rudimentary fitness checks. Compared to the open expanses of the Arctic, a cage this small could best be described as a polar bear's living hell.

The driver wound his way down through the basement car park levels where he arrived at the entrance to the underground laboratories on level B3. The crate came to an abrupt stop and the polar bear heard another pair of two-legs speak.

"Polar bears?"

"Yeah, where do you want them?"

"Lab 12, put them next to the benches."

The bear felt his crate move again until it finally came to rest against something hard. He sniffed at the air-holes and he could smell a two-leg getting closer. Above him, he heard the crate's wooden lid start to creak and one corner lifted up before the lid was flicked off by the two leg.

"Hello, there Big Fella," the two-leg said peering in through the top of the opened crate.

The bear could not move freely due to the lack of height in the cage but he still lunged at the two-leg, his teeth biting on the bars, making the whole cage shake.

"Whoa, there!" the two-leg said, jumping back, "We're going to have to give you something to calm you down."

The bear stared back at the two-leg with cold black eyes and let out a low continuous growl through his bared white teeth. From his time in captivity he had learned the hard way that if he barked or howled he would be beaten with sticks so he let the growl fade gradually away. Through the top of the cage, he saw the two-leg retreat backwards to a nearby desk where he picked up a pole. Three more two-legs appeared and they surrounded the cage, using poles to pin the bear in one corner. The two-legs removed the wooden sides of the crate, leaving the bear alone in his all-too-familiar small steel cage.

The bear looked out through the bars. He was in a large room, with long desks and stools and things he had never seen before. It was not at all like the farm where he had been kept for the past six months. To his left was his brother in a similar cage, a view that he had become accustomed to during this past year. On the opposite side of the room he saw three more polar bears, all of them appeared to be in a pretty poor shape. Probably had one too many beatings, he thought. He let out a short bark of hello but received no reply from any of them.

He watched them a little more closely. One of them continually mouthed at the bars of his cage with a vacant look in his eyes, as if he was focusing on something two miles away in the distance. Another sat slumped, leaning forward staring at the floor. The third bear was even more distressed. He swayed back and forth, rubbing the side of his head on the bars.

This was a sure sign that all of these polar bears were

suffering from deep depression, typical of bears kept in captivity.

"What do you make of those three?" he asked his brother.

"They are all in bad shape, every one of them. That one there, rubbing the bars with his head has really lost it."

A two-leg in a white laboratory coat walked into the room and picked up two pieces of card from a desk. Another two-leg joined him with a sharpened pole which he used to prod the bears to one corner of their cage while the other two-leg pinned the cards to the front of their cages. The bears fought bravely against the painfully sharp poles that dug into their ribs, not daring to fight back too hard because they knew that if they did they would receive far worse treatment.

The card labels on their cages read *'Control'* and *'Withdraw'*.

The two-legs stepped back from the cages and made a cursory check of their new test-subjects.

"They'll do fine, but you can get rid of the others, they've had it and their useless now. We'll start dosing these new ones up in the morning."

Three Weeks before the Power Crisis:

Monday 18:00Hrs

Martin Purnell opened the doors to Muller and Rathbone's offices in Grove Street, Exeter. Their fourth floor modern offices overlooked Cathedral Square and the busy Fore Street shopping centre. The marketing department had already been updated with the news of the extension to the MegaCorp contract and were waiting for him in the conference room.

"Good evening, everyone," he said, as he walked through the conference room's double doors. "Thank you for staying late, I take it you've heard the good news?"

He was greeted by a short burst of applause from his team that were already seated around a large wooden conference table. He smiled and placed his briefcase at an empty place at the head of the table and he took out the MegaCorp leather portfolio, placing it on the table in front of him. He tapped it for everyone to see.

"If you haven't heard already," he paused for a moment, "We have secured the MegaCorp contract for their cosmetics and over-the-counter medicinal ranges."

This news was greeted with another round of applause and a loud wolf-whistle. Martin held up his hand trying to bring the room back down to a professional level.

"What this means is hard work over the coming months so we may as well get started now."

The team settled down and the meeting started.

"First of all," Martin said, "We should congratulate Mark

and Stella for their excellent work on the MegaCorp *'Brite'* brand. Sales are up 23%."

"It was nothing to do with your daughter then?" said Pearson from a corner of the room. A mild ripple of laughter spread out.

"Ah, Mr Pearson," Martin Purnell smiled, nodding in his direction, "I'm glad you are with us. Yes, I agree my daughter using vast amounts of *Oven-Brite* on prime-time national television did have something to do with it, but credit goes to Mark and Stella for securing the *Star Struck* sponsorship in the first place."

Reluctantly, Pearson had to agree.

"As you've got so much to say, Pearson, perhaps you'd like to kick off the meeting with your marketing strategy for MegaCorp's medicinal ranges. Let's start with *'KwiknSlim'.*"

Two Weeks before the Power Crisis:

Wednesday 17:45Hrs

In the headquarters of Fusion Energy, a heated argument was taking place in the corporate boardroom. It was a meeting between the Head of Finance and the Head of Logistics and one man wanted what the other man could not give. Logistics wanted more energy resources, which cost money; finance wanted more money from the existing resources. No matter which way they sliced and diced the numbers, the numbers did not add up. Resources were stretched to breaking point with no funds to invest in development of new energy sources.

"If we don't invest in new energy sources now, we will fail to meet demand in the very near future. It's as simple as that," the Head of Logistics said, "We need more funding to develop new energy sources but even that would be too little, too late. We're already at breaking point."

His counterpart, the Head of Finance shook his head, "Funds from where, exactly? We have debts in the hundreds of millions and what funds were allocated to new energy development have been redirected to keep the company afloat."

He pointed to a map of Europe on the wall.

"We're buying nearly all of our gas for the power stations from Russia and believe it or not, we are sourcing energy from wind farms in Ireland and Norway and all of it at a cost well above the price we're charging customers."

He paused for a moment, his tone of voice contained a reluctant acceptance that the future was bleak.

"The Government are ten years behind on renewable energy and as a company we're haemorrhaging money."

Both men sighed because they could not find the answer. If Britain's overstretched power stations could not meet demand, the central grid would fail with catastrophic results.

The Head of Logistics knew that the next few weeks were critical.

"Unless we manage to squeeze every last kilowatt of power out of the power stations we currently have operational, we're going under and taking the power grid with us."

The Head of Finance sighed and reluctantly nodded in agreement, "That's it in a nutshell."

Both men knew the situation was critical and the immediate future of the country's power distribution now balanced on a knife-edge. The only question left was how to make the Government realise the severity of the situation and impress upon the people of Britain the harsh reality of the energy crisis they faced.

ONE WEEK BEFORE THE POWER CRISIS:

MONDAY 09:00HRS

Star Struck's producer, Grant Blows burst into his production room with a calculated, menacing stride. He stopped in the centre of the room and stared intently at the array of TV monitors showing live camera footage of the celebrities inside the house. In front of these TV monitors sat his production crew who monitored the live feeds from the cameras within the house. The crew tracked and recorded everything said and done, no matter where and when it happened.

Months before the celebrities had been announced to the public, he had already carefully hand-picked each and every one. He wanted celebrities that had once had fame beyond their wildest dreams, and then lost it. He wanted celebrities that had tasted fame and craved for more. He wanted disgraced celebrities. He wanted spoilt celebrities. He wanted them rude, opinionated, and outspoken. Most of all he wanted them desperate for fame. The more desperate they were, the more easily manipulated they were.

And Grant knew very well how to manipulate. Earlier in the day, he had sent one of the production team runners on an errand to a local book store to buy five sets of Key Stage 2 Maths SAT test papers. Grant knew that most, if not all of the celebrities, would struggle with basic maths and he had plans to expose this to his advantage. When the runner returned with the papers Grant was ecstatic as the plan hatched in his head; he could foresee hours, if not days, of rating-boosting TV coming out of this idea.

Grant stood in the centre of the production room. He tucked

the test papers under his arm and clapped his hands a few times to get everyone's attention.

"Production meeting in two minutes," he ordered, "Bring your thinking heads, not your numb-skulls!" he added.

The team of assistants, junior assistants and runners left their desks and headed for the meeting room. This room was sparse by design, there was no table and no chairs, everyone stood. Keeping the team on their toes, so to speak, was how Grant kept them sharp and on top of their game. At one end was a blank whiteboard, the width of the room. Across the top of the whiteboard were A4 size photos of the celebrities, held in place with sticky tape at the corners. The ones that had already been evicted had been crossed out in felt-tip pen with large red X's.

Every Monday morning, the production team was brought together to discuss and plan the next eviction. Agenda items for the meeting were the popularity of the celebrities, the show's viewing figures and which two celebrities would be put up for eviction. Strictly speaking, the decision on which two celebrities was made by the celebrities themselves. However, with some careful manipulation, the production team was able to influence their voting.

The production team's runners and assistants formed up in a rough semi-circle facing the whiteboard clutching their clipboards and notes to their chests. Grant was the last to enter the room, he walked to the front and placed the SATs test papers face down on the windowsill next to the whiteboard. He picked up a marker pen from the shelf below the whiteboard and tapped it on the board to get everyone's attention.

"Eviction Week Eight," he said, "Let's see what we've got."

Grant stepped back and surveyed the remaining celebrities, obviously deep in thought. After a few seconds he stepped forward to the leftmost photo, a black and white portrait of Opal.

Opal was 26 and from Hounslow, West London. Opal had

first come into the public spotlight when she sang her way to the final of Channel Nine's talent show, *Stairway to Stardom*. Opal had been catapulted from being an out-of-work nail art technician to pop star overnight. Professional critics would have commented that her voice was average at best and lacked any formal training for pitch and tone but the *Stairway* judges were not so focused on talent. What they required was a one or two hit wonder that would sell enough records to boost the show's profit margin and keep them in their very comfortable lifestyles for the next year. In the semi-finals, Opal had been the best bet for the most record sales, so for the final show the judges had chosen a song well within her karaoke-style capabilities and they had repeatedly broadcast a heartrending story about her being reunited with her estranged father to boost her popularity. Just to make doubly sure, the show's production team rigged the final votes in her favour, just to be certain she would win.

After winning the show, Opal had secured a record deal with Ethanol Records, and her first single, a cover version of Britney Spears' *'Baby One More Time'* was a Christmas number 1. Her first album, *'Zone 5'* went gold the following February. On the back of this success, Opal had enjoyed almost limitless media attention and she appeared regularly in celebrity and gossip magazines such as Heat and OK!

The next summer, she had released her second album. It had failed to chart in the top 50. The stresses of stardom started to manifest and the cracks appeared in Opal's persona. Soon she was coming apart at the seams. She had made a cameo appearance on the next *Stairway to Stardom* which went badly wrong due to her having had a few too many vodkas to loosen up. When she forgot the words to *'Baby One More Time'*, she let go a barrage of four-letter words live on TV. This was all the more catastrophic because she had been miming and the tape loop played on as she stormed off the stage. Media attention soon shifted from her music to her binge-drinking. She had been filmed by security cameras behind Hounslow Sports Centre, sleeping off another drunken night-out, slumped between two rubbish bins with the remains of a grease-stained fried-chicken bargain bucket in her lap. For Ethanol Records, it was a drunken binge too far and the threat of pulling her contract loomed dangerously over Opal's head. She met with her record company and they decided to release a safe-bet cover version from the eighties. A week before Opal entered the celebrity house, she had hurriedly recorded her version of the Human League's 1980 chart hit, *'Empire State Human'*. It was bound to appeal to a wide audience because it had been on the soundtrack of a long-running TV police drama, set in the eighties. Ethanol Records figured it was certain to be a sure-fire hit but unfortunately it wasn't a hit for Opal. It was the Human League's original version that climbed steadily towards the number one slot while Opal's poorer quality version floundered, failing to make the top 75.

Grant tapped the photo of Opal. After a few moments, he drew a large red circle around the photo and underneath he wrote in block letters:

VOTING?

And underneath this he wrote:

RECORD DEAL?

He turned and pointed to the assistant responsible for Opal, "Update us," he said.

"Last time she was up for eviction, she should have gone out. We kept her in with the footage of her clearing mines for UNICEF and that swayed the public vote."

"Yeah, yeah, I know that, we did some good work there but now it's time she went. I want her up for eviction this week. I hear her record's not doing too well and we can use that to shock her when in post-eviction interview."

"Yes, Boss," was the reply, "I've got some figures on her latest record sales and it's definitely not going at all well. If we got her voted out this Friday it would tie up with Ethanol dropping her. Good TV there, we can drop that bombshell on her live on Friday's post eviction show."

"I like it, make sure we drip-feed Rex some info so he can wind the stupid cow up."

Grant moved to the next photo. It was the photo of Rex Carrs.

Rex Carrs, real name Stan Woodbury, was 63 and he came from Dublin. Rex was the lead singer and front man of heavy rock group Blacksmith. Forty something years of a rock and roll lifestyle had taken its toll on Rex and he showed signs of being well past his rave-by-date. His once smooth good looks were now tobacco-hardened into a craggy, ragged, sun-dried face and his black thinning hair receded back almost as far as his pony tail which any sane man would have dropped as a bad idea twenty years earlier. He still wore the tight lycra, spandex leggings of his youth but he didn't fill them like he used to. They hung off his backside and sagged behind the knees, doing absolutely nothing to hide his scrawny, pencil-thin chicken legs.

Rex and his band had an extensive back catalogue of rock hits including seven platinum selling albums. There was a certain irony in this because Rex had been married and divorced by seven platinum blondes. His last divorcee, number seven, was a thirty year old, long-legged, bleached-blonde, silicon- implanted, collagen-enhanced, underwear model from Latvia, called Eva. She looked a lot like a fully-grown Barbie, or rather she looked a lot like a very scary version of Barbie, one that had been created from the *Barbie goes to the Over-Enthusiastic Plastic Surgeon* play set.

Before entering the *Star Struck* celebrity house Rex had been a contestant on Channel Nine's celebrity musician show, *Rock Bottom.* He was voted out in week two. His early ejection from *Rock Bottom* meant Rex had agreed to join the *Star Struck* house to boost the failing sales of Blacksmith's latest album, *Forge Ahead*, which was as usual, little more than a collection of re-mixed, re-released hits.

Underneath Rex's photo Grant wrote:

EX ????!!!!!

Grant turned from the whiteboard and pointed to the assistant that was responsible for Rex.

"What's happening with the EX Mrs Rex?" he asked.

"She can't make this weekend so we've got to keep Rex in for at least another week. I called her yesterday and she hates him. In fact, she despises him. Get those two together and we've got viewing figures through the roof. She just needs a week to recover from surgery."

"Surgery? What bloody surgery?" gasped Grant, "The woman looks more and more like an over-stretched plastic trout every day. Is she in for a lip reduction? She bloody needs one, that's for sure."

"She's having an eye-augmentation, Boss, we've got to wait for the swelling to go down."

"Swelling?" Grant asked, imagining the worst.

The assistant handed Grant a recent photo of Eva. Grant stared at the bruised and battered image in disbelief, "What the hell has happened there?"

Before the runner could answer, Grant continued, "Was her surgeon blind drunk at the time? Did he take a two kilo hammer to her cheek bones? It looks like he's rebuilt her face using spare parts from Mrs Potato Head!"

He pointed at the photo.

"What the hell are those? Are they eyebrows or eyelashes?"

The assistant started to explain, "I think they are...."

"No. Don't tell me, spare me the facts. Just make sure that when we put her in the house she's not looking like something from an episode of Doctor Who!"

Grant moved to the next celebrity and stared at the photo of Poppy Purnell. He rubbed his short goatie beard, evidently deep in thought.

Rachel 'Poppy' Purnell, 19 years old from Stoke Canon, in Mid Devon. Poppy was the fresh-faced, naturally pretty girlfriend of Dean Ashburn, the fast-footed, ball-curling, teenage football wonder-boy that ruled the right wing and was feared by every Premiership left-back. He had rocketed from Exeter schoolboy league to Premier league in less than a season and his new team, Liverpool FC, had hopes for a European trophy; England expected the World Cup. Ashburn's fame catapulted Poppy to A-list celebrity status and a lifestyle of glamour and glitz under the spotlight of an adoring media and public. Poppy became an advertiser's dream. Cosmetics companies fell over themselves for her endorsements. She became the face of *Naturesse*, promoting a range of cosmetic products aimed specifically at young women who wanted to be just like her.

However, this dream romance was not all it appeared to be, temptation soon reared its ugly head and Dean Ashburn's talent for scoring goals from anywhere between 18 to 30 yards soon became a talent for scoring girls from anywhere between 18 to 30 years old. The paparazzi were waiting for him to get caught with his pants down. Quite literally.

Overnight, Poppy ceased being the Teenage Footballer's Sweetheart and became the Teenage Footballer's Cast-Off. Demand for her endorsed range of products dropped away and *Naturesse* found a new face for their advertising. Poppy's celebrity rating dropped as fast as it had risen. She had once been in demand for Friday night peak viewing celebrity chat shows but within days of the news of Dean's affair, she found herself booked only for daytime gossip TV, facing questions about how it felt to be betrayed by the golden-booted wonder-boy *scumbag*. Poppy was now the face of the jilted generation. The call from *Star Struck* came when she was at her lowest point, she didn't even remember agreeing to appear.

Underneath her photo Grant wrote the word:

DIRT?

He underlined it twice for even more emphasis.

"Nothing, Boss," said the assistant in charge of Poppy, "There are no ex-boyfriends, no bad school reports and no criminal record. I've been down to her old school and no one's got a bad thing to say..."

"Yeah, yeah, I get it. She is a Miss Goody-Two-Shoes, but there's got to be something we can dig up on her."

"Our recent viewing figures suggest she's responsible for us hitting a much wider audience. We took a million viewers off Jamie Oliver last week and we picked up 30% more advertising revenue from B&Q when we let her loose with the toolkit."

Grant shook his head. For once he was stuck for words.

The assistant continued, "The network bosses say she's got to stay because she's TV gold apparently, they reckons she's keeping the show's viewing figures at an all-time high."

Grant drew a pair of glasses on Poppy's photo, he then added a moustache and freckles.

"Ok," he said, "Miss Goody-Two-Shoes-Popular-Poppy-Purnell stays in the house for now, but keep on digging."

"Yes, Boss."

Grant then moved to his right and tapped the next photo.

Double O-Zone was 22, from Bow, East London. Real name Matthew Mullins. He was a hip-hop rapper who had become famous for his hard-hitting rap style which focused on his life in the tough streets of East London. Unlike most rappers of his genre, he was white. He spoke, or rather rapped, in a tough urban style, a mix of black and Asian street slang delivered with sweeping hand gestures and pointed fingers, heavily loaded with knuckleduster sized bling-rings. He wore a tweed deerstalker hat and around his neck on a thick gold chain, he wore a gold-plated 9mm bullet, the one that had been removed from his left thigh after a drive-by shooting in Peckham High Street. The deerstalker and 9mm bullet-on-a-chain was his trademark, replicated by his wannabe gangsta followers.

His raps were filled with graphic detail of his experience of a hard upbringing, living on a tough estate filled with violence, difficulty, bullying and gang culture. Double O-Zone had been sent onto *Star Struck* by his manager, Tommy Todd. He didn't ask why, he just did what Tommy said and Tommy had said this would be a '*time for him to rhyme, a time for him to lay down his words to the burbs*'. For Tommy it was time for him to pocket the entire £50,000 *Star Struck* signing fee.

Underneath the photo of the rapper, Grant drew a stick man wearing a dunce's cap.

He turned to another assistant, "Tell me what we know about Double O-Stupid."

"You were right, Boss, he's from up market Royal Tunbridge Wells."

"I bloody knew it!" Grant was ecstatic, "What else have you found out?"

"He's not an orphan either, Mummy and Daddy are alive and well but on extended vacation. In other words, holed up at the family estate in the Cayman Islands. Something to do with off-shore bank accounts and tax avoidance. It looks like the whole family are loaded."

"What about the drive-by shooting?"

"Turns out that was a publicity stunt. He wasn't shot with a 9mm semi-auto Glock, he was shot with .22 air pistol. The Harley Street surgeon that removed the pellet was paid to keep quiet."

"Will he talk now?" asked Grant.

"Yeah, we've got him onside, he kept the airgun pellet in a specimen jar. He says he was able to remove it with tweezers but Double O insisted on general anaesthetic and seven stitches. I've got the interview all on tape, we're ready to break the news."

"How are his popularity ratings?"

The assistant checked her clipboard where she had already prepared the data on Double O-Zone's popularity poll. She handed a piece of A4 paper to Grant and he studied the graph she had prepared. The graph of popularity over time showed a steady downward trend which dipped at week three and then gradually declined indicating that O-Zone was the most unpopular celebrity with the voting public.

"His popularity dropped after the toilet block incident and it's falling steadily week on week," the assistant said.

"So the viewers don't like him and I bloody agree with them," Grant surmised, "He's an annoying, loathsome little turd and I'm not surprised Rex poisoned his tea, I'd have ground up a pint glass and put that in there as well."

Grant smiled at the events of three weeks earlier. O-Zone had been at his most obnoxious best, winding up the entire house with his argumentative, hostile attitude and unfounded assumption that he was always right. Rex had decided he'd had enough and he had taken it upon himself to put O-Zone right. Rex had offered to make everyone a cup of tea but while the kettle boiled, he had sneaked to the men's toilet, collected two toilet bleach blocks, ground them up into little pieces and added the tiny green crystals to O-Zone's cup. Grant had watched this situation develop from one of the house-cameras that had focused on O-Zone as he stood at a urinal. The camera had zoomed in on his face as he looked down with a confused look of curiosity at the fluorescent green coloured pee that was filling the urinal. O-Zone's look of mild curiosity had turned quickly to abject horror as the bleaching agent of the toilet cleaner sent both his kidneys simultaneously into shock. The bleach had then burned its way along the rest of his internal plumbing and by the time it had reached his manhood, it felt that he was trying to pee out the devil's own red hot razor blades. The toilet-cam zoomed in on the street tough gangsta, as he had slumped against the urinal and then collapsed in a heap on the floor, surrounded by an ever widening puddle of green pee. The camera had zoomed in on his little tears and snot bubbles as he sobbed loudly, whimpering for his mummy. Grant had wasted no time at all and the edited highlights were broadcast repeatedly throughout that evening's show. It was no wonder O-Zone's popularity had dwindled, he was now bad for viewing figures.

Grant underlined the photo of O-Zone, "It's time to get him out, he's the one we want up for eviction."

The team agreed with nods and grunts of approval.

Finally Grant turned to the last photo. He circled the photo a few times and then drew a large question mark under the face of Tony Tayburn, MP.

Tony Tayburn, Member of Parliament, was 46 and from Frimley Green, Surrey. He had stood as Labour candidate for Surrey North in the 2001 General Election. He had accepted that he had little chance of being elected because Surrey North was a safe conservative seat and the current Member of Parliament, Timothy Spalding, was destined to be re-elected by an overwhelming majority. However, fortune shone upon Tony Tayburn when his upper class opponent was arrested by police for shooting badgers with an unlicensed twelve bore at his Norfolk country estate. He protested his innocence saying that it was for personal reasons but animal rights activists were outraged. They became even more outraged when it was revealed that the police had searched Spalding's home and found Tupperware containers in his freezer labelled badger steaks and worse still, several more containers which were labelled kitten fillets.

The thought of filleted kittens turned the stomach of the voting public and the media labelled Spalding the Badger Butcher and the Kitty Killer.

As a result of the kitten fillets incident, Timothy Spalding's chances of re-election dwindled and support switched to Tony Tayburn who was duly elected the new MP for Surrey North with a landslide majority of 16,437.

Before becoming an MP, Tayburn had been a supervisor at Camberley Heath Sports Centre on a modest salary of £21,453 per annum. When he became an MP, his salary had tripled to £65,325 overnight.

Tayburn's contribution to debates in the House of Commons was minimal, in eight years he had never spoken in any debates and he had never raised a single issue. Tony was riding a gravy-train, the last thing he wanted to do was jeopardise his income, so he settled into being one of the many anonymous backbench MPs that followed the party line like overweight, dim-witted sheep.

However, he was not so dim-witted when it came to exploiting the unregulated expenses system. He started off small with a few fake claims for non-existent office equipment. These went through unchecked so he tried his luck with a few more fraudulent claims and they went through without question as well. Before long, he had claimed that he needed a second home, despite only living forty minutes by train from Westminster and he claimed for it to be fully furnished too. He sold that home for a profit and bought another, all on expenses. It was all so easy, he was doubling his already fat MP's salary through his exorbitant, fake expenses claims.

Tayburn knew he would not be able to rely upon his political reputation for re-election this time and his best hope was to gain popularity with younger voters so he had jumped at the chance to be in *Star Struck*. He figured he would be able to reach out and connect with more voters.

Grant circled Tony Tayburn's photo with his marker pen.

"Still on the fiddle is he?" asked Grant.

"Yeah, he's been a very greedy boy," said the assistant.

"Go on," said Grant.

"Two thousand pounds for a wide screen TV, eight thousand for an expenses paid, supposed fact-finding mission to the South of France. He's even claimed for fifty kilos of dog food as a necessary household security expense, and the only dog he ever owned was a miniature poodle and that died two years ago."

"Anything else?" asked Grant, shaking his head slowly in mock amazement.

"I've done some research at his Surrey place and I've got a meeting arranged with his builder who is ready to tell the world that Tayburn offered him five hundred quid to submit thousands of pounds worth of fake invoices for building work that he never did."

Grant nodded in approval and drew a huge pound sign under the photo of Tony Tayburn MP.

Grant stepped back and surveyed the remaining five celebrities. When the dirt on them was leaked to the media it would be on national TV and the internet within minutes. Whichever celeb he chose to expose would soon become public enemy number one and was sure to become the eviction victim on Friday. The bigger the scandal, the bigger the viewing figures and viewing figures meant advertising revenue.

"Right," Grant said to his team, "Eviction short-list, make some notes."

He tapped Tayburn's photo.

"Our greedy little MP stays in for another week until we get the builder's story confirmed, okay?"

The team nodded.

He moved to the photo of Poppy.

"Miss Goody-Two-Shoes stays for now, she's good for the ratings, so you're telling me, but keep on digging for dirt in case she makes the final."

He then prodded the photo of Rex with his finger.

"Wrinkly ball-bag chops stays in until we bring in trouty-pout Eva for a bit of an overdue family reunion. That will be solid gold TV fireworks for the final weeks, I guarantee it."

He then drew a large looping circle around Double O-Zone and linked it with the photo of Opal.

"So, this dozy pair are up for eviction, agreed?"

"Yes, Boss," the team replied in unison.

"Get hold of her record sales figures so we're ready for this Friday."

He then tapped the photo of Double O-Zone.

"Get on your phones and leak the news to the press about Double O-Jellyhead," Grant instructed, "And make sure we get the video of the surgeon and the air-gun pellet uploaded and online for the FaceTubers and the Twitterati."

The assistant that managed O-Zone thought for a moment before she asked Grant an important question.

"Have we got any ideas on how we'll influence the celebs into voting for these two to be up for eviction?"

Grant said nothing but his mouth twisted into a wicked grin.

One Week before the Power Crisis:

Monday 14:00hrs

Grant handed the five SAT test papers to the assistants standing opposite him. They looked at them with a mix of interest and puzzlement and they wondered where he was planning to take this idea.

Grant turned around, faced the whiteboard and in large red block capitals he wrote the words:

MATHS TEST

Some of the team squirmed thinking this was going to be aimed at them.

Grant added the words:

CELEB FORFEIT

The team breathed a sigh of relief. The celebs were in the firing line, not them.

Grant turned to face the team.

"We are going to make our lovely little celebrity housemates take a primary school maths test," he said with a wicked smile on his face. "We're going to find out which of these fame-hungry wannabes parked their brain in Year Five and left it in neutral till Year Eleven."

One of the team spoke up, "Did you hear what Opal said yesterday? She said she's not thick, she said she is really intelligent, it's just that she can't link up what she's thinking with the right words when she speaks."

The team burst into laughter because they all had their favourite Opal quotes.

"What about when she thought a sombrero was a posh orange ice lolly?"

"The best one was when she asked if Middle Earth was near the Middle East," someone else added.

"No, the best one was when she thought Boris Johnson was one of the wizards from Harry Potter."

"Yeah, yeah, yeah," interrupted Grant, "We all know she's so dense she affects the moon's orbit so what we're going to do is use her unbridled thickness to our advantage."

Grant went through his ideas with the team and as he added the finer details to his plan the mood in the meeting room turned from light-hearted mockery to amazed disbelief.

"They are never going to do that, Boss," one member of the team said, "They just won't."

"We'll see, won't we?" Grant replied, his tone of voice contained an almost sadistic glee, "They'll turn on each other and then we'll see just how desperate these D-List wash-ups are for a chance to be an A-Lister again."

"What's your name again?" Grant pointed at the assistant responsible for Rex, "Karen isn't it?"

"Katy," she replied. She had been on the show for two seasons and he still didn't know her name.

"That's it," Grant continued, "You need to get your backside down to the props department. I want to see what they've got that we can use."

"Yes, Boss."

A few of the assistants shook their heads. They did not doubt for one minute that Grant's idea would work, they just did not believe he was capable of dreaming up these ideas. Collectively, they all knew what was needed over the next few days, the aim was to alienate Opal and Double O-Zone to make the rest of the celebrities turn against them.

"Are we ready?" asked Grant.

The team nodded in acknowledgement.

"Get to it, then!" he ordered.

The production team filed out of the meeting room and returned to their desks where they continued to monitor the celebrities in the house. As a runner passed him by, Grant tapped him on the shoulder to get his attention.

"Rustle up some pencils and anything else they'll need and put it with the test papers in the Chat-Room."

Within a few minutes the runner had raided several desks and collected up five sets of pencils and rubbers. When he had finished he gave Grant a thumbs up. Grant nodded back in approval. The runner headed across the production room to a plain looking door in the corner of the room. To the right of the door was an illuminated sign that shone red with the words DO NOT ENTER. Grant looked down at the console on his desk and flicked the switch that unlocked the door. The sign turned green and the words changed to ENTER. The automatic lock clicked open.   The runner pulled the door open and stepped inside the Chat-Room and the sound-insulated door closed silently behind him.

The Chat-Room was a padded, sound-proofed room, about the size of a small bathroom. It was much brighter inside than the subdued lighting in the production room and it took a moment for the runner's eyes to adjust. In the middle of the room was a large, modern style armchair which was high backed and covered in a shocking purple velour fabric. Facing the chair was a small high definition video camera mounted on a tripod. Behind the camera, out of the public's view, was a large sign in bold print that warned the celebrities not to swear on live TV.

Throughout the day, whenever the production team wanted to talk privately with a housemate the Voice of *Star Struck* would announce to the house that one of them was required in the Chat-Room. Of course, the conversation was not strictly private, as it was either broadcast live or edited for later broadcast to an audience of millions. The Voice's aim was to ask questions that were designed to spark an emotional response from the celebrity, it took just a little provocation and soon the Voice would have the celebrities angry, upset and generally back-stabbing their fellow housemates. The no-swearing sign was often overlooked and a seven second broadcast delay was in place for expletive-filled outbursts that went out before the 9pm watershed that were not suitable for delicate, impressionable ears of the younger viewers.

The runner left the test papers on the floor in front of the camera and went back to the production room and the sound-proofed door shut silently behind him. Grant flicked the console switch and the door's mechanism locked it shut.

"We're in business, girlies, it's show time so let's make this work."

Grant clicked his fingers to catch the attention of the assistant that was the Voice, giving him the go-ahead to contact the house.

"Attention, housemates. *Star Struck* is going to set all of you a challenge," the Voice boomed through the house speaker system.

The celebs stopped what they were doing and stared blankly up at the nearest speaker.

"Would all housemates please make their way to the Chat-Room."

Grant watched as his little celebrity pets made their way over to the Chat-Room door. On the house side of the Chat-Room, the door had a button made up of coloured LEDs that shone red. Impatiently, Double O-Zone repeatedly pushed the button, as if he was waiting for a lift with the crazy notion that by pressing the button faster, the lift would arrive faster.

"Come on, come on, come on," he said impatiently, pressing the button faster and faster. Nothing happened.

Behind him the others were shaking their heads in disbelief at his lack of his intelligence.

Double O-Zone kept on pressing the button.

Tony Tayburn contemplated the back of Double-O-Zone and wondered what in the hell went on underneath that ridiculous hat that he wore because it sure wasn't intelligent brain impulses. Today, O-Zone had been wearing his trademark tweed deer-stalker hat with the side-flaps down, and he looked doubly-ridiculous.

"Give it a moment, it's not turned green…." said Poppy but was cut short by Opal who had pushed past her to see what the hold-up was.

"You're bloody useless," said Opal, "Let me do it!"

Opal tried to push O-Zone out of the way but he held firm and pushed her back. After pressing the button for a good twenty seconds, Double O-Zone realised that his button pressing was having no affect so he finally stopped pressing the button.

Grant viewed the celebrities with disgust. They really were like his little pet lab-rats. No, that was an insult to lab-rats because even the dumbest of rodents would have learned by now to stop pressing a red button. He flicked a console switch and the button's LEDs turned green.

"Idiot," said Opal.

"Don't you call me no idiot," replied Double O-Zone, slurring his words in a ghetto-gangster hip-hop style which matched his bad-boy rapper image.

"Well you are an idiot."

Double O-Zone sucked air through his teeth in anger, "I ain't no idiot, you is the only idiot around 'ere, sister."

"You are both a right pair of eedjets," said Rex in his deep Irish accent. He reached between the squabbling celebs, pressed the green button and pulled the Chat-Room door open.

The five celebrities entered the Chat-Room and the door closed softly behind them.

Opal jumped into the chair, staring expectantly into the camera, not noticing the test papers at her feet. The others huddled behind the chair in the cramped confines of the little padded room. Grant flicked the switch and the door latch locked tight, turning the LEDs red.

Opal bounced up and down in the chair, clapping her hands excitedly, "What's the challenge, what's the challenge?"

Then the Voice spoke.

"On the floor in front of you are five Key Stage 2 Maths test papers. These are the SAT tests that are set for Year Five, ten year old primary school children. Opal, please pick up the test papers and pass them to your fellow housemates."

Opal's excitement drained from her face. A maths test was the last thing she was expecting or had any hope of passing.

The Voice continued, "On the front of the test papers are the instructions, take your time and read them, do not confer with your housemates, you are now in exam conditions."

Opal reached down for the test papers and passed them back to her fellow housemates, keeping one set for herself. As she read through the instructions her bottom lip started to quiver. The camera zoomed in to capture her nervous expression in great detail especially for those viewers watching in high definition.

Double O-Zone, Opal's antagonist from a few moments earlier, stared at the paper, not really reading the simple instructions. He was like a startled rabbit caught in a car's headlights. He was not looking forward to this, he had never been very good at maths and wished he had spent a little more time figuring it out for himself rather than bullying brighter kids into doing his homework for him.

Standing next to the rapper was Rex Carrs. It was fifty long years ago since Rex had been in a maths lesson and he knew he was going to struggle. He said nothing, he just shook his head slowly from side to side.

Poppy was quieter than the others and she stood minding her own business in the back corner of the Chat-Room. She was pretty confident she would be okay and she was also smart enough to know this was not just a test. This test would lead to something else and that something else was probably going to be humiliating, degrading and more than likely both. She did not say anything, she tucked the pencil in the front of her dungarees and stared blankly back at the camera, arms folded.

Tony Tayburn had a look of relief about him. He was petrified that the show's producers had got hold of some of his exorbitant expense claims and he lived in fear of being called into the Chat-Room to explain his expenses live to twenty five million viewers. A maths test was a pleasant alternative.

"Housemates," said the Voice, "When you leave the Chat-Room you will all go to the breakfast table and wait for instructions."

Grant flicked the switch and the green LEDs signalled the door could be opened. The celebs filed out of the Chat-Room and walked to the kitchen. On the way, Opal and Double O-Zone pushed and shoved each other continuing their who-is-an-idiot argument from earlier, albeit in silence.

As soon as they were seated around the breakfast table the Voice spoke again through the house speaker system.

"Housemates, you now have forty five minutes to complete the test. You may turn over your papers and begin."

Grant was right to question what Poppy was up to. She had been a puzzle to him from the very first week and he often took a quiet moment away from the main production team to try to understand what made her tick. He left the production room and now stood alone in the empty meeting room, facing the photos of the remaining celebs. He wished he had something to throw at them and he made a mental note that for next year's *Star Struck* he would replace the whiteboard with a dozen dartboards.

He stared at the photo of Poppy, she puzzled him and it bugged him. He knew she was up to something, but what?

She was not behaving at all like the others, she didn't appear to crave fame and she never spoke about herself, not like the others who were *always* talking about themselves. He had booked her onto *Star Struck* expecting a momentous emotional break-down by about week two or three with the potential for a rebound, romantic liaison with maybe the dim-witted rapper but things had not gone exactly to plan. Grant had expected her to fall to pieces but here she was getting more and more popular.

"The Fall and Rise of Rachel 'Poppy' Purnell," he said to himself, "So how do I trip up Miss Goody-Two-Shoes?"

Grant stared at her photo and reflected on Poppy's first seven weeks on the show.

Poppy's Seven Weeks As a Celebrity on Star Struck:

Week one to Present Day

From Grant's perspective, Poppy's first few weeks in the house had been a reversal of what he had expected and he stood alone in the meeting room pondering what he could do with her. She's bound to pass this test he thought, what if I failed her as well? No, that messes up the eviction of Opal or Double O-Jelly Brain.

He thought about Poppy's early weeks and tried to figure out how he could manipulate her in the final weeks of the show.

From Poppy's perspective, the first week in the *Star Struck* house had been a blur and she had been on autopilot just to get through the daytime in one piece. She had felt flat and empty but had managed to put on a positive face and had bonded well with the other celebs. When the others had inevitably asked her about Dean Ashburn she had shrugged, smiled and politely replied that was life and that she wished him the best for the future and that she would, with time, move on. However, when she had been alone in her bed, she had pulled the covers tight over her head and sobbed uncontrollably into her pillow for four consecutive nights. On day five in the house, she had gone to bed before the others and when she had been sure she was hidden from the cameras, she had silently and secretly broken down. At around 4am, she managed to stop crying, she had cried herself out.

"That's enough," she had said softly to herself.

Very early on the morning of the sixth day of Week One in the house, she slipped out of her bed in the communal celeb bedroom and padded softly to the bathroom in her bare feet. She stood at one of the wash basins and turned on the cold tap, cupped her hands together and splashed cold water on her face. She rubbed her tired, sore eyes.

"Enough," she said again, quietly to herself, "That's enough now."

She regretted the last year where she had been a WAG and nothing more than a footballer's tag-along girlfriend. She had earned the nickname Poppy because she was popular and she now hated that name. She stared in the mirror and the girl she saw staring back was not Popular Poppy anymore and she did not want to be. In the dim morning light, the girl that stared back had returned to being Rachel. She just wanted to be plain and regular Rachel Purnell once more.

Rachel quietly left the bathroom and crossed to the large open plan kitchen to make a cup of tea. As the kettle boiled, she thought to herself, what do I do now? Do I tell them that coming onto this show was all a big mistake and that I'd like to leave? Would that work?

She thought about this as she crossed over to the large American fridge to get some milk. No, they'd never just let me leave, she thought to herself, and the media will be waiting to pounce the moment I step outside. What would they be saying about her and Dean? It did not bear thinking about and she shuddered at the thought.

She returned the milk to the fridge and headed across the living room holding her cup of tea in both hands while cameras automatically followed her through the house. She opened one of the large sliding glass doors that led to the patio and went outside into the chill morning air and sat on the edge of the hot-tub. The hot-tub camera mounted on the wall above the glass doors tracked her as she passed by, its red light blinking. The nightshift production team watched her intently as she slowly sipped her tea while tapping her foot on the wooden decking around the edge of the hot-tub, contemplating what was best to do.

A pair of junior nightshift assistants tracked her movements through the house.

"She's upset, try to focus in on her face," one of the assistants said.

"If she tries to drown herself in the hot-tub, one of us is going to have to go in," the other one replied.

"Not me, I'm not doing mouth-to-mouth, CPR live on pre-breakfast TV and besides Grant will have a fit if one of the celebs dies without his permission."

Their laughter was cut short when Rachel put down her tea and looked up at the camera.

"She's clocked us."

"Of course she's clocked us, she knows that we're watching her."

"I don't like it. It's like *she's* watching us."

Rachel contemplated the camera and contemplated her future. Perhaps being in here is a good thing for the time being, she thought because I'm better off not knowing what the media is saying about me.

"Yeah, that's right," she said to herself, "I'm better off in here. For now, that is."

She finished her tea and much to the relief of the nightshift assistants, she got up and went back inside to the kitchen area and washed her mug, placing it neatly back in the cupboard.

Right, that's it, she thought, I'll stay in here and show everyone I'm not the air-headed WAG they think I am and if they think I'm going out that front door to become media-fodder, they can think again.

Happy with this decision and her new positive outlook, she walked away from the sink to the cooking area and looked at the hob which was still dirty from last night's meal.

"Disgusting," she said out loud.

The sink was still piled high with crockery and cutlery. She searched in the cupboards for cleaning materials and she found an abrasive sponge and a spray container of *Oven-Brite*. Within minutes she had applied generous amounts of *Oven-Brite* and a vigorous amount of elbow grease to the dried-on grime that was stuck to the hob and it shone like new. She felt good. It felt good to take out her frustration on the hob. She felt very good.

Now for the dishes, she thought. She opened the dishwasher door and was reminded of last night's arguments that she had left behind her when she went to bed. The old guy, Rex had accused the rapper, she had forgotten his name, of breaking the dishwasher. The door did not open fully it was jammed. No problem, she filled the sink with hot water and added a dash of *Sun-Brite* washing up liquid to the sink. Within a few minutes she had washed all of the dirty crockery and cutlery, placing it in a neat pile to fully dry beside the sink.

She dried her hands on the tea-towel and crossed over to the Chat-Room door. She pressed the button to request a one to one with the Voice.

"What do we do?" said one of the assistants. It was 5am and they were not used to celebs being up and about on their shift.

"Best see what she wants, I suppose."

The button turned green and Rachel opened the door to the Chat-Room. She sat in the chair and faced the camera.

"What can *Star Struck* do for you, Poppy, is everything ok?"

"Everything is fine, thanks."

"Are you sure you are okay, *Star Struck* thought you had been a little upset earlier. Would you like to talk about it?" the Voice said, trying to open a soft spot to exploit an emotional response.

"I am fine," said Rachel, "I was wondering, do you have a manual for the dishwasher?"

"The dishwasher?" the Voice asked, quite taken aback.

"Yes, the dishwasher. The door is jammed and it needs to be fixed. I can do it, I think, if I had the manual."

The Voice went quiet as the assistants debated the pros and cons of making a decision without consulting Grant. In the end, they erred on the side of caution.

"*Star Struck* will look for a manual," the Voice said, "And we will let you know."

"Thank you," said Rachel.

"Anything else?" enquired the Voice, still probing for an emotional outburst.

"No, just the manual, please."

Rachel left the Chat-Room and returned to the kitchen. She found a cloth and a can of *Gleamin'-Brite* and set about cleaning the work surfaces.

At 6:30am, Grant entered the production room clutching the early tabloid papers and a black coffee in a polystyrene cup. He was not expecting to see anything on the monitors this early in the morning, except twelve celebrities dozing in their pits. He could see on the broadcast monitor they were on a commercial break, it was MegaCorp, the show's sponsors, advertising their '*Brite*' range of kitchen cleaning products.

"What's she up to?" he asked the first assistant to catch his eye.

"She's been up since dawn, Boss, she's been cleaning."

"Cleaning?" replied Grant. Oh well he thought, at least the sponsors would be happy.

"Yes, Boss, and she's asked for a manual for the dishwasher."

"And what did you tell her?" Grant asked.

"We told her we'd get back to her."

Grant contemplated this for a moment. Why would that Disco-Dolly want to fix the dishwasher? There's only one way to find out, he thought.

Within ten minutes, Rachel had been handed the manual via another visit to the Chat-Room. She left the Chat-Room and went back to her bed space and opened the locker by her bed. She opened her makeup bag and took out an emery board nail file and a black eye-liner pencil and then returned to the decked area of the patio.

Still wearing her pyjamas, she sat cross-legged and opened the manual. As she read through the pages, she started to file her long, well manicured nails. Garden-cam 1 zoomed in as she carefully and methodically filed each nail smoothly down to just above the finger tip.

"Aw look, the manual is too difficult for her," Grant said sarcastically, "She's given up on the big technical words and the poor little poppet is doing her pretty little nails."

He watched her intently though, he still was not 100% sure what was going to develop.

Rachel was filing her nails for a reason because she was getting ready for work. After reading the manual from cover to cover, including the trouble-shooting section, Rachel used her eye-liner to make some notes.

"Zoom in, show me what she's writing," Grant ordered.

"I think we're about to find out," said one of the junior assistants as Rachel jumped to her feet and headed to the Chat-Room for the third time that morning. She sat in the chair and listened to the Voice.

"*Star Struck* does not allow housemates to write things down, you know you are not allowed to communicate through written messages."

"I'm sorry," replied Rachel, "But I was making a list for *you.*"

A request for some new nails probably, thought Grant to himself.

"A list?" asked the Voice.

"Yes, a list of things which I will need to repair the dish-washer. I am going to need a medium size cross-head screwdriver, a small flat head screwdriver, a pair of needle-nose pliers and a tin of WD40, please."

Grant was not expecting that. He gestured to the Voice to go ahead.

"Is there anything else we can get for you?" said the Voice, in a slightly patronising tone.

"And a pair of overalls or dungarees in my size would be handy too," Rachel said.

Grant wasn't expecting that either.

Later that morning, one by one, the other celebrity housemates stumbled bleary-eyed from their beds into the kitchen to find a dungaree-clad Poppy repairing the dishwasher. She had released the jammed door an hour earlier, removed the hinges, re-oiled them and then rebuilt the door mechanism. Rex stood by the coffee machine and watched in amazement as she stood up and proudly opened and closed the door to test its new, smooth movement.

"There, that's fixed," she said, very pleased with her work, "Do you fancy a cuppa to celebrate, Rex?"

Grant had watched her from the production room monitors, this was definitely not what he had planned for. This was only week one and he had not bargained for a built in handyman or handywoman for that matter. He was happy to let this run its course but for now, he had eleven other celebrities to exploit and maximise viewers and advertising revenue. Poppy could wait.

As the first few weeks of the show passed and the early-round celebrities were evicted, Rachel kept herself busy with cleaning, tidying and general household chores. In week two of the show, the production team had watched her through one of the bedroom-cams, as she sat on her bed using a pair of nail scissors to cut the legs off a pair of her designer jeans.

"What's she up to now?" one of them asked.

"It looks like she's making a pair of cut-off hot-pants," one of the assistants replied as Rachel stood up and held the shortened jeans up to her waist.

She looked them up and down, sizing them up for further adjustments. Bedroom-cam 2 zoomed in for a profile shot of her backside.

It's about time she got out of those dungarees, that's for sure, thought the camera operator.

A small crowd of assistants, junior assistants and runners formed round the bedroom-cam 2 monitor in eager anticipation of Rachel modelling her new cut-off shorts.

She proceeded to cut the legs of the shorts even shorter. She then cut out the crotch seam and split the sides, right up to the belt loop. She then looped a belt through the waist band loops and put what was left of the modified jeans around her waist.

"Those aren't hot-pants anymore, she's making the world's smallest mini-skirt. Rex will have a stroke if she wears that round the house" a junior assistant said, not taking his eyes off the monitor, "We'll have every red-blooded male in the country from school to retirement home watching this."

The production assistants watched on through their monitors as the camera operators zoomed in on Rachel as she made some final adjustments to the jeans which were now not much more than the depth of the two back pockets.

"That's not going to leave much to the imagination," one of them sighed.

Rachel wrapped the belt around her waist over the top of her dungarees then she twisted the modified jeans around until the back pockets were at the front. She then reached down beside her bed and carefully placed her collection of screwdrivers and pliers into the pockets.

"I don't believe it," the junior assistant said disappointedly, "So much for the skimpy mini skirt, she's just made herself a bloody denim tool belt."

As the early weeks went by, Rachel was almost permanently in her pair of blue workman's dungarees and her tool belt was never far away, usually slung across the headboard of her bed or hanging in the kitchen ready for the next little job around the house. Squeaky doors, leaking taps and broken cupboards, she repaired them all. In her second week in the house, she had asked for the additional tools necessary to repair the house washing machine and with the aid of a technician's manual, she had soon identified the problem as a pair of soiled underpants jammed in the waste water outlet that had seized the drive mechanism. She replaced the broken drive belt and reassembled the washing machine much to the amazement of the production team and her fellow celebrity housemates.

Rachel added the pliers, adjustable spanner, hammer and duct tape to her growing kit of tools in her denim tool belt.

At the start of week three, Opal had mistakenly left the freezer door open before going to bed and the celebs awoke the next morning to a flooded kitchen and a freezer full of defrosted food. The week's supply of frozen microwave ready-meals and pizzas was ruined. In Opal's defence, it was a genuine mistake but the other celebrities ganged up, turned on her and a spiteful row of accusations and counter accusations broke out. Grant had fuelled the flames even further by having the Voice announce that there would be no resupplies that day.

While the verbal slanging match ensued in the living room, Rachel quietly went through what was left in the kitchen cupboards and fridge-freezer, placing items of food in front of her on the kitchen work-surface next to the hob and oven. It didn't amount to much. Most, if not all of the frozen food was inedible now and would have to be thrown away. There were a few packs of defrosted beef mince but that was about all that was safe to eat. There were half a dozen eggs and a few tomatoes, some left over salad and some mixed herbs. The vegetables amounted to two onions, a lettuce and a bag of potatoes. In the bread bin she found some buns and an unopened packet of Jacob's cream crackers. She stepped back and summed up what was there to make a meal.

Grant checked the monitors and flicked the live TV feed between the argument in the living room and Rachel in the kitchen. Kitchen-cam 2 zoomed in on Rachel as she sorted through the mixed herbs and vegetables.

"Stay with kitchen-cam 2," Grant instructed, "Focus in on Miss Goody-Two-Shoes but keep the living room argument in view."

Kitchen-cam 2 focused on Rachel while living-room cam 3 monitored the Opal argument and Grant switched the live feed between the two cameras. Most of the language from the living room was silenced out due to the multitude of four-letter words while the sound from kitchen-cam 2 was of Rachel quietly humming to herself as she started to cook. Rachel found some parsley and chopped it into fine pieces on the chopping board and then placed it in a large mixing bowl. She then took the cream crackers out of their packet and broke them into very tiny pieces before placing them into the mixing bowl with the parsley. She added a dollop of mustard to the mix and added three eggs for good measure. Kitchen-cam 2 zoomed in on the mixing bowl as Rachel used a wooden spoon to mix the ingredients together. Rachel sliced the potatoes into wedge shaped chunks, leaving the skins on and sprinkled on a dash of salt and pepper and what was left of the parsley. She then placed the seasoned potato wedges on a lightly greased tray and put them in the oven.

Rachel then added the beef mince to the bowl, added a touch of salt and pepper and mixed all of the ingredients together with her hands. She separated out ten equally sized portions and gently pressed and squeezed them into round shaped meat patties about ¾ of an inch thick. She then spread a thin layer of olive oil over them and put four of them into a griddle pan that she had been pre-heating on one of the hobs. The patties sizzled in the olive oil and their delicious, herby aroma drifted from the kitchen to the living room. The argument soon came to a stop as the celebs' noses led them towards the kitchen. Opal took the opportunity to retreat from the living room argument and joined Rachel at the worktop where kitchen-cam 2 zoomed out slightly to capture Opal watching Rachel with interest as she flipped the patties.

"No time to stand around, Opal, would you mind slicing up those onions and tomatoes for me?" Rachel said as she flipped the meat patties over again.

The aroma that filled the house was absolutely mouth-watering.

"Okay", replied Opal, relieved that at least one person was not shouting at her.

"Knives and forks are in the drawer over there and plates are in the cupboard," Rachel added.

Opal soon became a willing sous-chef and the pair of them worked together preparing the meal, while an ever growing number of celebrities crowded around the kitchen. Grant switched the live feed between kitchen-cam 1 and 2, following the pair as they moved around the worktops, hobs and oven.

Rachel then split the bread rolls by hand and lightly toasted them in the frying pan before arranging them on the plates that Opal had prepared. She then took the lettuce, tomatoes and onions that Opal had sliced and placed them between the toasted rolls. Finally, she flipped the meat patties over one last time until they were perfectly cooked.

"I've done enough for all of us," she said to the crowding celebs, "Grab a plate!"

From natural ingredients she had just created live on TV to an audience of tens of millions, the perfect hamburger. Grant sighed, he had not achieved the emotional breakdown he had expected, what he was witnessing was an emotional bounce-back of epic DIY and culinary proportions.

By week four, the official viewing figures indicated that

Rachel had a huge following from regular *Star Struck* viewers who had tuned in to see what she had been fixing or cooking that day. In addition, the polls indicated that she was attracting a huge number of viewers from demographics that would not have usually watched the show. Pensioners on tight budgets switched over from daytime quiz shows to copy her simple but delicious recipes for their evening meals and The Daily Mail had recently printed Poppy's best ten recipes, with her lasagne voted the best dish for value and natural goodness.

Busy housewives no longer had to nag their husbands, they learned from Rachel how to disassemble toasters, unblock vacuum cleaners and change fuses for themselves. Sales across the nation's DIY stores increased considerably after Rachel had taken up one corner of the celeb-house decked patio and repaired the wooden sub-frame live on primetime TV. A million and a half new *Star Struck* viewers watched, learned and planned decked patios of their own.

When she was not fixing things or cooking meals, Rachel had kept herself busy in the garden. She had asked the Voice for some gardening tools and she tended to the flowerbeds around the perimeter of the artificial grass lawns. She had even planted a small vegetable patch next to the garden shed which in turn attracted a new audience of keen gardeners who had switched over from their regular gardening programmes to watch Rachel's unique and rather fresh approach to gardening.

Week on week, Rachel had drawn in a wider and ever increasing number of viewers. Channel Nine estimated that viewing figures were up by 35%, which in turn meant 25% additional revenue from advertisers and the key sponsor, MegaCorp.

The pressure from the network to keep her in the show annoyed Grant. In the first seven weeks she had become a one woman viewer-magnet and not for the reasons he had planned. Ok, he thought to himself, Poppy can wait, I'll at least get one of the idiots out this weekend, then we'll get Eva Carrs in the show for some matrimonial sparks with Rexy-boy. Then I'll figure out some way to expose some dirt on Miss Poppy-Goody-Two-Shoes.

Grant left the meeting room and returned to the main production room, where he watched the live-camera feeds of all five of the celebrities taking the test. He scanned through the monitors, checking on their progress.

Opal and O-Zone were clearly struggling. He looked at the monitor displaying the camera-feed of Poppy and he zoomed in on her test paper.

Bugger, he thought, even her bloody handwriting is neat.

One Week before the Power Crisis:

Monday 16:15Hrs

Standing in front of the production room monitors, Grant watched the celebrities fidget uncomfortably as they worked their way through the test and he watched them scratch their heads and chew their pencils in frustration. He smiled to himself as they feverishly crossed out their answers and scribbled in new ones.

After fifteen minutes, Grant instructed the show's Voice to make an announcement to the house.

"*Star Struck* hopes all of you pass the test because this is a team task. If the team passes the test, there will be a reward. If you fail, there will be a forfeit for you all. You have thirty minutes left."

Opal started to panic at the thought of a forfeit. She realised she had spent fifteen minutes doing next to nothing. One of the house high-definition video cameras zoomed in on Opal and focused on her test paper. Doodles of love hearts and little flowers adorned the test paper where there should really have been answers to maths questions. She furiously started to rub out her kindergarten art-work and stared at the first question.

Question 1.

> A radio costs £7.65.
>
> Sanjay buys a radio and two batteries. Sanjay pays £8.85.
>
> How much does one battery cost?

Opal knew she was way out of her depth and knew she had next to no chance of guessing the right answer. The numbers were way too complicated so she reverted to counting on her fingers. She had one eye shut and her tongue pressed firmly inside her cheek as she concentrated on her counting. She worked her way from little finger to thumb as she mouthed the numbers to herself but she lost count and had to start again.

It was not looking promising for Opal and neither was it looking good for Sanjay and the price of his batteries.

Double O-Zone hunched over his test paper and wrapped one arm across the top of it in an effort to stop the others from seeing his answers, not that this would have done them any good, his answers were a muddled mix of smudges, crossings out and random guesses. Grant spotted him looking over at Opal's paper and he clicked his fingers to get the attention of the Voice.

"Star Struck will not tolerate housemates copying from one another!" the Voice boomed through the house. Opal caught Double O-Zone looking at her answers.

"Oi, what did you have for breakfast, Cheatabix?"

"Bugger off," hissed O-Zone, "I ain't that desperate, you is a Grade A thicko, not me, innit."

"Talk to the hand," Opal said, as she gave O-Zone the stereotypical US Chat-Show diva head-shake.

Rex and Tony were not doing much better than Opal. As they worked through the test paper, they tried to remember something from all those wasted hours they had spent doodling and daydreaming their way through school. The time passed very quickly as they struggled with the basic geometry, algebra and arithmetic questions.

Rex had made better progress through the test paper than Opal and Double O-Zone and he was up to question nine. At the expense of being considered un-cool, he had replaced his trademark wrap-around yellow tinted sunglasses for his prescription reading glasses, but it made the answers no clearer, he was clueless. His brain just did not engage.

Question 9.

Three matchsticks have the same length as five bottle tops.

How many bottle tops will have the same length as 12 matchsticks.

Rex especially struggled with this one. Matchsticks and bottle tops, he thought to himself, they are kidding, right? His life had been one all-night party after another and he had crashed out unconscious many, many times, surrounded by overflowing ashtrays and empty beer bottles and now that wild lifestyle had come back to haunt him. Bottle tops and matches? He had often woken up in a pool of spit and vomit with bottle tops stuck to the side of his face but that was no help to him now. It dawned on Rex that all those years of inhaling cigarette smoke had slowly kippered his brain and his alcohol induced semi-comas had evidently destroyed what remaining functioning brain cells he had. Simple multiplication was beyond him, he took off his glasses and rubbed his eyes in despair. He felt very old and very dull.

"You have five minutes left," said the Voice.

The celebrities frantically scribbled down their last attempts at guessing an answer.

Grant loved all this because he loved picking on them. They were his special little lab-rats in a big glass cage and he could prod them whenever he wanted to, with a metaphorical large pointy stick. The best bit was that twenty five million people watched him do it.

After five minutes the Voice boomed out new instructions.

"Housemates, the test is over. Please stop writing."

The housemates put their pencils down. Opal glanced at Double O-Zone and then at his paper. "You've not put your name down so just put *idiot*, they'll know whose it is."

Double O-Zone threw his pencil at Opal which hit the table and bounced harmlessly away.

"And you throw like a girl!" she added.

The pushing and shoving started up again between them but was interrupted by the Voice.

"Housemates, your papers will now be marked," the Voice said, "Please make your way to the Chat-Room."

The five celebrities made their way to the Chat-Room and huddled together in the confines of the small padded room. This time Rex had won the battle for the comfy chair and they all stared at the TV camera in silence, waiting for the Voice. The TV camera stared silently back at them.

"Place your papers through the communication hatch," the Voice said.

The celebrities passed their papers forward to Rex, who put the papers through the hatch. It was the type of hatch used in banks and petrol filling stations where money is passed into a chute under a glass window, except in this case, the window was a one-way mirror. They never saw the production crew on the other side.

In the Chat-Room, they waited anxiously. Double O-Zone tried the door to get out but it was locked.

"The lights tell you it's locked, you idiot," scorned Opal.

Double O-Zone sucked air through his teeth and pointed both index fingers with thumbs up like little pistols at Opal in the standard hip-hop gangsta pistol pose and snarled "I ain't no idiot!"

Before Opal could respond with more name-calling, Rex interrupted.

"That's grammatically a double-negative," corrected Rex, "So that does make you an idiot," he laughed.

Neither Opal nor Double O had any idea what a double-negative was. Double O-Zone switched from picking on Opal to picking on Rex.

"You is too old and fragile to be patronalising me, grandpa!"

Rex threw his head back and laughed, "It's patronising, not patronalising!"

"Whatever," Double O-Zone sneered, "But you better watch your mouth, old-man, you is proper testing my patience."

"If you could spell *patience* I'd be worried," snorted Rex.

While Rex and O-Zone argued with each other, Opal's mind clicked into gear and it dawned on her this was a team challenge and because she was pretty confident that she had failed, she thought a bit of diplomacy would be a good idea. Perhaps she should promote some team solidarity.

"Look," she said, "Under the circumcises, I fink we should all stick together, it's a group test...."

A confused Rex interrupted Opal.

"Under the what?" he asked.

"The circumcises," said Opal.

"The circumcises?" sniggered Rex," That's a bit of a *cutting* remark, isn't it?"

"Yeah, grandpa, under the circumcises, innit."

Tony Tayburn stepped in to help Opal, "I think you mean *'Under the circumstances'*, Opal, dear."

Team solidarity and diplomacy was forgotten in an instant, Opal opened up a new offensive on the Tayburn front.

"Don't you call me *'dear'* in your hoity-toity stuck-up toff voice, who the bloody hell are you anyway? Who are you, eh, Mister I'm a big MP, I talk all posh an' all that!"

A taken aback Tony Tayburn tried to defend himself.

"I assure you I was merely trying to....."

"Yeah, well, don't, alright?" interjected Opal with a blunt, to-the-point threat backed up with her usual U.S style diva head shake and wagging finger.

The mood darkened in the Chat-Room with nerves and tempers on a knife-edge. It was rare for Rachel to get involved in their squabbling, but in the tight space of the Chat-Room she had no choice.

"I think the test was just the first part of something bigger and there's more to come," she said quietly, "Some of us, probably all of us, are in for a rough time."

"You're not wrong there, luv," said Rex.

These profound words struck home and the others went silent as they considered what could be in store. Rachel's mind didn't dwell too much on the test, she was preoccupied with finalising plans she had long been preparing. If all went to plan, she would be out of this celebrity mad-house very soon.

Meanwhile, in the production room, the housemates' test papers were given to five crew members who checked through the answers before passing the final grades to Grant. He thumbed through the papers, shaking his head in disbelief at the scrawled attempts to answer primary school maths questions.

Only one celeb had passed their Key Stage 2 SAT test, the other four had failed. Grant's initial disgust soon turned to delight. Instinctively, he put his tongue over the front of his bottom teeth, pushing his bottom lip out from the inside. As his face contorted he made a deep, patronising 'Durrrrrrrgggghhhhhhh' sound, the universal playground gesture used by kids to mock another kid's stupidity.

"You over-rated, underachieving, brain-less numb-skulled, bunch of idiots," he scorned.

He turned to his team.

"Get into the house and collect up all their alcohol and cigarettes. Check the video archives for their secret stashes, we already know Double O-No-Brains has got half a bottle of Smirnoff under his mattress and that old codger, Rex, has got a week's worth of Marlboro's hidden in his cowboy boots."

While the four celebs stood huddled together around the chair in the tiny confines of the Chat-Room, a small army of house-operatives searched through the celeb's belongings. Their hidden stashes of fags and booze were collected up into two large bin bags and removed from the house. All that was left in the fridge was milk and orange juice.

Satisfied that the house was now clear of nicotine and alcohol, Grant put the next stage of his plan into action. Having four celebs fail the test was better than he had hoped for, he had just needed Opal and O-Zone to fail. That had been the plan and he stuck to it.

"Housemates," the Voice said sternly, "*Star Struck* is disappointed in your results. Two of you have failed the test so therefore, as a house, you all failed the task."

The Voice paused for dramatic effect while the celebrities considered their fate.

"As a result of the poor test results, all cigarettes and alcohol have been removed from the house."

It took a moment for the stark announcement to filter through to the celebs still enclosed within the Chat-Room.

"Oh my god", shouted Opal, "That's *soooo* unfair!"

"You is kidding me, right? That's bang out of order, innit!" added Double O-Zone.

Tony Tayburn turned sideways and faced the soft padded wall of the Chat-Room and started to bang his head on the sound-proofing. "Heavens," he softly moaned, "That's just too much."

"Well, I isn't standin' for it, it's infringement of my eurohuman rites or summin, innit!" Double O-Zone added as he kicked the soft padded wall beside Tony.

Tony continued to bang his head, "No, no, no," he moaned, in time to the self inflicted blows.

Opal pushed past the others and sat on the arm of the chair next to Rex, staring into the camera.

"What we gotta do to get them back?" she demanded from the silent staring camera in front of her. "What we gotta do?!"

The camera stared silently back with its unblinking eye.

"What we gotta do?" she pleaded.

"Keep it real, you is embarrising yourself," Double O-Zone said to Opal who was getting angrier by the second.

"Don't tell me to keep it real, it's your fault we failed!"

"My fault it ain't. I is well in with the maffs, you is the one with no clue what to do," O-Zone was quite surprised he managed to rhyme a rap that nearly made some sense.

"Are you calling me fick?" Opal stood up and pushed O-Zone hard in his chest, "I ain't the fick one 'ere, I passed the test, proper like."

The enormity of the no-nicotine prohibition slowly dawned on Rex and he jumped up from the chair and launched at Opal. He could hardly contain his temper.

"Let's face it, you really don't know your arse from your elbow and you sure as hell don't know the first thing about maths. You wouldn't know algebra if it crept up behind you and booted you up your backside!"

Opal retaliated.

"Algebria! What's algebria got to do with maths? Algebria's in Africa innit?"

Rex shook his head in a mix of pity and disbelief, "That would be Algeria. Algeria is a country in North Africa. Algebra is what you missed when you bunked off school to watch daytime kid's TV. I can't believe you are so thick, I reckon you must still struggle with the plot of Pingu."

"I may not be able to speak proper but I'm more intellingent than you, grandpa."

"Yeah, of course you are, luv," Rex laughed, "I must have missed seeing you on University Challenge."

"More like Universally Challenged," Double O-Zone added with a sarcastic laugh, pleased with his clever play on words.

Opal gave up on words and tried to slap Double O-Zone across the face, he dodged backwards and Opal's palm followed through and caught Rex a stinging smack on his left ear. Deafened and slightly shocked, Rex stood up and lunged for Opal as she ducked behind the back of the chair. Double O threw his head back and laughed at Rex.

"You is gonna need to be quicker, old man."

Tony Tayburn made a feeble gesture of diplomacy and tried to get in between the fighting pair but only succeeded in pushing them tighter together. He gave up and pinned himself back in a corner to avoid getting caught up in the brawl.

"Oh, right, I suppose this sort of thing is funny in your '*hood,*" Rex said.

He poked Double O hard in the ribs causing Double O to double up.

Through clenched teeth he hissed at Rex a veiled threat of revenge, "I ain't forgotten what you did with those toilet blocks, I is going to knock you into next week, Grandpa!"

"Yeah, yeah, yeah," said Rex, "I'm quaking in me boots. You're the bad-boy gangster rapper, a rapper with a silent C."

"That's it, I ain't taking your disrespect no more, you is going to get the beats that you is long deserved."

Double O-Zone threw a left jab at Rex but in the confines of the Chat-Room his elbow caught the soft padded wall and most of the force from the punch was lost. Rex was ready for him and blocked the blow as they pushed and pulled at each other like six year olds in a playground.

Tony and Rachel pinned themselves into the corners of the small room to avoid getting caught up in the mêlée. A wayward kick from Rex missed O-Zone and knocked the tripod mounted camera over and it landed on the floor sideways, still filming the action, albeit at a ninety degree angle. This added a new perspective to the action and a somewhat gritty ambience to the O-Zone v Carrs wrestling match.

In the production room, Grant was barely unable to suppress a sadistic smile, as he watched Rex and O-Zone rolling around on the floor trying to land punches on each other while Opal took opportune pot-shots, stamping on both of them with her bare feet.

Grant switched the live TV broadcast feed to the fallen camera.

In the far corner of the room, Rachel watched as her fellow housemates pushed, pulled, shoved, shouted and screamed insults at each other.

Grant tilted his head to one side and watched her through the fallen camera with interest, he still hadn't quite figured out what made her tick. He had been trying to work on her, to expose her worst traits but the more he tried, the more she excelled. He needed to figure out what motivated her so he could manipulate her. That could wait though, he had more than enough video footage to work with from the other four.

Rachel squeezed passed the flailing arms of Opal and stepped over the writhing bodies of Rex and O-Zone to get to the fallen camera. While the close-quarter battle raged around her, she carefully picked the camera up and placed it upright on its tripod. She took a clean cloth from the top pocket of her dungarees and looked closely into the lens of the camera. The camera continued to film her as she gently breathed on the lens and wiped it clean.

I really don't get what she's up to, Grant thought to himself.

Behind the close-up shot of Rachel, Opal had engaged in the fighting and she had hold of Tony by a handful of his wispy ginger hair, while she stamped repeatedly on Rex's groin. Grant decided that Opal battering Rex's private parts was too much for a TV live feed but it would make a perfect highlight for the later shows so he flicked the Chat-Room door release button and switched the live-feed to the living room.

Rachel was first to notice the door had been unlocked and she quietly left the Chat-Room for the living room, leaving the chaotic celeb-battle behind her.

ONE WEEK BEFORE THE POWER CRISIS:

MONDAY 16:45PM

Peter and Brian's dad, Joe Marshall, had finished work on the farm earlier than usual so that he would not miss the five thirty kick-off. England were playing Poland in a last ditch attempt to qualify for the World Cup tournament and it was one of those nail-biting situations where England, as was usual, had left it all to be decided on this last game. The points table was a muddle of ifs, buts and goal difference permutations. In essence, it boiled down to these hard facts: if it was a draw or a loss, England would fail to qualify for next year's World Cup.

Max was at Peter and Brian's house, their conversation centred on the upcoming game and the new widescreen TV which filled most of the wall above the fireplace.

"What do you think of the new TV, Max?" Peter asked.

"Not bad, it's a lot bigger than ours at home."

"Dad got it for the World Cup next year, he's optimistic, eh?" Peter said laughing.

"Yeah, he's hoping," Max replied, "But I'm not too sure about tonight though, with Ashburn injured we're going to be stuffed up front."

From the living room doorway, Joe joined the conversation.

"The trouble with you youngsters is that you have no faith. You've got to have a little faith. You're both too young to remember Beckham's unstoppable free kick against Greece in '02. It's all about faith, boys, it's all about faith."

"Yeah, dad, is that why you've kept the receipt for the telly, just in case we don't qualify?"

"We won't be needing Curry's fourteen day cooling off period, son, I'm confident we'll win this one. Anyway, enough about the telly, can I get you a beer, Max? A can of Fosters, perhaps?"

Max was puzzled, was he asking this for real?

"Oh, silly me," Joe laughed, "I forgot you're only seventeen. Maybe next year you can have one, for when we win the World Cup."

"Really funny, Mr Marshall," said Max, "You should be on telly."

Joe pointed at the TV.

"Talking of the telly, what's that nonsense you're watching? It looks like tag-team wrestling in a padded cell."

"We're just waiting for the football to start, it's that celebrity TV thing," Max replied, "You know, they all get put in a house together, we're trying to work out if we know any of them."

Joe stepped a few paces forward to get a closer look at the screen to see if he could identify anyone.

"Well that one there, the old guy wrestling with the chap in the deerstalker, looks a lot like a bloke that used to be in a band called Blacksmith."

"Who's that hitting him?" Peter asked.

"I've got no idea, son."

"Nor me," added Max, "But whoever he is, he's just lost his stupid hat."

"I just don't understand who'd be watching this tripe on a daily basis," commented Joe, "They've knocked the camera over with all their bickering. It's a blatant disregard for other people's property, if you ask me. If this is the way primetime TV's going then the TV *can* go back to Curry's."

Peter tilted his head to one side so he could follow the action on screen. He was noticeably distracted and unusually quiet as Rachel moved towards the camera.

"Who's that?" he just about managed to ask.

"She was going out with Dean Ashburn, I think," Max replied.

Peter didn't say anything.

"I saw it on the news," Max said, "They split up because he was playing away from home, if you know what I mean."

"Well he must be a prize chump," was all Peter said, lost in his own little daydream watching Rachel in extreme close up as she lifted the camera and cleaned the lens.

Max nudged Peter out of his daydream and pointed past Rachel to Opal.

"Who is that, Pete?"

"Oh, her, er….I've no idea who she is," mumbled Pete, having been rudely woken from his happy daydreaming.

Joe watched the TV and shook his head.

"I don't get it," he said, "I don't see what the fascination is with watching this nonsense. I could understand people watching it if the people they put in there were properly interesting."

"Like who?" asked Max.

"Well, I'd be more interested in watching it if they put in people like what's-his-name, the one that does QI."

"Stephen Fry?"

"That's him, and that professor who did the series on the solar system."

"Professor Brian Cox?"

"Yeah, just imagine the conversations those two would have. If you then put Chris Packham or Kate Humble in there you would get some intelligent conversation, rather than all that bickering. Perhaps then even your mum would watch it. Mind you, people like that would never go on it, they're out doing something a bit more worthwhile with their lives rather than bickering on TV like a pair of big girls' blouses."

The boys laughed out loud at the big girl's blouse comment.

"Anyway," said Joe, "Where's your mum?"

"She's gone round Aunty Pauline's to watch Springwatch," Peter replied, "She said she's not missing her favourite TV tonight."

Peter returned to his enchanted dreamy world watching Rachel in the celeb-house kitchen. Max thought about what Joe had said and wondered what it would be like on *Star Struck* if Stephen Fry and Brian Cox were discussing the finer points of the universe along with Chris Packham and Kate Humble. It would definitely be a more stimulating conversation than what was happening on the show right now because Opal had joined Rachel in the kitchen and was trying to help her prepare the evening meal. Opal's contribution so far was to ask Rachel if there were pips in potatoes.

This made the two boys roll about with laughter.

"Did she just ask if there were pips in potatoes?" Joe asked, but they were laughing too much to answer.

Joe shook his head in disbelief and went upstairs to change out of his work clothes before the game started. As he passed Brian's room, he stopped at the doorway. Brian was sat, with his back to the door, at a large wooden desk with a row of plastic storage trays spread across its width. The trays were filled with odd lengths of thin coloured cable, various electronic components and a multitude of printed circuit boards. At one end of the desk a large PC monitor was balanced upon a pile of RS Components electronics catalogues and the distinct smell of hot solder filled the room.

"What you up to, son?" asked Joe.

Brian spun around in his swivel chair, in one hand he held a slightly smoking soldering iron and on his head, he had a pair of magnification glasses with small LED torches on either side. In his other hand, he held a pair of tweezers that were gripping a striped resistor with what appeared to be a small red bulb on the end held in place with a small blue crocodile clip.

"Hey, Dad, I'm just finishing this off before the football. These were the bits I was waiting for, I wanted to just check I can get this infra-red module to communicate with the receiver from this……"

It was at this point his dad lost the technical thread of the conversation and he nodded in agreement, trying to look as though he understood what it was that Brian was telling him.

"….and then if that works it should be easy to connect this….."

His dad nodded again and tried to look as though he was keeping up with Brian. He saw something on the desk which looked like a calculator.

"Is that a calculator?" he dared to ask.

"Yeah, if I can uprate the PCB and get a cross polarised diode……"

Joe was lost again. After a short while, Brian had to pause for breath. Joe pointed at a piece of equipment he felt confident he could safely identify.

"Is that a pager?" he asked.

"Dad," Brian sighed, "That is what I've been trying to tell you, the pager and calculator will be able to link together."

"Oh, I get it now. And what will you use it for?"

"Free messages for one thing," Brian replied.

Joe shook his head in mild disbelief at what his younger son was capable of. He ruffled Brian's hair and gave him an approving pat on the back.

"Well done, son, that's great," he said, "But don't forget the game's on. Kick off's in ten minutes. It's England, you know."

"I'll be down after I've done this, ok?"

"Good lad, see you downstairs."

ONE WEEK BEFORE THE POWER CRISIS:

MONDAY 17:15HRS

Near Exeter Airport, in the basement laboratories of MegaCorp's Research and Development building, the bear marked '*Control*' watched with growing concern as his brother swayed gently back and forth, rubbing his left ear on the metal bars of his cage. He remembered the constant ear rubbing he had seen on the three other bears that had left a few weeks ago and he became even more worried. He called out but there was no response, his brother just moved to and fro in time to a steady, silent rhythm that was only in his head.

He was helpless to intervene as his brother had slipped from his usual grumpy self to this terminally depressed state in a matter of weeks and there had been nothing he could do about his decline. He had tried to keep his brother's spirits high but nothing he said could stop him from spiralling into a deeper and deeper depression. The two-legs had been giving his brother special treatments that had helped for a while but they stopped those and his condition had dipped drastically soon after.

It was too much for him to watch this.

He called again and again but his brother did not hear him, he just continued to sway from side to side, drifting further and further away.

One Week Before the Power Crisis:

Monday 19:30Hrs

In the celebrity house a different kind of madness had resulted from the maths test, all of the celebrities were in panic mode, all of them except Rachel.

She felt quite confident that she had passed the maths test, although if her plan worked it did not really matter if she passed or failed because she was now ready to leave the show. After seven weeks of cooking, cleaning, DIY and gardening, Rachel felt quite pleased with her new self, not due to the viewing figures, because after all she was cut off from the outside world and had no idea that she had become the show's main feature. No, Rachel felt pleased with herself for another reason, she felt confident that during the past seven weeks she had shown the world she was not just an air-headed bimbo or just a footballer's WAG. She had proven she had talents of her own.

That had been the first phase of her plan, it now was time to test phase two.

Rachel stepped outside onto the patio, collecting up the gardening tools that she had been using earlier in the day and she headed across the lawn towards the small shed in the corner of the celeb-house garden. As she opened the shed door she glanced over her shoulder at garden-cam 3 which had tracked her walking across the lawn. She went inside and the door swung closed behind her. With the shed door shut, garden-cam 3 lost her from view and the camera operator instinctively tracked the camera around the garden to find another celebrity to film.

Rachel carefully peered out through the shed window. She had already worked out the shed area was not covered by garden-cam 1 and garden-cam 2 was monitoring Opal and Rex as they talked idly, lounging about beside the hot-tub. Garden-cam 3 slowly panned round and found a new target in Double O-Zone as he sat on a sun lounger, picking his feet.

Rachel slowly opened the shed door and stepped out into the garden closing the door behind her. She carefully measured out ten paces keeping tight against the wall heading towards the wooden wheelie bin store. By her calculations, if she stood still, she was now in a camera dead-zone between the arcs of garden-cam 1 and 2. With garden-cam 3 tracking O-Zone, she was now invisible to the outside world and more importantly, the production team. Week eight was going to be different. Now all she needed was a diversion.

One Week before the Power Crisis:

Tuesday 18:00Hrs

Twenty four hours had passed since the house was cleared of cigarettes and alcohol.

Grant had decided he would wait a full day to coincide with primetime viewing before he revealed to the house which of the housemates had failed the test. For now, he was more than happy with the effect the imposed 'no booze and no fags' embargo was having on the celebrities.

Even Rachel wasn't happy. She rarely drank alcohol but she knew it would be hellish without the others having alcohol to calm their nerves and take the edge off their constant bickering. The kitchen cam zoomed in on her and Tony as they sat on the sofa in the living room. Opal and Double O-Zone rushed past them from the kitchen and headed outside into the garden.

Grant tracked them on the monitor for garden-cam 2. O-Zone and Opal had taken their *who-is-the-idiot-debate* to another level and a storm was about to break.

He barked instructions to the production team.

"Get ready for prime-time edit material, focus on Opal!"

"Your mum must have dropped you on your thick, ugly head when you were a baby!" Opal screamed at Double O-Zone.

She overturned one of the sun loungers and launched it at him. He dodged the lounger as it skidded across the wooden decking, hitting the hot-tub with a loud crack.

"Leave my mother out of it, you is the thick one! You spelt your name wrong on the test and it went downhill from there!"

O-Zone wasn't taking any more attitude from Opal, he was teetering on the edge of going nicotine cold-turkey and he picked up a heavy sun lounger cushion and swung it at Opal, she ducked but he caught her with his second attempt.

Grant watched the fight develop on the monitors, "I bloody hate him," he said, under his breath.

Rex came into camera shot with a menacing look in his eye.

"Listen," he said, "If you two don't stop the bickering, I will strangle you both with my bare hands, got it?"

Opal was about to say *"He started it"* when she realised Rex was in no mood to be messed with. The hollow look in his eyes brought on by cigarette and alcohol deprivation had given him the terrifying look of a madman with homicidal tendencies so she did not risk antagonising him. Double O-Zone pushed Opal out of the way and he sulked off to his bed. At least he had a bottle of vodka there he could secretly open later, or so he thought. Rex stared at Opal. She got the message and sulked off to the kitchen, muttering obscenities under her breath.

In the production room, Grant had switched back to living-room cam 3 which was tracking Tony and Rachel who were chatting on the living room sofa.

"When those three start rowing even I could do with a drink," she sighed.

"You're not wrong there," Tony replied, "Anyway, who do you reckon failed the test?"

"I'm not sure, exactly," said Rachel, "I think we'll find out soon enough."

Tony looked outside and watched Rex pacing up and down the patio.

"This is not going to be good," he said, "I can't see those three lasting another three hours, let alone three more days."

Grant reluctantly had to agree with Tony. It was time to

dangle the carrot. He clicked his fingers to get the crew's attention.

"Production meeting room in two minutes," he said, as he tapped his watch.

Grant was already in the meeting room as the rest of the crew filed in and formed up in a semicircle around the whiteboard. Grant was ready to unveil the second part of his plan.

"Right, we all know it was only Miss Goody-Two-Shoes that passed the test but we're going to tell them it was Opal and Double O-Dunderhead that failed."

The crew nodded their approval.

"Then, if our little Darling Buds of May want their fags and booze back then they are going to have to work for them."

"We're putting them out to *work,* Boss?" said one of the junior assistants.

"No, not exactly *work* in the true sense of the word because that would probably kill them. What they are going to have to do is wear this."

Grant's smile turned to a wicked grin as he picked up two zippered suit bags from beside his feet and held them up in both hands. On the front it said '*Elstree Fancy Dress Hire*'.

He then continued to brief the crew. As they listened, some shook their heads in disbelief. The meeting dispersed and the second part of Grant's plan to alienate Opal and O-Zone was put into place. Within ten minutes, the Voice made a general announcement to the house.

"Rex, please come to the Chat-Room."

Rex slowly made his way to the Chat-Room and made himself comfortable in the chair while he waited for the Voice to speak.

"How are you finding it without your cigarettes, Rex?" the Voice asked.

"It's hell and you know it is."

"It must be worse for you not having your secret stash of Marlboro's. Were you planning to smoke them under your duvet, Rex?"

Rex gave the camera the stinky-eye look.

"You bloody know I was."

"So, how are your housemates doing without their cigarettes and alcohol, Rex?"

"Look," said Rex abruptly, "It's a living hell for all of us, not just me. You've made your point, why not give them back?"

"That's what we plan to do, Rex."

A huge feeling of relief washed over him. It was as if two concrete blocks were lifted from his shoulders and he relished the thought of getting some good old nicotine back in his crusty lungs.

The Voice continued, "There are two bags in front of you, Rex. Please open them and take out what is inside."

Rex leaned forward in the chair and unzipped the first bag. He reached inside and produced the front end of a pantomime horse. He looked more closely at the grey tufty, matted fur, the big buck teeth, and the huge eye-lashes.

"It's a bloody donkey," he said, struggling for words, "It's a bloody pantomime donkey."

He reached further into the bag and produced a large white pointed cap with a large red capital D on it.

"That's right, Rex. It's a pantomime donkey suit. The back half is in the other bag and it's for the two housemates who failed the test. They have to wear the suit and the dunce's cap for the next twenty four hours. You and the other two celebrities have to groom the donkey and take it for regular walks around the garden."

Rex stared at the camera with a hollow look in his eyes, he was too old for this nonsense.

"If the donkey is well groomed, you will get your cigarettes and alcohol back. In fact, *Star Struck* will double the amount of alcohol and you and your fellow housemates can have a party after eviction night this Friday."

"And what happens if they won't wear it?"

"Then the ban on cigarettes and alcohol will be extended for another week. You will have to convince them to wear the suit, Rex."

Rex shook his head.

"Rex," asked the Voice, "Do you understand?"

"Yes I bloody do!" he said.

"Then if you understand what's required to reinstate your cigarette and alcohol allowance, you'll need to know who failed the test."

The Voice paused for a few seconds before it gave Rex the results.

"Rex, the two housemates that failed the test were Opal…"

"That figures," said Rex under his breath.

"….and Double O-Zone."

"No surprises, there, then," said Rex as he got up to leave.

Rex left the Chat-Room and returned to the main house and broke the news of the donkey-suit forfeit. He explained that it was the fault of the two people who had failed the test and that if they didn't wear the suit, there would be no booze and no fags for a week for any of them.

Rex then told the group who had failed.

In an instant, each celebrity had decided who was going to be put up for eviction. Opal and Double O-Zone's fate was sealed.

One Week before the Power Crisis:

Wednesday 16:00Hrs

Throughout the previous night, Rex had kept everyone awake with his smoker's cough as he attempted to dislodge the compacted tar in his crusty grey lungs. He had hacked his way almost incessantly through the night into Wednesday morning and the whole house had woken up in a bad mood. Already fragile nerves were dangerously close to breaking point.

Rex, faced with another whole day and night without a good-night fag, had turned his frustration repeatedly upon Opal and the resulting arguments had been particularly spiteful. On several occasions, Opal had sulked off to the bedroom telling anyone that would listen that the whole world hated her. The house cameras had been busy all day zooming in on her puffy, tear-reddened eyes and her smudged *'Stunning Eyes'* mascara.

Twice, the Network bosses had phoned Grant with formal complaints from MegaCorp officials that were concerned with the poor representation of their eye makeup products. Grant had reluctantly agreed to edit out the worst of Opal's makeup disasters but he would however, be keeping in all the day's juicy arguments compacting them into a three-minute perfectly-edited explosion of hate-filled anger and temper tantrums. This edit would be perfect for broadcast before and after the advertisement breaks. It was a sure-fire, guaranteed ratings booster.

For the most part of Wednesday morning, the celebrities had fought off their cravings by drinking copious amounts of black coffee, replacing their nicotine addiction with caffeine. At midday, Grant had pulled them all into the Chat-Room to remind them that all they needed to do was convince Opal and O-Zone to wear the donkey suit and dunce's cap. An argument broke out in the Chat-Room and Grant kept the best bits of the fight for editing, mixing it into the previous edits of the Rex v Opal explosive arguments. While the celebs fought in the Chat-Room, Grant sent a runner into the kitchen to empty out the last of the remaining coffee from the house. He then let the celebs back into the main house.

Grant stood in front of the array of monitors and watched with barely suppressed glee as Opal made herself a cup of coffee with the very last granules from the jar. Before she had a chance to take a sip, Tony and Rex had accused her of drinking *all* the coffee and the fighting and name-calling broke out again, further alienating Opal from the rest of the group.

Tempers remained on a knife's edge all through Wednesday afternoon. There were a few calm periods when the celebrities dozed on the sun loungers but this peace was shattered with outbursts of accusations, recriminations and death threats whenever Rex brought up the subject of Opal wearing the donkey suit.

As the afternoon slipped angrily into early evening, Grant zoomed in on a secretive conversation between the usually mild-mannered Tony Tayburn and the less well-mannered Rex.

"I propose," said Tony diplomatically, "That we use a carrot and stick approach with Opal."

"Good idea. I'll hit her with the stick, you ram the carrot up her…..!"

"Nice thought, but no, I'm not suggesting that at all, Rex," interrupted Tony, "We need to convince her by offering her an incentive."

"I've given up trying to convince the stubborn cow so I say we're going to have to use force, if you get hold of her arms then me and Double O-Clueless will force her into the top half of the suit."

"Right," conceded Tony, "And then I'll do the zip up?"

"Exactly, Tony, my boy, you do the zip up bloody tight."

Rex laughed at their plan, then started coughing and couldn't stop.

"Give her one last chance and then we'll do it, ok," said Tony, patting Rex hard on his back to loosen up the tar in his lungs.

"Okay," Rex hacked, "One last try."

One Week before the Power Crisis:

Wednesday 19:30Hrs

Rex, Opal and O-Zone were on the patio. It had taken Rex no time to convince Double O-Zone to get into the bottom half of the suit. Messing about by the hot-tub, O-Zone was already one half of a donkey, the huge baggy grey furry trousers hung from oversized braces over his shoulders and he looked even more of an idiot.

"These new trousers are the bizness, Rexie-Boy, they is well wicked, geezer, innit. LOL!"

"'ello, what?" replied a confused Rex who chose to ignore the nonsensical words of the strutting rapper, returning to focus on Opal.

"Look, luv, there's no point fighting it, if you don't wear the top half, we're not getting any booze or fags for another week."

"I ain't doing it, no way am I wearing that, I've got my dignitude, ain't I?"

Opal held her hand out for Rex to talk to, pursed her lips and shook her head, diva-style.

Grant watched O-Zone through the monitor of hot-tub cam. Garden-cam 2 picked up on Rex who was way past the end of his nicotine-deprived tether. He pointed at the top half of the pantomime donkey suit lying on the back of the sofa in the living room.

"Look, just put the bloody thing on, you stroppy mare!"

The irony of calling her a mare was wasted on Opal.

"Get stuffed, old man, I still ain't doing it," she replied and sat down on a sun lounger.

She instinctively reached into her pockets for a cigarette because she really needed one. Just one puff to take the edge off. She put her head in her hands and wailed.

"I don't see what the problem is, I've got the rough end, ain't I?" said Double O-Zone, "I've got to put my head up close to her fat ar.."

"That's not going to help matters, son," Rex interrupted.

Kitchen-cam 3 focused in on Rachel who had walked from the sofa to the kitchen. She finished loading the dishwasher and started to clean the worktop surfaces. She sprayed *Clean-n-Brite* on the surfaces and wiped them down, she glanced over at the pantomime donkey suit that was draped over the living room sofa and decided it was time for one final check.

She opened the cupboard below the sink and the waste bin swung out as the door opened. She flipped open the lid and lifted the full black bin liner out, placing it on the kitchen floor. She sealed up the top of the bin liner with a quick knot and shut the cupboard door and glanced up at kitchen-cam 2. She then picked up the bin bag and headed out of the kitchen. Kitchen-cam 2 had seen her take out the rubbish many times before and slowly tracked her as she made her way out of the kitchen area to the living room where living room-cam 2 took over coverage. Rachel passed by Rex and Opal who were still arguing by the sun loungers with O-Zone strutting in a hip-hop style, prancing around in the bottom half of the suit.

Hot-tub cam focused on Rachel as she made her way past the hot-tub heading towards the bin store at the end of the garden where garden-cam 3 filmed her as she opened the bolt that secured the doors of the bin store. With the bolt unlocked, she swung the doors open wide and pulled one of the black wheelie-bins out of the store and lifted the lid, placing the bin bag inside. She pushed the wheelie-bin back but it appeared to be stuck and would not budge. It was not actually stuck at all. As Rachel bent down to see what fictitious object had blocked the wheel, she checked the back of the wheelie-bin store.

At the far end of the store was a set of double doors, identical to the ones on her side and this was where the bins were collected from the other side of the garden's perimeter wall.

She gave the wheelie-bin an extra hard shove as if to free it and pushed it back inside the wooden bin store. She closed the doors and bolted them shut. She glanced up at garden-cam 2 that was tracking her and she made her way back across the garden.

"I need a smoke, so bad. Please put the suit on," Rachel heard Rex say as she walked past.

Rachel headed to the communal bedroom. Bedroom-cam 2 tracked her as she bent down beside her bed and changed from her flip-flops to her trainers. Inside her left trainer she had hidden an item of Opal's clothing and she deftly transferred this item from her trainer to the palm of her hand in one slick movement. She continued to tie her laces with the item scrunched tight in her fist, hidden from view. She stood up and walked towards the bedroom door next to Opal's bed, keeping her hand hidden from the camera. As she walked past the bed, she dropped Opal's bikini bottoms on the floor.

Rachel headed back outside towards the patio, as she passed by the kitchen table she picked up Rex's reading glasses and smoothly slipped them into her dungaree pocket. She walked over to the arguing Rex and Opal and came to an abrupt stop as though she had just noticed something important.

"Your back looks a bit red, Opal, you need some after-sun lotion. There's some on my bed, help yourself."

Opal twisted round and tried to look over her shoulders at her back.

"You don't want to peel," added Rachel.

"Cheers, Pops," Opal replied.

She left a flabbergasted Rex in mid-argument and headed off to the bedroom. Rachel sat on the lounger and joined Rex in conversation.

"Do you think she'll wear it, Rex?" she asked innocently.

"Honey, I need a smoke real bad," Rex said, "Soon she'll be wearing it whether she likes it or not."

Suddenly, there was a loud noise from the bedroom as if someone had overturned a bed. Several beds in fact.

"You utter bastard!" Opal screamed as she stormed out of the bedroom heading towards Double O-Zone at full speed like a demented banshee waving her bikini bottoms wildly above her head.

O-Zone figured she was coming for him, but he had no idea why, he looked even more clueless than usual.

"Look what he's done, look what he's bloody done!"

She held up her bikini bottoms. Across the back of them in big eye-liner printed letters was the word LARD ARSE. O-Zone could see that Opal meant business. He quickly backed away but he tripped up in the baggy donkey suit trousers and fell over backwards. Rex forgot about his nicotine craving and laughed out loud.

"You've done it now, lad, she's gonna kill you."

His laughter brought on a smoker's uncontrollable coughing fit and he bent double, hacking and coughing up phlegm.

"It wasn't me," O-Zone blurted out, getting awkwardly back up onto his donkey-feet, "Why do you always blame me?"

"I believe him, Opal," Rex quipped, "He can't spell lard, let alone...."

Opal cut him short, she wasn't listening.

"Two can play at that game!" she screamed and stormed over to the kitchen and opened up the cutlery drawer where she found a pair of scissors. She then marched into the bedroom, scissors thrust forward, opening and closing the blades, cutting through the air.

"What have you done this time, you eedjit," Rex was still laughing, "She's lost it, good and proper."

"I ain't done nuffink!"

"There you go again, with that double-negative," Rex said sarcastically, "You'd better check on what she's up to."

But O-Zone didn't need to because flying out of the bedroom doorway came his deerstalker, missing one of its ear flaps, closely followed by Rex's Armani jacket which had been roughly remodelled into a sleeveless waistcoat.

Tony, Rex and O-Zone looked at each other in panic and they fell over themselves as they ran to the bedroom to rescue the rest of their clothes.

Rachel stayed where she was because her diversion was going to plan. She glanced up to check that the cameras followed the others and then picked up her tool belt and headed over to the garden shed. She stopped at the shed door, opened it and went in. Peering out of the window she checked the position of the wall mounted cameras. The remote operator of garden-cam 2 soon lost interest in filming the shed door and panned around to provide a long distance shot back towards the house where it filmed Rex wrestling the scissors from a kicking and screaming Opal. Garden-cam 3 tracked O-Zone as he hopelessly searched for his other earflap on the patio.

Tony intervened and tried to hold onto Opal's legs but he took a well-manicured toe-punt to the chin.

This was the total diversion she needed. Rachel opened the shed door and followed her planned route to the camera dead-zone beside the bin-store. She knew she did not have a lot of time, she bent down and released the bolt on the bin doors. She opened the doors and wedged herself in with the bins and reached around, closing the doors behind her. Using her pliers, she gripped the bolt through the wooden slats and locked the doors from the inside. She then squeezed between the bins to get to the doors at the back of the bin store where she used her pliers to unlock them in the same way. She peered through the wooden slats to check it was clear and then pushed one of the bin-store doors slowly open. When she was sure no one had seen her, she shut the doors behind her and closed the bolt. She looked around to get her bearings and saw she was in the *Star Struck* staff car park, exactly as she had figured. With her back pressed firmly against the perimeter wall she edged along keeping out of view of the security cameras but these were focused on keeping members of the public out, not celebrities in, so they pointed away from the perimeter wall.

Rachel headed to her left keeping in the shadows. She figured somewhere along this wall was a bike shelter because when she had been in the garden, she had heard members of the production team cycling past, the rear wheels of their bikes clicking as they freewheeled on the other side of the wall. She moved slowly and steadily along the wall and reached the edge of the shelter without crossing the field of view of any of the post–mounted cameras.

She slipped inside the bike shed and found a rather nice mountain bike but opted for a shopper type bike with a basket on the front. It was unlocked so she would not need to force open a padlock with the pliers after all. She quickly took off her dungarees and underneath she had on jeans and a plain green sweater. She tied back her hair into a tight pony tail and she put Rex's reading glasses on, which were a bit too large and needed to be pushed right back to stop them slipping off her nose. It was the best she could think of as a disguise.

It took a moment for her eyes to adjust to the lenses then she backed the bike out of the shelter, leaning down to turn on the bike's front and rear lights. She had planned out to the nth degree how to get this far but she did not know what was on this side of the perimeter wall so she had no plan on how to get past the car park security hut and barriers.

"I'll have to bluff it," she said to herself.

She rode steadily towards the security hut weaving between the arcs of the security cameras as best she could. Fifty metres from the hut, she flicked the front wheel up and mounted the pavement and rode at a fair pace towards the barrier. The security guard glanced up and saw her.

Here we go, she thought, it's too late to turn back.

She rode one-handed and reached into the basket on the handlebars. She rummaged around and pulled a cleaning cloth from her dungarees that were stuffed in the basket. She put it up to her face as if she was blowing her nose.

The security guard had seen her so he stood up and walked a few paces to the door of the hut with his clipboard in his hand. He shone his torch in her direction as she wobbled towards him, still riding one-handed, with the other hand covering her face with the cloth.

As she cycled closer she put on her best phone-in-sick voice, "Feel awful. Gudding dome early," she mumbled through her pretend blocked nose.

"Oh, you'd best get off home, love," he said as he waved her through the barrier, "And wrap up warm."

"Dank you," she said through the cloth as she passed by him, "I will do."

Once through the barrier, Rachel did not look back. She had avoided the media and left the show on her terms. She picked up pace and when she was a safe distance from the hut she took off Rex's glasses and threw them into the bike's basket. It took a while for her eyes to refocus on the road ahead but she soon recognised Elstree High Road.

She was now heading west and towards home where she could start her new non-celebrity life.

One Week before the Power Crisis:

Wednesday 21:00Hrs

Grant was apoplectic and the veins in his forehead throbbed dangerously close to bursting. His anger was vented like the exhausts on a harrier jump jet in the direction of the junior assistant that stood before him.

"Why have you suddenly become a master of the bloody obvious? I know she is missing, you mindless cretin. What I want to know is how she got out and where the bloody hell she is now!"

Rex, Double O-Zone, Tony and Opal had been sent to the bedroom and locked in, while the house was searched. The live feeds focused on them as they sat on their beds discussing Poppy's disappearance and what it could mean for them.

Grant peered over the shoulder of the assistant monitoring garden-cam 2. On the screen was another assistant who spoke to them through a walkie-talkie.

"No sign. The last we saw was her go in the shed and now she's disappeared."

Grant snatched the walkie-talkie and shouted, "She's got to be somewhere. Bloody find her!"

Another assistant called over to Grant, "The Network's on the phone, Boss, they want to know what's happening."

On the other side of London, Rachel had already boarded the first Inter-City train that was leaving Paddington and heading for Exeter.

Grant swore and kept swearing until he went blue in the face and was forced to stop and take a breath. He then swore some more for good measure. With only four celebrities and no chance of the ex-missus Rex coming in next week he was a celebrity short, not enough to finish the show's next three weeks.

"Get me Rex's Ex on the phone now!" he shouted.

Grant had taken over the search for Poppy and had already narrowed it down to the wheelie-bin store when news over the walkie-talkie reported that a bike was missing. The search widened and the security guard at the car park entrance was questioned. It all was too late though, by the time they had figured how she had escaped Rachel was already walking up the driveway of her dad's house. It was well past midnight when she rang the doorbell.

When he opened the door, Martin Purnell could not believe his eyes and he struggled for words. "Poppy, are you alright, is everything ok, aren't you supposed to...."

She interrupted him with a huge hug, "I've had enough of that madness, Dad. It was time I left the show."

"But how did you get out?" he asked.

"On my own terms," she said proudly, "I got out without them noticing, I escaped through the bin-store in the garden."

"No way, that's my girl!" he said, stepping to one side to let her through the door.

"So what now for Poppy?" he said, shutting the door behind them.

"Ummm, I think I prefer Rachel, Dad."

He was glad to have his Rachel home, "I think I do too," he said.

One Week before the Power Crisis:

Thursday 11:00Hrs

Grant paced up and down the production room. Pacing helped him think and he had to come up with an answer to the missing celebrity pretty soon or the future of the show was in the balance. What he needed was celebrity eye-candy to keep the viewers watching. What he needed was to bring forward the planned entrance of Eva Carrs. Earlier that morning, Grant had despatched one of his senior assistants across London to meet with her management but the four-way phone conversation was not going at all to plan.

Eva was relaxing on a leather-clad reclining chair wrapped in a fluffy white bathrobe, having a pedicure at her plastic surgeon's health and fitness spa located deep within the Malvern Hills. She still had crêpe bandages around her face and soft cooling gel pads on her puffy, bruised eyes and eyebrows. (Or were those eye-lashes, it was still hard to tell the difference).

Eva lay on the chair while a specialist team from the spa pandered to her every need. Two nail-technicians delicately manicured Eva's fingernails while a third beautician held a mobile phone to Eva's ear. Another hovered close by with a pre-lunch double gin and tonic on a silver tray.

Eva purred into the mobile phone, "I'm just not ready for my public, darling."

Her manager relayed the message to Grant's assistant that Eva was still in rehab.

The assistant updated Grant.

Grant didn't have time on his side, his patience was wearing paper-thin.

"I don't care if her manager says she is in rehab, I want that bleached-blonde, bubble-headed, pout-mouthed trollop in this studio within twenty four bloody hours!"

The production assistant on the other end of the phone relayed Grant's words to Eva Carrs' management who delicately put Grant's request to Eva.

"Dahhhling," said a pampered Eva, "I am just so not ready for an appearance, it will have to be next week, Doctor McNutt says I need to rest."

The assistant then relayed their response back to Grant, who was not accepting no for an answer.

"I don't care what Doctor-Bloody-Numb-Nuts says, whoever the bloody hell he is. She's signed a contract and she's going to be on the bloody show. Tell her management that we'll sue!"

Grant was bluffing.

The assistant relayed Grant's message to Eva's manager. There was a pause while the manager spoke with Eva.

Then the assistant updated Grant.

"What?!" snapped Grant, "They reckon they can back out of the contract due to health reasons? Plastic bloody surgery is not a health reason!"

Grant was losing control, "Tell her bloody management that if she's not….."

"Boss?" the production assistant said, trying to get a word in edgeways.

"….in our make-up room and in pre-…." Grant ignored the assistant and continued with his threats against Eva Carrs

"Boss?" tried the assistant.

"…production briefing ready to walk down those bloody stairs to the house, I'll…."

"Boss," pleaded the assistant.

"What is it?"

"Boss," said the production assistant, "Eva's hung up."

Grant threw his phone across the production room where it narrowly missed a cameramen filming from behind one of the mirrors overlooking the celeb bedroom. The sudden noise startled Opal and Tony who were still in their beds talking about the missing celebrity, Grant watched them on the monitors as they got up and crept over to the mirror to see if they could see through.

"Bloody idiots," Grant sighed, "Thick as fairground goldfish, all of them."

A junior runner plucked up the courage and dared to tap Grant on the shoulder.

"Boss?" he said.

"What now!"

"The Network management are on the line, they want to know what we're doing about…."

"I know, I know, I bloody well know what they want to know, they want to know where our bloody missing DIY Diva is. That's what I bloody well want to know as well! Has anyone found her yet?"

Grant was met with silence and shrugs.

"Go on make my bloody day, one of you please tell me that you know where she is."

"Er….no, Boss," said the junior runner, "But the Network's still on the line, what shall I tell them?"

One Week before the Power Crisis:

Thursday 11:30Hrs

Rachel was still in bed at her dad's house.

Martin Purnell had called into the office to say he was working from home and that he would be in later in the afternoon.

Rachel came sleepily downstairs, yawned, and joined her dad in the kitchen for a late breakfast.

"Did you sleep ok?"

"Great thanks," she replied, stretching, "I was out like a light, what time is it?"

"It's nearly midday."

"Really? Aw, I'm sorry I must have been pretty tired. Aren't you late for work?"

" I said I would be in later, I wanted to make sure you were ok first."

"Thanks, Dad," she said opening the fridge, looking for some orange juice.

"Everything's still in the same place, cereal in there, teabags in there. You know where it all is, don't you?"

"Yes, Dad, thanks."

"So what now, Rachel?"

"Well, I was thinking I'd stay here for a while, if that's ok with you, just in case the show or the papers are looking for me."

"I think that it goes without saying that they'll be looking for you!"

"Yeah," she said with a deep sigh, "So I'll stay here if that's ok?"

"Of course you can," he said, "Stay as long as you like. What else have you got planned?"

Rachel was rummaging through the cereal cupboard.

"Erm….perhaps we should get some decent breakfast cereal for a start," she said, shaking a bright primary-coloured yellow and blue cereal box with a cartoon chimp on the front. The cheeky-looking chimp held a spoon in one hand and appeared to be enjoying tucking into a bowl of multi-coloured cereal.

Rachel shook the box and checked inside.

"What exactly are *'Mornin' Stars'*?" Rachel asked as she poured what appeared to be brightly coloured pieces of cat litter into a breakfast bowl.

Martin Purnell looked a bit embarrassed.

"It's a MegaCorp kid's cereal," he explained, "It's supposed to get kids up and raring to go in the morning."

Rachel started to read from the back of the box.

"'*Mornin' Stars*'," she said, "Let's see what the ingredients are…"

Martin Purnell looked even more embarrassed.

Rachel read through the list:

"Wheat, ok that's good."

"Maize, that's good too."

"Glucose syrup, that's not so good, is it?"

"Fat Reduced Cocoa Substitute, I don't think that's good at all," she said.

As she read further her frown deepened.

"Hmm, what exactly are *Trisodium Phospate E339, Calcium Phosphate E341, Aspartame and Phenylanine*?"

Rachel read further from the recommended helping guide of 100 grams.

"It says here that these have one gram of fibre and there are twelve grams of sugar per 100 grams!"

Rachel shook her head and sighed.

"Dad, that's the same as three teaspoons of sugar, you are so bad, you're not looking after yourself!"

"They were free from MegaCorp," he tried to explain, "They gave them out as promotional packets."

"That's no excuse. Let me do some shopping, do we still get deliveries out here?"

He nodded that they did.

"I'll place an order for delivery tomorrow evening, as long as you're here to answer the door, ok?" she said, "I'd like to stay hidden for a little while longer."

"That's fine by me," said Martin Purnell, he was enjoying having Rachel back home, "But sooner or later you're going to have to change out of those pyjamas, perhaps you should order up a change of clothes or two as well?"

One Week before the Power Crisis:

"No, we haven't found her yet," said an exhausted Grant, "When we do, I'll let you know."

The voice on the other end of the phone was clearly not pleased and was demanding answers.

"We're working on it, we'll have something for the five o'clock news," promised Grant, who had no idea what he would come up with by then.

He hung up the phone. He had been up for nearly forty eight hours straight, trying to think of a way out of this mess. If it had been a *'standard'* house, he would have had ten thousand wannabe members of the public clamouring to get in the house for their *'fifteen minutes of fame'*. As it was, he just couldn't rustle up a half decent celebrity out of nowhere.

In the far corner of the production room, two assistants had been on the phone to every B-list, C-list and D-list agency trying to find a suitably desperate celebrity who was willing to come into the house on an hour's notice. Even for the most desperate, low-grade celebrity that would be a bridge too far. Grant called over to the assistants for an update. They shrugged and shook their heads.

That option was closed.

Grant had pressured the management of Eva Carrs and he had got as far as her solicitors. That option was closed too.

Time was ticking away, their 7pm to 9pm prime-time slot loomed closer and closer and he had to make a decision.

"The network's on the phone, Boss," said one of his assistants, cupping his hand over the receiver.

"What do those blood-suckers want now?" sneered Grant.

"They're getting more pressure from MegaCorp about viewing figures, they want to know what we're doing."

"Let me think for a second," Grant rubbed his head, hoping a fresh idea would burst forth.

"The network statisticians are saying this morning's figures are down by fifteen per cent and dropping," the assistant added.

That was it, Grant made up his mind.

"Tell them I'll call them back," he said.

The assistant stalled their network bosses.

Grant called out to the assistant called Katy, "Karen, have you still got your man-friend at the Beeb?"

"Yes, Boss, and it's Katy."

"Yeah, whatever, get onto him and leak the news that we've got a celebrity joining us before tomorrow's eviction and the eviction is still on. Drop the hint that it may be Poppy-Goody-Two-Shoes coming back, that should get the viewing figures back up while we sort this mess out."

The Power Overload

Friday 18:35Hrs

At 43 Battersea Road, SE1 2TA, the Reynolds family eagerly awaited *Star Struck* and any news of the missing celebrity.

"What do you reckon, then?" Stacey Reynolds asked her husband.

"It's all planned for publicity isn't it? They used time delay cameras or summin to get her out the house."

"Messes up this eviction and the final show if one of 'em goes early, there's not enough left."

"I heard they are putting someone else in next week to make up the numbers," Gary said, "Rex's ex-missus apparently or they might have got Poppy back."

"Aw," Stacey said patronisingly. She patted Gary's knee, "Eva won't replace your little Poppy will she, love?"

"Laugh all you like, but your bloody cooking's improved these last few weeks," he said, "And get us a beer while you're up, luv."

Stacey sighed, muttered under her breath, pulled herself up from the sofa and headed to the kitchen. Gary leaned forward from his seat and turned the electric fire up a notch. He settled back in the sofa and watched the pre-show MegaCorp-sponsored adverts.

As Stacey walked through the hallway to the kitchen she passed the wall thermostat and instinctively turned the dial up a few degrees to make sure the heating was on. The kitchen's spotlights illuminated an untidy worktop covered with empty ready-meal cartons. She flicked the switch on the kettle. In the opposite corner was a portable TV that was already on and tuned to Channel Nine, ready for *Star*

Struck at 7pm. Stacey opened the fridge door and picked up a carton of milk, reaching deeper into the fridge for a can of beer that was tucked behind a plate of yesterday's pizza. She paid no attention to the TV that was showing the last few minutes of the evening's news.

A Channel Nine news reporter and film crew were broadcasting live from the control centre of Fusion Energy. In the background, behind the reporter, several people at computer terminals were standing up and talking feverishly on their phones. Some had a phone at both ears while they read from their computer terminals and shouted instructions. Behind them, amber warning lights started to flash on a huge map of Great Britain. The reporter faced the camera and warned that power in the grid was at maximum and approaching critical levels. A graphic overlay came up on the TV screen showing a steep graph of energy consumption figures. Behind the reporter, on the large map, one of the warning lights in the South London area turned from flashing amber to a solid red.

The warning was missed by Stacey and twenty five million other viewers, all of them preoccupied with the upcoming drama of a celebrity eviction with the added drama of one of the celebrities missing.

Stacey emptied a few damp tee shirts from the washing machine and placed them into the tumble dryer. Turning the dial to high heat for 60 minutes she slammed the door shut and the dryer started its cycle. The kettle boiled and Stacey returned to the worktop to make her cup of tea. Upstairs in her bedroom was their 14 year old daughter, Kylee. Like most teenagers, Kylee was a devotee of *Star Struck* and her TV was already switched to Channel Nine. She was too busy updating her status on several social networking sites to notice the Channel Nine news report.

Stacey walked down the hall and called from the foot of the stairs to her daughter to remind her that *Star Struck* was about to start. As usual, there was no response. Stacey then took the beer through to her husband who acknowledged it with a grunt of thanks without taking his eyes from the TV. He was watching an advert for a product called 'KwiknSlim'.

"That reminds me", she said, "We need some more of that."

Gary grunted again.

Stacey returned to the kitchen, took a frosty pizza from the freezer, unwrapped it and placed it in the oven, turning the dial to full. She then sat down with her cup of tea at their kitchen table, reached out for the remote and turned the volume up on the portable. The Reynolds family settled down in three separate rooms, to watch an hour and a half of *Star Struck* punctuated, of course, every twelve minutes by commercial breaks. As with most of the viewers across the country, the Fusion Energy warnings went unheeded.

While the three family members sat transfixed and motionless in front of three televisions in three separate rooms, everywhere in the house a multitude of other electrical appliances hummed away, drawing kilowatts and kilowatts of electrical power from a national power grid that was rapidly approaching its limit. While the Reynolds family slowed down to a near stationary sloth-like state in front of their televisions, the only thing moving with any speed in the house was inside the electricity meter. Behind the meter's glass viewing window, a small silver disc was spinning round and round at high speed measuring the rate that electricity was being consumed. Number 43, Battersea Road was just one home amongst the five million other homes in the Greater London area and the Reynolds's irresponsible attitude to energy consumption was replicated millions of times over across London. The city's total energy consumption was at a critical level. As the demand for more and more energy increased, the power grid moved closer and closer to overload.

At 6:54pm, an alarm sounded at Fusion Energy's West London Headquarters. Fusion Energy's computer system had been monitoring the increased demand from London and automatically started the process to transfer additional power from the national grid to the London sub-stations that were demanding more power. Except this time the power did not automatically reroute to London, the national grid, already overstretched by other cities increased power consumption, was at full capacity with no reserve power available.

Back at Number 43 Battersea Road, behind the living room TV cabinet, the over-loaded, eight way extension socket showed signs that things were about to go seriously wrong. The tiny neon power light on the side of the extension socket flickered and dimmed as the power supply to the house abruptly stopped. Two minutes into *Star Struck* the TV's picture flickered then disappeared. Simultaneously, the house was plunged into total darkness and the background hum from a multitude of electrical appliances faded away to an eerie silence.

Stacey broke the darkened silence first.

"Gary!" she shouted, "What's happened to the TV?"

Gary was too preoccupied to answer, under normal circumstances, the priority would have been to find a torch but these were not normal circumstances; it was eviction night. What the Reynolds's needed most was a working TV.

Within seconds of the living room TV going off, Gary levered himself up from the sofa and into the darkness. With surprising agility for a man of his bulk he dodged the coffee table and headed blindly for the kitchen, arms outstretched feeling for the doorway that he knew was somewhere in the inky blackness. With the same urgency, Stacey was up from the kitchen table, heading at speed for the living room. Kylee reacted even quicker than her parents, she had already made her way from her room, feeling along the wall for the banister rail and the first step of the staircase. Once she had found the top of the stairs, she instinctively knew where the next steps would be so that by the time she reached the foot of the stairs, she was travelling at literally break-neck speed to find a working TV.

"Mum?"

"Stace?"

"Gaz?"

With a dull thud and a crack of heads, Stacey, Gary and Kylee collided in the total darkness of the hallway. Winded and dazed all three of them slumped to the floor alongside the broken remains of their TV remotes. It took a moment for Gary to regain his senses and his priorities. He struggled to his feet, slipping and sliding on sharp pieces of broken plastic and half a dozen AAA batteries. With arms outstretched into the darkness he found the doorway to the kitchen and stepped through into the lightless room. He reached out for the worktop and cursed as his knee caught the edge of something hard. He groped along the worktop to the place where he remembered he had left his laptop computer and he prayed he still had some battery life left. He opened the lid and switched it on. He figured he could connect his laptop through his mobile phone to the 3G broadband network so they could see live coverage of the eviction at the *Star Struck* website. The computer's start up sequence seemed even slower than usual. As each agonising second passed by, he knew they would be missing the build up to the eviction. Stacey saw the faint glow of the start-up screen and made her way through the half-light to join Gary in the kitchen. Both of them waited nervously in the darkened silence watching Windows boot up, willing it to go faster.

"Come on, come on, come on," Gary said to the computer as he repeatedly tapped the icon to open the web browser.

Meanwhile, Kylee's head was still thumping from the collision in the hallway and she was seeing stars of a different kind when she flipped open the case of her mobile phone. Alone in the total blackness she stared at its screen, willing the YouTube webpage to open.

Across London, four million people had the same idea. The London segment of the 3G mobile network was immediately overstretched and within seconds it ground to a halt. The network was designed to be fail-safe and to automatically distribute network demand by re-routing IP traffic to data centres in Birmingham and Manchester. Soon, every media server, in every data centre was running at 100% drawing tens of thousands of kilowatts from an already over-stretched power grid. In an instant the rest of the national power grid overloaded and the country's fate was sealed.

Four minutes after the power went off across London, Birmingham was without power. Manchester went down thirty seconds later. One by one, like stacked dominoes toppling over in a line, every city and major town lost power. Within eight minutes, the entire country was plunged into darkness.

Day One after the Power Crisis:

Saturday 08:30Hrs

Most of the village of Witheridge was without power except the outlying farms which had fitted solar panels and wind turbines to generate power for the milking machines. It was ironic that while the country was effectively shut down, it was business as usual for dairy cows.

"If the power isn't back on soon, dad said we'll have to run the house from the cowshed supply," said Brian.

"It's never been off for this long before," replied Peter, "Mum said she heard on the radio that most parts of London are still without power."

"Bristol and Manchester too."

"Yeah, but forget them," said Peter, "What about Tiverton?"

Brian laughed at his rugby-mad brother. Most of the country was still without electricity and Peter's only concern was rugby and his practice that had been cut short when the club's floodlights went out at 7:15pm.

The two brothers continued to walk towards the village square on an errand to get their father a newspaper with any news on the power outage. The people they passed on the way were all discussing last night's power shortage. Across the square was Max. He was waiting for the number 155 bus, sitting on a bench outside the Mitre Pub. Peter and Brian crossed the village square and walked over to join Max at the bus stop.

"Hey, Max, have you got your power back?"

 "No, not yet," Max replied, "My dad went into work early, he was called out to an emergency at the studios."

"The power is down there as well?" Brian asked.

"So my dad says but he called home just before I left to say parts of Exeter are getting power back so I'm going to meet him at work."

"We're off to the newsagents, Dad wants a paper to find out more about the power cut."

All around them in the village square, the conversation was about the power cuts. People swapped stories about what they were doing when the power went off and how they had managed to get by. It was no surprise that *Star Struck* was not mentioned at all.

The number 155 bus appeared and drove past the church towards the square, Max gave the driver a wave and the bus started to slow.

"Are you back later, Max?" asked Brian, "We're ready to test the pagers."

"Professor Brains and his science lab strikes again!" Peter interrupted, "Just head for the smoking solder and smell of burnt circuit boards, Max!" he laughed.

"I should be home about four, guys, I'll see you then," Max said as he boarded the bus and found an empty seat next to a window. He watched as his friends walked off to the newsagents. He tapped on the window to get their attention as he pointed at the sign outside the shop.

"Power Cut Across UK. No Papers Today"

Brian and Peter shrugged then they headed back home across the village square. Max tapped his watch and held up four fingers. Brian gave him the thumbs up.

As the bus wound through the countryside towards Exeter, Max wondered how his dad would be getting on at work. His Dad was a senior technician at the local TV studios of South West TV and he would be working hard to have the computer and video link systems back up and running. Max often went to his dad's work at weekends and he had become a useful, albeit unpaid, extra pair of hands in the IT department.

The bus had to stop for a few minutes to let a convoy of Fusion Energy Land Rovers pass over the narrow bridge at Stoke Canon. Max kept them in view as they took a farm track across the fields driving towards a group of men in fluorescent orange jackets that were standing beneath a large electricity pylon. Half way up the pylon a team of men in harnesses were making their way to the top while the team below loaded toolboxes and equipment into lifting cradles. Max checked further down the valley, following the line of pylons, and saw other teams of engineers busy at work checking and repairing the power cables.

The bus was soon on the outskirts of Exeter but the city seemed very different this morning. There was not the usual Saturday morning shopping rush and it was a lot quieter than normal, except for a chorus of shop alarms that sounded somewhere off in the distance. The bus slowed down to a stop behind another convoy of Fusion Energy Land Rovers so Max decided to get off a stop early and he walked the rest of the way along New North Road towards the offices of SWTV.

"Hi, Max," said Rose the receptionist as he went through SWTV's reception, "Your Dad's up on the third floor, head over to the news studio."

"Will do," replied Max, giving Rose a wave.

"Use the stairs though, we're still getting the odd power cut."

As he passed by the reception desk, Rose handed him a clipboard.

"Can you take this up to your Dad, he left it down here earlier," she said, "And you'd better wear a visitors badge today, we've got Channel Nine and a few other nationals here planning to do a nationwide broadcast. It's all getting a bit hectic up on the news floor!"

"No problem, I'll keep out of their way," Max said as he clipped the SWTV badge to the lapel of his Berghaus waterproof jacket. He put his dad's clipboard under his arm, waved goodbye to Rose and headed over to the stairs.

Max quickly climbed the stairs up to the third floor. As he opened the stairwell door and turned towards the news studio he was immediately swept up by a chaotic group of over thirty reporters and photographers that he didn't recognise, they were definitely not regular SWTV news reporters.

Max was bunched in amongst photographers on the outside of the crowd that held their cameras at arm's length to take photos over the heads of the reporters closer to the centre of the crowd. Flashes from their cameras lit up the corridor making the swirling mass of bodies look like a mini thundercloud and Max was swept along in the storm. Max struggled to keep his balance as he was pushed along with the reporters as they squeezed through the corridor towards the SWTV news studio. To his left, one of the reporters was pushed out of the pack. In a split second the man regained his balance and with a surprising turn of speed and determination, he pushed his way back to the centre, knocking Max to one side. The unmistakable logo of The Sunday Mirror was on his microphone. In the centre of this swirling chaos of cameras, microphones and reporters Max caught a glimpse of a man in a navy blue suit that was being shielded from the press onslaught by an SWTV security guard, both of them were struggling to make headway through the news crews. As he disappeared from view, Max saw the badge on his jacket. The man was from Fusion Energy.

"What are you doing to get power back to London?" the Sunday Times reporter shouted.

"When will the grid be operational?" the man from the Telegraph demanded.

"Why were we not told about the potential overload?" shouted a reporter from the Sun.

The man from Fusion Energy resisted the temptation to tell the reporter from the Sun Newspaper that there had been many, many warnings but no one had listened. He just kept his head down and tucked in behind the security guard.

The reporter from the Sunday Mirror thrust his microphone towards the Fusion Energy spokesman and demanded the question he thought his readers would want to ask.

"When will it be possible to broadcast last night's eviction?"

The Fusion Energy spokesman ignored the questions and stuck closer behind the bulk of the large security guard.

"Move back, please!" the security guard ordered. He knew he had to get the spokesman to the live TV studio in one piece and on time.

"Move back!"

The security guard firmly guided the spokesman using his body and right arm to block the cameras and microphones that were being thrust forward. With his left arm he reached out for the studio door.

Like sharks in a feeding frenzy, the reporters were hungry for answers and the moving mass that surrounded the spokesman closed in even tighter and Max was squeezed against the studio door, his father's clipboard clutched tightly to his chest. Fearing that their exclusive interview opportunity was about to reach the safety of the studio, the reporters made one last desperate attempt to get an exclusive sound-bite from the spokesman.

Without any warning, a stray elbow, probably from one of the photographers, knocked the security guard's hat clean off. The guard, fearing the worst, reached with both hands to check his wig was in still in place. His eyes opened wide as both his hands slapped bare skin and he watched in horror as his hat spiralled to the floor, followed less elegantly by his cherished hairpiece.

"My hair!" he screamed, "Don't step on my hair!"

The security guard had already decided that his pride was more important than protecting the Fusion Energy spokesman so he dived amongst the crowd's sharp stilettos and heavy brogues to rescue his lost hair and dignity. Tripping over the diving guard, a reporter kicked the hairpiece upwards where it landed upon the shoulder of the Daily Mail's most ruthless female reporter who had recently spent two weeks reporting live from the slums and shanty towns of New Delhi. She still had recurring nightmares about unnaturally large and ferocious sewer rats and fearing that she was under attack again from an oversized ginger rodent she instinctively lashed out with a well aimed karate chop that glanced off the hairpiece but caught the spokesman square between the eyes, knocking him to the ground in a crumpled heap with blood pouring from his nose.

The guard, already on all fours, followed the new trajectory of his wig and with arms outstretched, he launched himself after his flying hairpiece. Despite his best aim, he grasped nothing but a handful of fresh air as it slipped through his fingers. The spokesman, semi-dazed from the karate chop, was trying to get back to his feet when the guard's empty, but very heavy fist, caught him square on the chin. His mouth fell open, his false teeth came loose and he slumped to the floor in a crumpled heap. His bottom lip quivered and his loosened dentures dropped to the floor, skipping and bouncing along between the stampeding feet of the reporters.

Determined in his quest to regain his hair, the guard desperately continued his frantic search. He turned to his left and right, slamming into the ankles and knees of the reporters. The Daily Star's reporter managed to avoid the semi-prone guard weaving in between his legs but in doing so, stepped on the slippery bottom plate of the false teeth and he skated head-first into the photographer from the Independent, blind-siding him with a tremendous crack of heads. The Independent's photographer was a hardened professional of twenty years. He had been assaulted many times by the country's best (arguably worst) celebrities so he definitely wasn't going to take being hit by someone from the Daily Star.

"Who the bloody hell do you think you are, you clumsy

clod-footed oaf!" he shouted as he landed a retaliatory blow with his camera on the top of Daily Star's head.

"Don't you bloody hit me!" was the reply, "Just because you come from a lah-dee-dah posh paper doesn't mean it gives you the right to push me....!"

But his threat was cut short by a right-hand jab from the Independent that hit him square on the chin.

For a moment, both men looked at each other in amazement then they started pushing and slapping each other like eight-year-olds fighting in morning break.

On the floor, the guard continued to weave left then right, recklessly bashing hard into legs and ankles.

"Don't step on my hair!" he shouted, pushing out at shoes and ankles that came close to his prized toupée "Get off my bloody hair!"

The crowd of reporters swayed back and forth as they did their best to avoid the frantic guard beneath their feet. Some of them managed to break free of the chaos, the remainder had to fend off blows from fists full of cameras and kicks from heavy shoes that struggled for grip on the shiny corridor floor. Small fights broke out in the centre of the storm and soon spread outwards. The spokesman, disoriented and totally dazed, found himself an unwilling participant in what appeared to be a no-holds-barred wrestling match between the Mail on Sunday and Hello Magazine who were fighting it out, tooth and nail.

"Get your bloody camera out of my eye!" Hello Magazine shouted as he tried to lock the Mail on Sunday into a half-nelson submission while applying a two-fingers-up-the-nostrils death-grip.

"I've got every right to be here, more than you and your tripe-filled glam-mag!" screamed Mail on Sunday breaking free long enough to poke the metal spiked end of his camera tripod deep into Hello Magazine's groin.

As the two of them wrestled, gouged and kicked each other, both of them inadvertently stamped repeatedly on the luckless Fusion Energy spokesman. In desperation, he summoned his last ounce of strength and with one final effort to escape this madness, he managed to get up onto his knees. Through his blackened, swollen right eye, the spokesman saw Hello Magazine get kicked in the shins by a well-aimed size ten toe-punt causing the reporter to squeal with pain, clutching his throbbing shin, hopping on one foot like a scalded flamingo. Mail on Sunday pressed home his advantage with a well aimed jab to the ribs but Hello Magazine spun round on his good leg, in a circle to dodge the blow. His camera swung in a wide arc around his body and the well-worn nylon strap gave way. Two kilograms of top-of-the-range Nikon SLR camera and telephoto lens flew through the air on a direct collision course with the spokesman's left eye. The last thing the man from Fusion Energy saw was his battered, bloody and bruised reflection in the lens, then he hit the tiled floor for a third time and he was knocked out cold.

It wasn't just the energy spokesman that took a battering, Max was also caught up in the carnage that was unfolding around him. The guard's frantic wig-search had knocked Max into the midst of the reporters, pointed elbows clipped his ears and jabbed him hard in the ribs. Max dodged left and right, stepping over the fighting reporters, broken microphones and pieces of camera that littered the floor.

Max spotted his clipboard and badge underneath the kicking, screaming Daily Mail reporter. Evidently, she had put the rodent trauma behind her and she had switched from self-defence to all-out attack. Rolling around on the hard tiled floor, she was engaged in a hair-pulling, arm-biting battle with the Daily Star's photographer.

"You don't like it, do you, you gutless little mommy's-boy," she hissed through gritted teeth, "Why don't you photograph this with your bloody camera!" she added, gripping him tight in a crushing head-lock.

"Get off me, you crazed, demented witch!" the suffocating photographer managed to gasp.

"Take this, and this!" Daily Mail shouted in time with the blows of her microphone which she was using as a make-shift club, pummelling him repeatedly on the ears, which grew redder and redder with each blow.

The photographer tried desperately to break free of the Daily Mail reporter's death-grip, his legs kicked wildly, and he twisted and turned on the floor, attempting to shake her off. This made it worse and she clung on like a limpet, determined to batter him into submission.

Max dodged the swinging arms and legs of these would-be WWF wrestlers and the rest of the kicking and punching madness that surrounded him. He saw a gap in the bodies and reached down for his clipboard and badge. He grabbed them both and turned to run but as he took his first step he planted his left foot firmly on the ragged remains of the guard's hairpiece, slipped head over heels and fell backwards through the TV studio door.

Day One after the Power Crisis

Max adjusted his Berghaus jacket and tucked his check shirt into his trousers. He looked back at the studio door that had closed behind him and he shook his head. That was way too extreme, he thought to himself and laughed at the thought of the security guard's wig.

He was still laughing to himself as he clipped his visitor badge back onto his lapel. He checked it to make sure it was straight and his eyes opened wide when he realised it was not his visitor's badge, it was the badge of Mr S Devonshire. Below the name it read, *'Fusion Energy'*.

Max looked up suddenly when one of the TV runners grabbed him by the arm. The runner spoke into a headset.

"Here he is, I've found the Fusion Energy guy!"

Someone on the other end of the headset was evidently shouting at the runner, Max could hear it through the runner's headphones.

"I *am* on my way!" he shouted as he half-pulled and half-dragged Max by the arm to the centre of the studio, heading towards a small table and two formal looking office chairs.

In one of the chairs sat Peter Michaelmore, a reporter for Channel Nine News.

"But I'm…." protested Max to the runner.

"Yeah, you and me both, man," the runner said pulling Max along, "But we're going to be in even worse trouble if we don't get you on TV in the next ten seconds!"

The runner pushed Max back into the chair opposite Michaelmore and gave him a quick once over, straightening his hair and jacket.

"There, you're all good!" said the runner, who spun quickly away and disappeared behind the cameras.

Max recognised Peter Michaelmore from Channel Nine news and stared at him in disbelief. Peter Michaelmore stared back. He looked Max up and down and he checked the badge on Max's jacket. It clearly said Fusion Energy. Michaelmore touched the earpiece in his left ear and spoke softly into his microphone.

"Are you sure this is the right person?"

Across the studio, in the production room, the producer watched the second hand on the studio clock ticking away. With seven seconds to go before a live broadcast he didn't have time to check, he had to make a decision.

"Go with the questions, Peter! Go! We are live in five..... four.........three......."

Michaelmore took a long look at Max.

"Are you sure," he said in his microphone, "I don't think he is...."

"Live in one!" the voice in his earpiece said.

"But...."

The studio went silent and a red light on camera one indicated that they were now broadcasting live to the nation. Michaelmore smiled into the camera and read from the autocue.

"Good morning, I am Peter Michaelmore, live with you from the studios of SWTV, our hosts for this national TV broadcast. Power is back on in Exeter and we don't know yet know how many of the population will have power to view this but we hope you have been able to join us, wherever you are."

He paused for a moment, looked at Max and he thought about stating the obvious but a voice from the producer in his earpiece stirred him on.

"Just ask the questions, read the autocue!"

"With me today is Simon Devonshire from Fusion Energy, who will *hopefully* be able to provide the answers to the questions on everybody's mind. What happened to the power grid and when will electricity be reinstated to all homes?"

A red light on camera 2 came on as it focused on Max. Max quickly glanced over his shoulder, desperately hoping that the real Simon Devonshire from Fusion Energy had made it to the studio. He hadn't.

Max stared at Michaelmore and Michaelmore stared back. It was only a few seconds but it seemed like an eternity. On live TV to the entire nation, this was more than an awkward gap, it was a rapidly widening canyon.

"What are you waiting for? Go with the questions!" the producer shouted in Michaelmore's earpiece.

Michaelmore knew he was interviewing the wrong person but he asked his question anyway. He leaned forward in his chair and rephrased his first question.

"Can you tell our viewers what happened to the power grid?"

Max thought for a second. Why is he asking me? He racked his brain for an answer and he remembered the Fusion Energy statement from the previous night.

"The grid couldn't supply enough power and it overloaded," said Max trying to help Michaelmore who seemed to be asking him pretty obvious questions.

Michaelmore had taken on a rather strained look and was turning a nasty grey colour despite his studio make up so Max offered some more information, hoping it would help Michaelmore in some way.

"There was no more power available, all of the country's power stations were at maximum output," Max added.

Michaelmore tried to get back into his stride.

"And what is being done to get power back to those households without electricity?"

"Everything that Fusion Energy can," replied Max, "I saw teams of engineers hard at work on the way here this morning."

Michaelmore was a little perturbed with the direct answers and tried to take the advantage.

"And what do you suggest is done to ensure this doesn't happen again in the future?"

Max thought for a moment and remembered a college project he had completed last year on energy conservation.

"Well, perhaps it's an opportunity for us all to take a moment and think about our own energy usage."

Michaelmore was taken a little aback at this unexpected shift in direction.

"Go on," he said, trying to squeeze something controversial out of the interview.

Max thought back to the figures he had calculated about energy wastage.

"My report on energy consumption identified that in the average household we waste over 35% of the energy that comes into the house."

"35%, you say?"

"Yes, over 35%. If you consider an average household, you would find a multitude of unused electrical appliances left on. Lights are the obvious one but it's also other smaller things, for example, phone and laptop chargers, people rarely switch them off even though the phone or laptop is fully charged."

"I hardly think the odd phone charger accounts for 35%," said Michaelmore, in a slightly smug tone.

"No," replied Max, "But it all adds up. For instance, how many people boil a full three litre kettle with a two kilowatt element for just one cup of tea? It is the same with three kilowatt immersion heaters that are left on all day. What about high-energy consuming tumble dryers that are used to dry clothes that could go out on a washing line?"

Max was on a roll, he knew quite a lot about energy efficiency, "May I ask you a question?" he said.

"Er, yes," replied Michaelmore.

"Do you use energy efficient light bulbs in your house?"

Michaelmore had meant to fit them but he had never got round to changing his 100watt and 60watt bulbs for 10watt low energy ones.

"I have started to," he lied.

"Well, if you changed them all, you'd save up to 80% on the energy you use in lighting your house. And the money saved would pay for the new low energy bulbs in no time."

Max changed tack slightly and switched to heating energy.

"May I ask what you have set your boiler thermostat to? Is it still set at twenty two degrees even though you're not at home this weekend?"

"Ermm...."

"If it is, then your boiler will be running all weekend, heating an empty house. What about your TV equipment, do you switch it off or just put it on standby?"

Michaelmore was getting more and more uncomfortable, he should be the one asking the questions.

"Are you trying to tell me that the country has come to a standstill because a few TV's were left on standby?"

Max referred to the figures he had calculated for his energy project.

"An average TV on standby consumes roughly 5 watts of power and if it's on standby for 20 hours a day that costs £30 a year. If you then multiply that £30 by all the households in the country that's a phenomenal figure that's estimated to cost tens of millions of pounds each year. Plus it takes a lot of resource from the powerstations. In 2005, it was estimated one million tonnes of coal was needed just to provide the power to keep electrical appliances on standby."

"Really?" said Michaelmore. A moment later a voice in his earpiece confirmed the figures were pretty much correct.

"I'm not saying that is the only reason why the power failed because there are loads of other things we waste energy on. What I am saying is that perhaps TV as a whole does have something to do with it."

"Such as?"

"Well, thirty million people were watching TV last night across the country and they all would have probably left their TV's on standby, but don't you think it would make more sense not to watch so much TV in the first place?"

Michaelmore floundered, he didn't have a response ready.

"What I mean is, take that celebrity reality show..."

"*Star Struck*?" offered Michaelmore.

"Yes, that's the one. Why do so many people watch it? The celebrities in there have very little to say that's of any value so it's a waste of time watching it and a waste of energy running a TV to watch it. If you must watch TV, there are much better programmes on at the same time."

"Such as?" asked Michaelmore who was losing control of the interview.

"Springwatch for one," answered Max, "Instead of watching a bunch of mindless celebrities gibbering on about nothing, you could turn over and learn something interesting about what's going on outdoors and then turn off the TV and *go outdoors* and see it for yourself."

"But *Star Struck* is reality TV!" Michaelmore struggled with Max's simple but oh-so logical argument. He had lost all hope of getting this conversation back on track.

"But it's not reality TV is it? Those celebrities aren't real people and they don't lead real lives. Don't you think it would make more sense to once in a while turn off this so-called reality TV and go outside into *actual* reality and do something a lot more interesting? I mean, when was the last time you took a moment to look up at the stars and wonder how the solar system works, or took your kids to the beach and checked out the contents of a rock pool?"

Max was tempted to add that the combined IQ of the average rock pool was probably higher than that in the celebrity house but he stopped himself. Max now had the upper hand and he forced his point home using some advice his mother had drummed into him from an early age.

"Or perhaps go outdoors and speak to a neighbour and ask them how they are, better still, take the time to stop and ask a stranger how they are. That would be a better kind of reality for a start."

"But....but...." Michaelmore tried to answer but he couldn't argue with that logic.

Across the nation, millions of people listened to Max and they couldn't argue with his logic either.

One Week after the Power Crisis:

The first seven days

In the *Star Struck* house, the four remaining celebrities sat around contemplating what had happened. When the power first went off in the celeb-house they had all assumed it was a trick to start with then it gradually dawned on them that things were not right. Opal had noticed it was quiet outside and she had gone into the garden to listen for the crowd outside the house. There had been screaming as was usual on eviction nights but that had stopped suddenly and now it was deathly silent outside the house. On her way back indoors she stopped and gazed up at the stars. Because the street lights and exterior floodlights were off, there was no light pollution and she had never seen so many stars before. She was awestruck as she saw constellations from far off distant galaxies that were usually hidden from view by the background light of the city. She was joined by the other celebs and they all gazed upwards in wonder. Every now and again one of them would point out a shooting star but apart from that, it was the quietest the house had been for eight weeks, and the most civilised. The awe-struck celebrities experienced the wonders of the solar system and the galaxies beyond. So did many of the residents of London and other large towns and cities.

In the production room, Grant had successfully directed his cameramen to switch from the mains-powered cameras inside the house to battery powered portable ones in an effort to keep filming. He had then commandeered one of the outside broadcast power generators to divert power back into the production room and celeb-house but the power was out at the Channel Nine network broadcasting centre so despite Grant's efforts, the show was off the air.

Grant threw a fit when he figured out the show was not being broadcast. In the darkness, his crew took cover trying to avoid being in his firing line. When his temper reverted to a more approachable level, one of the crew mustered up the courage to pass him a hand-written memo. Channel Nine's Chief Executive of Broadcasting demanded a meeting.

The meeting had not gone at all well for Grant, the Chief Executive wanted reassurances from Grant that plans were in place to reinstate the missing celebrity so that an eviction could be announced to boost the show's declining popularity. Grant had banked on Rex's ex-wife and gambled on Poppy returning and both options failed to materialise. He was left hanging high and dry. Without another celebrity joining the house, the show could not run for another three weeks and still have a grand three-celeb final. To make matters worse, Max's *'Switch off Star Struck and switch over to Springwatch'* message had crippled the show. The Chief Executive had up-to-date viewing figures for the show which were drastically low, they were less than two million. Even though power had been reinstated to most areas and people had the opportunity to watch *Star Struck,* they clearly chose not to. By the end of the week viewing figures were down to one point two million.

A large percentage of the country still had no power four days after the power outage. The remarkable thing was that people managed without heating, hot water and electricity by helping each other. Neighbour helped neighbour, and more importantly, strangers helped strangers. Across the nation, those without any cooking facilities arranged barbeques to cook the meat that was defrosting in their freezers and invited their neighbours to join them, a lot of whom they had never really spoken to before.

Dust was blown off the boxes of long-forgotten board games and families settled down to play candlelit games of Scrabble, Mousetrap and a hundred other old favourites. People left their sofas, they opened their front doors, went outside and were met by other people doing the same. Games of football started up in streets and parks and people talked to each other over fences. Even dogs that were rarely walked were taken out and the dog owners stopped and talked with the people they met.

The older generation said the spirit of togetherness was similar to how it was during the blitz. The younger generation asked their elders what it was like in the blitz and new friendships and bonds were made across age-groups.

The major news networks, hungry for any story they could get, ran and re-ran the Michaelmore interview. Like a pebble dropped into a pond, Max's logical comments and refreshing ideas rippled across the nation and boosted the general feeling that it was time for a drastic change of lifestyle. When the power gradually returned to the country, people did not return to their sofas. The new friendships made, remained intact. While people's TVs and computers had been without power, they had found other things to do and found them a lot more interesting.

Across the country, a huge number of *Star Struck*'s viewers had taken Max's advice and discovered better things to do with their time than watch the idiotic banter of three dwindling celebs and an MP that was on the fiddle. Gary Reynolds was at the sports centre, playing five-a-side football in a local league that had sprung up from the football in the park on the day of the power outage. Stacey and Kylee had taken Max's advice quite literally and they had switched over to Springwatch earlier in the week. They were now avid nature spotters rather than avid TV watchers.

Most of the population had left their sofas and were out doing other things, anything but watching TV.

Within a week, the national grid had returned to providing power to all homes but it now operated at 28% less than its total capacity, way below the critical levels it was running at before the crisis. The difference in energy consumption was due to people throughout the country assessing their own energy usage and simply turning electrical appliances off that were not being used. The difference this made was nothing less than remarkable.

At MegaCorp, it took a few days for the weekly sales figures to come through to Bishop but there had clearly been a drop due to lack of advertising. Bishop wasn't sure if this would just be a blip or a downward trend. He studied the sales figures for two key products in the MegaCorp medicinal range. *'KwiknSlim'* was down 8%. This was usually a strong seller. Bishop would keep his eye on that one but the most concerning was *Pro-Retanzin*. This was their over-the-counter non–prescription anti-depressant. It had shown a steady increase in sales since it was launched and was another strong seller and profit-maker for MegaCorp but since the power outage sales had dipped by 45%. Bishop considered this from a sales and marketing perspective and couldn't find the reason for the sudden drop in sales. What he overlooked was the fact that since the power outage, people were more active hence they had no need for slimming drinks and likewise, with a more outward-going lifestyle, people did not need MegaCorp's anti-depressants.

Rachel had spent the first few days of her freedom lying low at her Dad's house. After a while reporters had figured out she may be there and had arrived at the house in droves looking for her and a juicy story. She had stayed indoors with the curtains and blinds drawn. Towards the end of the first week the media moved off following up on a false tip-off that she was back in London. Her father was pleased he had made that anonymous call and he was even more pleased to have her home.

Towards the end of the week, Rachel removed the blonde highlights from her hair returning to her natural mousy brown colour. She wore her hair tied back in a simple ponytail and switched from her contact lenses to a pair of her old brown rimmed glasses. Rachel looked more like a secretary than a celebrity and the change was quite remarkable. Her dad couldn't help teasing her when he came home from work that evening.

"Who are you?" he demanded, "And what have you done with Poppy?"

"Shut up, Dad!" she said, whacking him on the arm, "It's my new look."

"It's your *old* look," he said with a smile.

"Daaad, please. Just tell me what you fancy for dinner, okay?"

He had not been particularly happy with her moving to London with Dean Ashburn in the first place and he had hardly approved of the rash decision to go on *Star Struck*, although he had watched some of the show and noticed the change in her as the weeks went past. Now that she was home he saw those changes for himself, she was brighter, more enthusiastic and she really was the old Rachel again.

"Have we got any beef mince in the fridge?" he asked.

"I think so."

"Then I fancy lasagne, I've heard you're pretty good at making those!"

One Week After the Power Crisis:

Saturday 09:45Hrs

For Max, following his impromptu TV appearance, he had been in demand for more TV interviews due to his common-sense advice which had dramatically changed people's attitudes. His father had agreed that he could appear on South West Television's Saturday morning chat show, so exactly one week since he first appeared, Max was back at the studio for another interview, this time with Sally McMahon, one of SWTV's up-and-coming presenters.

His dad was in the studio with him and they had a last minute chat just before Max went on.

"Remember, Max, don't be pushed into talking about anything you're not comfortable with."

"Okay, Dad."

"And if it's not going well and you want out, just give me a sign."

Max nodded.

The show's runner came over and asked Max if he was ready. Max said he was and before long, he was being led onto the studio and was seated on the sofa next to Sally McMahon.

The news and weather segment of the show came to an end and the cameras switched live to Max and Sally.

"With us this morning," said Sally to camera one, "Is Max Chambers, someone you all probably know very well. It's very good to have you here, Max."

"Hello," Max said with a smile.

"It's nice to have you here as *yourself* this time," said Sally building up to her punch-line, "And not impersonating someone from Fusion Energy!"

"I wasn't exactly impersonating him, it was a simple mistake," replied Max.

Camera two cut to a quick cameo shot of the runner who had been responsible and he looked severely embarrassed. Sally continued with the interview.

"What you said about reality TV appears to have had a huge impact on that type of TV show. Viewing figures for *Star Struck* have dropped to an all-time low of one point two million."

Max didn't respond, he was lost for words because he certainly hadn't meant to do that.

Sally tried a more probing question.

"*Star Struck's* viewing figures have dropped to just over a million and the show's main sponsor, MegaCorp, is threatening to cancel their advertising contract. What do you say to that?"

Max thought for a moment.

"Well that wouldn't really be a bad thing would it?"

"Wouldn't it?" countered Sally.

"Well, no, I don't think it would, would it?" said Max, "In our house, if we are watching TV programmes we've recorded that break for adverts, we fast forward through them and if we can't do that we have a good laugh at them. Some of the adverts on TV are so false they border on being ridiculous."

"Such as?" said Sally, hoping that if she gave him enough rope he would either trip or hang himself with it.

Max took a moment to compose his response.

"Take yoghurt adverts for example, the ones that say they have a special ingredient Bioactivus Harmonium, those are not real words."

Sally was taken aback, she drank one of those yoghurts every day.

"Yes it is, it's Latin," she said triumphantly.

"Er...Latin for what?" questioned Max, not really wanting to upset Sally but he felt he had to ask.

"Well, bio means biological and the activus means active and it's all in harmony so that's the harmonium."

Evidently Sally had not studied Latin at school, Max wasn't sure if she was being serious or not so he gently questioned Sally's Latin skills.

"Are you sure that's right, Sally?"

"Yes, I'm pretty sure that's right," confirmed a now less confident Sally.

The voice from the producer in her earpiece told her that it wasn't.

"I've just been told it's not, viewers," she said, her cheeks beginning to blush a little.

Max didn't want to appear smug, it wasn't in his character, but when he was faced with untruths he felt he had to speak his mind.

"I'm sorry, Sally but that must make you wonder if the made-up ingredient is actually beneficial. It's the same with shampoos. One shampoo adverts claims it uses Regeneris Reinforcium but that's not a proper Latin name either."

Sally said nothing, she didn't want to risk disagreeing again.

"It does sound like a Latin name so we assume it means something like regenerating and reinforcing but that's not correct, it's just a regular shampoo."

Sally tried to get a word in and failed.

"And the adverts show people using a handful which is subliminally telling the viewers that's the recommended amount to use when all you need is a much smaller amount, about the size of a ten pence piece."

"Perhaps that's enough about shampoos, Max," Sally tried to interject but Max wasn't finished.

"And I'm pretty sure they put a dye in some of the shampoos so that when you look down in the shower you think the water is dirtier than it really is, so you feel you need to wash your hair again and use more shampoo."

Max was picking up momentum, he had more to say about shampoo but switched to another Chambers family favourite, make-up adverts.

"Sally?" he asked, "Have you ever noticed the small print they have to show in some make-up adverts?"

"Er..no..." she started to say.

"Take a look when you next see an advert for mascara and eye makeup. There's one on TV at the moment, I think it is called *Stunning-Eyes*, which claims to strengthen and lengthen lashes but if you read the small print that comes up at the bottom of the screen it tells you the model's eyelashes are digitally enhanced. They are fake computer-generated eyelashes. Me and my dad always have a good laugh at that one."

Sally shook her head, not just in disbelief but also to clear her head in an attempt to get the interview back on track.

"Max," she said forcefully, "We have quite a few interesting emails from viewers who would like to ask you some questions."

"Okay," said Max.

"This email is from Mary in Solihull. She would like your advice on how she can keep her weekly food shop within budget. She says she always chooses the supermarket offers but her shopping bill increases every week. Any ideas on that Max?"

Max thought about this for a second. His mum always took a calculator when she went to the supermarket which she used to work out the best deals.

"Perhaps it would be a good idea to take a calculator to the shops and compare the deals and offers. That may save you some extra cash and keep you within budget."

Sally frowned and looked a little puzzled.

"Don't the supermarkets highlight the items on special offer? They do in the one I go to."

"They do," said Max, "But quite often the items that are marked as being *'value pack'* or *'Buy two and get one free'* are not the best deals for *your budget* and they can be misleading. Sometimes it's better value to choose the *non-value pack*. You need a calculator to work out the true unit cost by breaking it down by weight or volume."

"So what you're saying is that the special offers sometimes hide the true cost," added Sally.

Max thought of an example from when he had been shopping with his mum.

"Okay," he said, "Let's say we're buying some minced beef and there is a choice between an 800gram pack and a 500gram pack. The mince is the same, just the pack sizes are different. The 800gram pack costs £3.79. The 500gram pack is usually £2.69 but there's an offer to buy two packs for £5. Which one is the best deal? Is it the 800gram pack or the offer of two 500gram packs for £5? The two for £5 offer appears to be the best deal, but is it?"

"Erm….I don't know," said a puzzled Sally.

"To be honest, neither do I without a calculator," said Max, "The price per kilo on the 800gram pack is very hard to work out, I can't divide 3.79 by 0.8 in my head."

"Neither can I", said Sally with a rather intrigued look on her face.

"The other one to always check is cans of fizzy drink. They come in sixes, eights, tens, twelves and even twenty four packs. Some of them are branded as special offer bulk packs, some are offered as two packs for the price of one but it's not clear which is the best deal until you've worked out the unit cost of a can in each pack."

(A voice in Sally's earpiece advised her that Max's example of the mince proved the 800gram non-offer pack was better value because it was 26 pence cheaper per kilo.)

"I've some interesting news, viewers," said Sally to camera one, "I've just been told by my producer that the two for £5 offer on mince is *not* the best deal. The 800gram non-offer pack is twenty six pence *less* per kilo."

"Oh, yeah, I must admit, I've got a bit of a confession to make," said Max, "My mum spotted that one when we were shopping last week, she chose the 800gram *non-offer* pack."

"And that's why you need the calculator," said Sally, "I get it now."

"Yep," said Max, "I'm not trying to undermine the supermarkets but you have to keep in mind their ultimate goal is to make us spend more in the store."

Max explained what he meant by using an example of a loaf of bread that cost £1.00 with an offer to buy two loaves for £1.80. He explained it was in the supermarket's best interest to sell more bread but the offer only worked in your favour if you really needed two loaves. If one went to waste because you didn't eat it then you had just spent £1.80 on one loaf.

"Good point," agreed Sally.

"The other thing to watch is the way they use percentages, it can be quite confusing," continued Max, "*50% off* sounds better than *33% extra*, but it's actually the same."

"Ah," said Sally, "I never really noticed that before."

"And three *for the price of two* sounds better than *50% extra*, but again, it's exactly the same except for one important thing."

"What's that?" asked Sally.

"Three for two makes you spend *twice* as much, *50% extra* gives you something *extra* for free."

"And getting three for two can be wasteful if you don't use all three."

"That's right, the *three for two* offer is designed to influence us into buying more than we really need, it's there to boost sales and profit for the suppliers and the supermarket."

Sally encouraged Max to explain further so he picked up a pen and a spare piece of paper from her interview notes and did some examples. Soon, Sally was getting stuck into some percentage calculations to put Max's examples to the test. After a few moments, a pleased looking Sally held up the piece of paper where she had worked out the percentages longhand.

"Pretty cool, eh?" said Max.

"No calculator, either!" said Sally, who was very proud of her longhand arithmetic and showed it off to camera two.

"So we need to be careful of the *three for two* offers and we should check around for deals that give us *33%* and *50% extra* instead."

"That's it, and don't forget it's very important to always work out the unit cost," said Max, "I hope that's of some use to Mary from Solihull."

It certainly was, and to millions of other housewives who were also watching.

This interview had not gone exactly to Sally's plan and they were way off topic but she had to admit what he said was interesting and it made sense. The next question for the show came in by email from a Mrs Jane Bennett from Salisbury. She wrote that she had seen Max's first time on TV where he had suggested switching off *Star Struck* and switching on Springwatch. She added that she had done just that and was now planning to take her family on a nature walk but first she wanted to ask if Max could offer any advice on how to reduce her home's energy consumption.

ONE WEEK AFTER THE POWER CRISIS:

SATURDAY 10:00HRS

Rachel was having a late breakfast with her dad while they watched Max's interview live on their kitchen TV. Rachel had steered clear of the TV since her escape, especially the news and media channels and she had never seen Max before.

"Who's that, Dad?" she asked as she finished her cereal.

Her father nearly choked on some toast as he laughed out loud then he explained to Rachel who Max was.

"Well, after the power crisis, he ended up live on TV in an interview that was broadcast nationwide."

"So why is he back on this week?" Rachel asked.

"It was the day after you disappeared from reality TV. He said some things about power consumption but more importantly about how people live their lives."

"Really?"

"Yeah, I think it's fair to say that you and that young man are both jointly responsible for the demise of reality TV!"

"Did we really do that?"

"Yeah, he's certainly changed the way people look at things, especially TV. For a young lad, he has a lot of common sense between his ears."

Rachel watched the TV as Max gave Mrs Bennett from Salisbury some advice on reading her electricity bill and also some excellent tips on where to look for Kingfishers.

"He's pretty smart, isn't he?" Rachel said as Max moved onto another caller's question.

Max was back onto the topic of how to work out what are the best deals in supermarkets. He then answered another question about what telescope he recommended for astronomy beginners.

"He's got a switched-on way about him, that's for sure," added Martin Purnell, "And he's not afraid to tell it how it is."

ONE WEEK AFTER THE POWER CRISIS:

SATURDAY 10:30HRS

Meanwhile, on the other side of Exeter in the MegaCorp Research and Development building, Bishop and Nina Glover watched Max's interview on a large LCD screen in Bishop's office. Bishop pointed at Max on the screen.

"To start with, that little toe-rag has cut our target TV audience from twenty five million to less than two million," Bishop snarled, "We're now sponsoring shows that no one is watching and we can't switch sponsorship to that bloody Springwatch because it's on the BBC."

Nina nodded in agreement while Bishop continued to rant.

"Then, he takes apart the scientific belief in our products, live on TV, to a nation that now hangs on his every word. If that's not bad enough, he's just shown the country how to buy our products for less money!"

Nina Glover turned the TV screen off and Bishop continued ranting.

"Have you seen last week's sales figures? More importantly, have you seen the sales forecasts for the next three months?"

Bishop handed Nina a spreadsheet with a bar graph. The trend line dipped dramatically downward.

"We have stock piled high on the shelves in supermarkets and it's not selling. We have more stock, backed up in distribution depots, because supermarkets are not reordering."

Nina nodded. She knew this already because she was the person that had prepared the reports.

"And we've got our own manufacturing plants backed up with surplus stock with nowhere to store it and nowhere to ship it too because the distribution depots are full!"

"The Board of Directors will not be pleased," Nina added, "Revenue is down 30%, profit down by 22%. The MegaCorp share price is down by 18%."

"If we don't do something now the share price will tumble even further than it has already. We have no option," Bishop said with a commanding tone, "We will implement X-Ingredient immediately."

"Yes, Sir!" Nina smiled, she knew what that meant.

"And get me our advertisers on the phone, I need to have a word with Mr Purnell."

One Week After the Power Crisis:

Saturday 10:45Hrs

Rachel was tidying away their breakfast things when Martin Purnell's mobile vibrated on the kitchen worktop. He picked up the phone and read the message. It was a memo from his assistant that said Mr Bishop from MegaCorp had called and they had requested a meeting by conference call later that afternoon.

Martin Purnell sighed, an impromptu business meeting on a Saturday afternoon was not what he needed.

"What's up?" Rachel asked.

"Just work, Rach, it looks as though I have to go into the office this afternoon for a conference call with one of our clients."

"I guess it's important, yeah?"

"Pretty much," he replied, "What have you got planned for today?"

"Nothing really," Rachel said as she loaded the dishwasher, "Maybe I could tag along with you when you go into town, I won't get in the way and it's time I got out of the house."

"Right," he said, "We'll leave at about twelve thirty and I'll have the team on pain of death and docked pay if they spill the beans where you are."

"Okay, thanks," said Rachel. She knew sooner or later she would have to get out of the house and someone was bound to recognise her, despite her new appearance.

Martin Purnell picked up his mobile and made several calls to his team of advertising executives. He apologised for calling on a Saturday but explained this was an urgent meeting and he asked them to be at the office for two o'clock, to prepare for the three o'clock conference call.

Martin Purnell and Rachel drove into Exeter and arrived a little before two o'clock. Gradually, the rest of the team arrived. Some of the team members made a bit of a fuss about Rachel but they were soon down to business and the first sales report to come off the printer confirmed what they feared. The products they promoted for MegaCorp had falling sales figures and the forecast did not look good at all, not one MegaCorp product was performing to target. At least they could now anticipate what the agenda would be for the upcoming conference call with Bishop.

Rachel had expected to wait in her father's office and quietly read a book but she soon became involved in the marketing team's hectic pre-meeting preparations. She had started by running a few errands but as the deadline for the meeting approached she was asked to do a lot more. She had cleared paper jams in printers, helped prepare sales reports and had assisted the IT department in the setting up and testing of the conference call equipment.

She now sat quietly in a corner of the meeting room and watched as the meeting with Bishop got underway.

ONE WEEK AFTER THE POWER CRISIS:

SATURDAY 15:00HRS

Martin Purnell's team arranged themselves around the speakerphone positioned in the centre of the meeting room table. Dead on three o'clock, the speakerphone clicked and Bishop came on the line. His sharp, direct voice echoed through the speaker. As they expected, he was quick to apportion blame for the downturn in sales and demanded that they come up with a revised marketing strategy.

Pearson, the exec in charge of *'KwiknSlim'* was first to respond. He had prepared a presentation for the meeting which included his ideas to rebrand the product with revised packaging and a new marketing campaign in key outlets. This, he assured Bishop, would revitalize the sales of *'KwiknSlim'*.

Bishop cut in after just two minutes into his presentation.

"Our market research suggests otherwise," said Bishop curtly, "It needs something more than your usual re-branding. It needs something that is going to get people back buying the product."

Pearson tried to think on his feet and come up with a new plan but Bishop cut in again.

"I do not want to hear half-baked ideas, what I want to hear are solid plans on how you intend to regenerate sales in our medicinal and cosmetic products."

Duane Rogers, who managed several MegaCorp cosmetic brands, including the *Stunning-Eyes* range of eyelash conditioner mascaras, entered into the meeting with his proposals. He put forward his ideas of a new model with a new advertising slogan. He went on to recommend they develop a marketing strategy using the ever popular Eva Carrs as the new face of *Stunning-Eyes*. He didn't get far until he was cut short by Bishop again.

"Young man," said Bishop, not hiding the tone of sarcasm in his voice, "Do you keep up with current affairs?"

"Um…yes," replied Rogers, thrown off balance by Bishop's direct question.

"Well, I am very surprised to hear that, because if you did you would be aware of two facts. Firstly, Eva Carrs' face is so swollen after her most recent surgery it looks like she's been in a fight with a particularly angry swarm of African killer bees. Secondly, master know-it-all, the kid from the power-outage, was on breakfast television earlier today and he exposed the fact that your '*Stunning Eyes*' adverts use fake models with even more fake, computer generated, eyelashes."

Rogers was dumbfounded.

"And if you are about to come up with a bright idea of three for two offers then think again because he exposed those as well."

Rogers struggled, the wind had completely left his sails.

"I….er…I think…"

"I believe you need to reassess your whole approach, don't you?" said Bishop, going for the jugular.

Rachel listened to the conversation from her seat in the corner of the room and she thought back to earlier that morning and the way Max had won over Sally and the viewers by telling the truth. She looked at her father who was gesturing to his team to be quiet while he spoke with Bishop.

Martin Purnell leaned forward towards the speakerphone.

"Mr Bishop, this is Martin Purnell. I believe it's clear we need to completely re-think our strategies moving forward."

He was stalling, he had no strategy in mind.

"Evidently," said Bishop, "I am all ears, please go on."

Martin Purnell was now faced with thinking on his feet and he scanned around the room for an answer. His team had portfolios full of old ideas which were no use when faced with a need to be spontaneous. From the back of the room, Rachel caught his eye and she mouthed something to him. He couldn't make it out. He shrugged and mouthed back, "What?"

She quickly reached for a notepad and pencil and scribbled out a note which she held up for her father to read:

How about a marketing strategy that tells the truth?

She raised her eyebrows to emphasise the point. She then wrote again on the pad:

What about that guy Max - It might be what people want to hear

Purnell seized on the idea.

"Mr Bishop, I believe we have a plan to take MegaCorp products into a new direction of advertising, a new direction where we tell the plain and simple truth about the product. We will emphasize the genuine features and benefits of the product and we will sell at a fixed no-nonsense price."

"Go on," said Bishop.

"This honest, down-to-earth campaign will capitalise on the change of attitude that's sweeping through the country."

On the other end of the line, Bishop considered this novel idea.

"I suggest we reconvene to discuss this further later in the week, when you've formulated your ideas."

"Of course," said Purnell. A click on the speakerphone indicated Bishop had left the conference call.

Purnell turned to his team and considered what needed to be done because this was a radical idea for them all. He briefed them to develop marketing strategies based upon telling the truth and they would discuss them further on Monday morning. He thanked his team for coming in to work at such short notice and wished them a good weekend, what was left of it.

When the team had left, he and Rachel locked up the offices and headed back to their car.

"So how do you reckon we're going to recruit this Max Chambers then, Rach?" he asked.

"Erm…..aren't you the ideas-man?"

"Ah, not so fast, this was your idea, remember?" he replied, "We'd better make it work, hadn't we?"

"He was on SWTV earlier, right? Their offices are at the other end of town. Let's see if they've got a contact number for him."

Bishop was also pleased with the outcome of the call. He had forced Muller and Rathbone into re-thinking MegaCorp's marketing which would be the push necessary to clear old stock which would then be replaced with new stock.

Stock with X-Ingredient.

Two Weeks after the Power Crisis:

Monday 17:00Hrs

Martin Purnell had called SWTV on Saturday afternoon and had been put through to Max's dad who was still at work. They had a brief chat where he explained he had been impressed by Max's appearances on TV and he wanted to offer him the opportunity to work for Muller and Rathbone in an apprentice/consultancy role. At first, Max's dad was sceptical but Martin Purnell assured him that Max's role would be to provide comment and advice on their marketing strategies and that it would not affect Max's college work. He suggested meeting at the Muller and Rathbone offices on Monday evening where they could discuss the opportunity in greater detail.

Max and his parents arrived at the offices and were lead to Martin Purnell's office by a smartly dressed young girl, wearing a business suit, brown rimmed glasses and with her hair tied back in a neat pony tail.

"Can I get you anything to drink? A tea or coffee perhaps?" she said.

Max's parents accepted the offer of a cup of tea and Max went for a glass of water. It puzzled him where he had seen the girl before, her face was vaguely familiar.

Before long, Martin Purnell joined them in his office. The young assistant brought him a fresh cup of coffee and placed it on the desk in front of him.

"Thank you, Rachel," he said with a tiny hint of a smile.

That's it, thought Max, as he put two and two together and figured out where he had seen her before. That's Rachel 'Poppy' Purnell so that makes her Mr Purnell's daughter.

Martin Purnell noticed Max's enlightened expression and figured he had recognised Rachel, despite her recent change of hair colour, ponytail and glasses.

"That's right, Max," he said, "I see you've figured out that Rachel is my daughter and she's missing from quite a famous TV show."

Rachel blushed a little.

"Sorry, I didn't recognise you, dear," said Max's mum, "What was it like in that dreadful house?"

Rachel told them a little about her time on *Star Struck*, especially how she had made up her mind very early on to leave of her own accord. Max's dad was interested to know how she got out of the house so she told him about the diversion and the camera blind spot.

"Very impressive," he said, "I'm surprised you didn't tunnel out of that mad-house weeks earlier."

"I did think about cutting through the wall behind the washing machine in week three but the bin-store was a better option," she added.

"Well I'm just glad she is out of there," said Martin Purnell, "But the knock on effect of Rachel's unplanned exit and Max's openness in recent TV interviews has meant viewing figures for *Star Struck* and shows like it have dropped drastically. This affects the efficiency of our advertising campaigns and that is why Muller and Rathbone are interested to have Max on board. What we need are fresh ideas to take us in a new direction, and we believe Max is the right person to do that. It was actually Rachel's idea that we contacted you."

"It wasn't just my idea," Rachel protested.

"Don't be too modest, I'm pretty sure it was," Martin Purnell replied, "Anyway, *Star Struck's* fall in popularity and of course Max's recent TV exposure is what we're here to discuss. To put it bluntly, Max has a certain way about him that people are responding very positively to. Muller and

Rathbone would like Max to work with us on a new *'tell it how it is, plain and direct'* advertising style."

He went on to explain further that he was offering to employ Max on a six month contract to attend the advertising team's brain-storming meetings where his input would become a key factor in influencing the team's creative productivity.

Max's mum was concerned with Max being involved in an industry that she knew little about but Martin Purnell reassured her that he would keep a close eye on Max. Max's father brought up the subject of salary and it was decided Max would receive the full market rate of pay for an advertising consultant with a proportion paid as a monthly allowance and the remainder invested into a fund towards the rest of college and then university.

"How do you feel about this, Max?" Martin Purnell asked, aware that Max had let his parents do most of the talking.

"So, what you want me to do is attend meetings after college and give my opinion on marketing and advertising ideas?"

"That's it exactly. We want your input, is that okay?"

"Okay," said Max.

"If it's fine with your parents then I think we have a deal. Welcome aboard, Max."

Martin Purnell stood up and offered Max a handshake to seal the deal. Max stood up and shook his hand.

"So, when can you start, is tomorrow too soon?"

"Tomorrow is fine," said Max, "I finish college at three thirty, I could be here for just after four o'clock."

"Good. I will arrange a meeting for four thirty, dress code is smart casual and I'll have our IT department set you up with a laptop and email address ready for when you arrive. Are you a Mac or a PC?"

Max could not believe this, he had not only just got the best after-college job in the world but he also was being offered a laptop.

"Er... a PC, please," he said.

"Excellent, I'll see you tomorrow at four thirty when I'll introduce you to the team and we'll get started straight away on our current projects."

The meeting drew to a close and Martin Purnell walked down to reception with the Chambers family, Rachel following a few paces behind.

As they were about to leave, the pager/calculator device in Max's pocket vibrated. Everyone instinctively checked their pockets for their mobile phones.

"Er, I think it's me," said Max.

"When did you get a mobile phone, Max?" his father asked.

Max took the device out and showed his father.

"Brains.....I mean Brian designed it. It's a pager and a calculator joined together."

Max's one was held together with two cable ties and thick rubber bands.

"I can see that, what does it do?"

"It means we can keep in touch with each other by sending short messages. It's like texting but with no mobile phone charges."

Martin Purnell looked intently at the device.

"Perhaps we need to be employing this Brian in our IT department as well as you Max," he said with a smile, "How does it work?"

Max gave them all a quick demonstration on how to receive and send messages. Brian's message had said:

`'in ex with pete any chance of lift home'`

"Pete and Brian are in Exeter, Dad, can we give them a lift home?"

His dad said of course they could.

Max showed everyone how to send a reply using the

calculator's keypad. It worked in the same way as a mobile phone without predictive text. Brian had moved the number keys and replaced them so they were in the same layout as a mobile phone with 1,2 and 3 at the top. If you pressed the 2 key once you got an A, if you pressed it twice, you got a B, three times, a C. Press 3, and you could enter D, E and F and so on through the number keypad where multiple taps on the 9 button produced W, X, Y and Z. The 0 was a space.

Max was getting more skilled at inputting messages through the number keypad and he quickly tapped out the multiple key presses required.

Within a few seconds a reply came back. `meet at cathedral ok'

Max's mum had only just mastered using a mobile phone and she looked at Max with a puzzled look on her face as he sent back a reply using multiple taps on the calculator's keypad.

"You boys and your toys," she said as she ruffled Max's hair.

Two Weeks after the Power Crisis:

Tuesday 16:30Hrs

Max arrived on the first day at his new job and was immediately whisked off to the 4:30pm advertising brainstorm meeting. He had expected to take a back seat role but Martin Purnell ushered him to a leather swivel seat at the end of the meeting room's long wooden table. The seat was so high-backed, it was almost as tall as Max. Already in the room were two advertising executives wearing designer jeans, designer shirts and designer glasses, not that Max knew what designer labels were. All he knew was his idea of smart casual was a lot different to theirs. He took off his dad's borrowed tweed jacket and placed it on the back of his chair then he rolled up his shirt sleeves and loosened his tie in an attempt to look less like an über-geek.

Martin Purnell took his place at the head of the table.

"Mr Pearson and Mr Mitchell, I trust you've read the memo. This is Max Chambers."

Pearson and Mitchell nodded a hello. Pearson made a gun shape with his thumb and finger, winked and made a *chuck-chuck* sound which was his trendy way of gun-slinging a welcome to Max. Mitchell held out his fist at arm's length for a fist-bump and waited for Max to do the same. Max had no idea what a fist-bump was, so he politely shook the out-stretched fist instead, much to the puzzlement of Mitchell.

"Pleased to meet you both," Max said as he took a seat next to the advertising executives.

"Max is here to add an edge, a different view, an angle, call it what you will," said Martin Purnell, "The public seem to like what he says and we're going to use that in our advertising campaigns."

Pearson and Mitchell doubted that Max would offer much but they nodded in approval all the same.

Martin Purnell wasted no time getting the meeting underway.

"We'll kick off with *'KwiknSlim'*."

Pearson stood up. He had prepared a PowerPoint presentation earlier that day and within a few seconds his opening slide was projected onto the white screen opposite the table. Pearson's presentation was in a storyboard style outlining the contents of the thirty second commercial. The opening few seconds featured a woman in tight lycra fitness clothes and she claimed she had lost over fifteen kilograms in three weeks using *'KwiknSlim'*. The following set of slides included the woman holding up a photo of what she used to look like compared to what she looked like now, while she commented to the camera, *"Can you believe this used to be me?"* The storyboard then included shots of the woman drinking *'KwiknSlim'* from a tall glass. The commercial closed with the slimmer version of the woman and her proud husband who made the closing comment, *"I can't believe it's her either."* The commercial ended with both of them looking rather pleased with each other, walking along a golden-sanded beach, silhouetted in a perfect, picture-postcard, tropical island sunset.

Pearson was pleased with his work. It was solid gold advertising.

"Of course," he explained, "We'll have to include the usual product disclaimer in small print at the bottom of the screen, *blah, blah, blah, only works if used as part of a calorie controlled diet, blah, blah, blah* but otherwise I reckon this is good to go."

Mitchell spoke up and praised Pearson's work.

"Good strap-lines," he said, "And who did the airbrush work on the before and after shots?"

"That was Ahmed in Design, he's a wiz with Photoshop."

"And the supports?" asked Mitchell.

"That was Demi from Make Up, she worked wonders with surgical tape and strapping bands to pull in, tuck up and support all the wobbly bits."

"And what about the gastric band operation?"

"That's all sorted as well, our actress has signed a non-disclosure agreement so she's not going to blab to anyone that her weight loss is due to having her stomach stapled shut."

Martin Purnell turned to Max and asked if he had any thoughts.

Max had quite a few but didn't think it right that he commented. Martin Purnell asked him again but this time he reassured him that he was part of the team and that his thoughts were important. He then stressed the point that Pearson and Mitchell were grownups and could handle a little constructive criticism.

"Okay," said Max with a little trepidation in his voice, "My first thought is that this is the same style that all slimming products follow."

"Of course," Pearson interjected, "It's a tried and tested format."

"Maybe it is a *tired* format as well, Pearson," Martin Purnell interrupted, "Let Max finish."

"Well, no one actually believes those before and after shots anymore do they? It's hard to see any resemblance between the two. The first photo shows her in a loose baggy black vest which does nothing to hide her bulges. The after photo, she is clearly a lot thinner due to whatever a gastric band is and the Photoshop editing work of Ahmed. He's airbrushed so much of her away it almost looks like a different woman."

Pearson and Mitchell looked at each other and then stared at Max with disbelieving eyes. Max realised he had probably said way too much.

"Erm...." said Max, "All I meant to say was that no one really believes this anymore."

"Go on, Max," encouraged Martin Purnell.

Max paused for a moment and thought about how he and his father pulled these type of adverts apart.

"The other thing is the disclaimer that states that *'KwiknSlim'* doesn't help weight loss unless you're on a diet in the first place."

Martin Purnell smiled, "And what would you suggest, Max?"

Max started off being cautious in what he said because he did not want to criticise Pearson's work any further. He began by suggesting that they removed the before and after photos. He also proposed a re-think of the actress, swapping her for a more typical mum-type in typical mum-clothes. The sort of everyday mum that tried to diet but because she was busy she did not have the time to eat healthily and got by on snacking instead of healthy square meals.

Martin Purnell stepped in and helped Max along.

"So what you're suggesting is we approach this from the perspective of a typical mum who has tried diets before and she knows there isn't a quick fix. What she wants is something that fits in with her busy lifestyle and stops her reaching for snacks."

"I guess so," said Max, "Maybe in the advert we show that she replaces snacks with *'KwiknSlim'*. Maybe our mum-type actress keeps a tin of *'KwiknSlim'* by the bread bin, another by the biscuit tin, another tin in the fridge maybe so that when she reaches for a snack she can have her low-calorie drink instead."

"Not a bad idea," said Purnell, "And the upside is that we don't need to use the disclaimer. We can have the actress say she's tried other diets and they didn't work. What she needs is a snack replacement and that's *'KwiknSlim'*."

Pearson was not overly happy. Max continued with his thoughts.

"What about if it was promoted in packs of three smaller tins marked fridge, breadbin and biscuit tin? That way you could place a tin beside the places where you keep your snacks."

Purnell was pleased, selling three tins instead of one in a snack-busting pack was a stroke of genius. He directed Pearson to re-think the advertising campaign using Max's input.

Next up was Mitchell's proposed campaign for MegaCorp's shampoo for men, the one that contained Regeneris Reinforcium. His proposal referred to the fake ingredient twice. The advert showed plant extracts and waterfalls with computer generated images of hairs rebuilding themselves through using the shampoo. *(The disclaimer stated it was a computer simulation and that using the shampoo may not repair real hair)*. It finished with a good looking male model liberally applying a handful of shampoo in the shower and closed with a shot of attractive women running their fingers through his hair and commenting that it felt soft and smelt citrusy fresh.

Max's solution was simple. His experience of shopping for himself and with his dad suggested the choice of shampoos was totally confusing for anyone who just wanted to wash their hair. He added that the average man didn't want their hair to smell of citrus, apples or any type of fruit or oriental tree blossom. Martin Purnell picked up on the idea and it was decided that Mitchell's advert would be redesigned. It would be focused on being a no-nonsense shampoo. No need for a disclaimer because they were dropping the Regeneris Reinforcium. The advert would show that you needed to use exactly this much shampoo, you rub it on, no dandruff, no citrus smell, just no-nonsense shampoo for men.

"Okay," said Mr Purnell, "That's enough for today. Mitchell, you'll get the shampoo redesign done and circulated to the production team by close of play tomorrow. Pearson, you know what to do with *'KwiknSlim'*".

"Yes, Boss," they said in unison.

"And we'll reconvene tomorrow, same time. Agenda for tomorrow will be *Pro-Retanzin*, the over-the-counter, non-prescription anti-depressant and *Itchbegone*, which I believe is your baby, Pearson, the athlete's foot powder and cream."

"Okay, Boss."

"And don't forget to copy in Max on your emails."

The meeting ended and Mr Purnell led Max back to the main entrance.

"Thanks, Max, your insight was invaluable."

"Thanks, but I didn't really do much more than say how I see things."

"You keep doing that, and we'll all be fine," said Mr Purnell with a friendly smile on his face, "We'll see you same time tomorrow, yeah?"

"Okay, sure. Same time tomorrow." replied Max, still not really understanding what he said that Mr Purnell liked so much.

Max opened the office door and stepped out into the cobbled alleyway that led to Fore Street. He hurried along the busy shopping street towards the offices of SWTV where he would meet up with his dad and get a lift home.

Four Weeks after the Power Crisis:

Tuesday 18:30Hrs

Max had settled into the routine of leaving college, catching the train into Exeter and working for a couple of hours at Muller and Rathbone. Initially, the advertising executives had been dismissive of his plain and simple approach but after time, they came around and incorporated Max's ideas and comments into their own work. It had not taken long for Max to have had a definite influence on all of the executive's projects, with some remarkable results. Slowly but surely, week on week, the new advertising approach was re-building the sales figures for MegaCorp. It was a more confident Max that left Muller and Rathbone each evening.

He stepped out of the main office doors and slung his satchel-style courier bag over his shoulder and headed at a quick pace along Fore Street to meet his dad at SWTV.

"Hey there, Office Boy!" said a voice.

Max turned around, it was Peter and Brian.

"Hey, what are you two doing here?"

"We thought we'd come into town and meet you, do you fancy the cinema? It's the new Bond film, it starts at seven fifteen."

"Too right," said Max, "Lead on, Brothers Grimm!"

"We've let your Dad know," said Brian, "He's going to pick us up from the station later."

The three of them headed along Fore Street which was still full of early evening shoppers. Heading towards them from the opposite direction with a file of papers under her arm was Rachel.

"Hey, Max," she said, "Are these two hooligans kidnapping you or something?"

"No, it's okay, this is Brian and this is Pete, they're my friends."

"If you say so," joked Rachel.

Brian was quick to point out that Peter was not actually his friend, he was his brother and therefore he was forced to tolerate him. Pete had a witty response ready, it was a joke about Brian being adopted but the sentence didn't leave his mouth. All he managed to mumble was a clumsy, 'hello', when Rachel smiled at him.

"Anyway," said Max to Rachel, "What are you up to?"

"Running some errands for my da.. *our* boss. What are you up to?"

"We're going to see the new James Bond film, do you fancy coming with us, there's plenty of time?"

Rachel thought about it for a second.

"I do, yeah, that'll be good, give me a moment to drop these files off and tell *our* boss where I'm going, okay?"

"Fine, no worries, we'll meet you back here."

Rachel hurried back to the Muller and Rathbone offices. A puzzled Brian watched her as she walked away.

"She looks familiar, what's her name, Max?"

"Brian, you are not going to believe me if I tell you. That is, or was, Poppy Purnell."

"No way, what with the ponytail and glasses?"

"Yes way, with the ponytail and glasses."

"No way!"

"Way."

"It's not."

"It is."

"Really?

"Yes, it really is."

"Pete? Max here is saying that was Poppy Purnell. Pete? Pete?"

Pete had already recognised her and was struck dumb.

"Just do me a favour, guys, try not to call her Poppy, she prefers Rachel okay?"

"Does she live round here?"

"She lives in Stoke Canon, you know, in the cream coloured house on the other side of the bridge."

"No way!"

"Yes, way!"

After a short while, Rachel reappeared and joined the three of them walking along Fore Street's crowded shopping precinct. Max and Rachel chatted about work for a minute or two but soon the conversation changed to a much more pressing topic. Who was the best Bond?

Rachel said she preferred Daniel Craig with Dame Judie as M, but Brian dismissed him out of hand due to the lack of gadgetry. Roger Moore, they all decided, was out of the running due to the dubious safari suits in his later films. Max was quick to defend Roger by mentioning the speed boat chase in *Live and Let Die* and that kept Roger close to the top of the league table until Brian raised the painful issue of the terrible *Moonraker* film. Roger was then definitely out of the top three. Rachel put Pierce Brosnan into the mix and they all agreed he was not bad, until Brian pointed out the improbable, unbelievable, invisible Aston Martin. Pierce was relegated to a respectable third place, above Roger Moore. Pete said he preferred Connery, saying he was more ruthless. Max threw a wild card into the debate and mentioned George Lazenby but none of the others knew who he was and despite Max's determined backing of *On Her Majesty's Secret Service*, poor George was dropped.

The Bond-banter continued the length of Fore Street and became more and more animated the closer they got to the cinema. Rachel soon felt totally at ease with these three somewhat unique and colourful characters. Max and Brian were the type Dean Ashburn and his hanger-on mates would have picked on and bullied constantly but Max and Brian had a confidence about them, secure in the protection of their larger muscle-bound friend and big brother.

As the four of them crossed Fore Street, checking for traffic from their left, Pete automatically placed a gentle arm across Rachel's path, stopping her from stepping out into the road. It was no big deal, Pete just did that sort of thing naturally and without thinking about it.

No one has ever done that for me before, she thought.

The Bond-debate heated up when Pete asked who should be the new Bond. Rachel fuelled the flames with a rash opinion from out of left-field.

"I think Clive Owen would make a good Bond," she said, deliberately provoking outbursts of derision and support from different corners of their group.

In no time, they had reached the cinema and were walking up the steps to the ticket office where Pete held the doors open for Rachel.

No one has ever done that for me before either, she thought to herself.

Six Weeks after the Power Crisis:

Monday 17:00Hrs

Bishop and Nina Glover stood chatting in the lift lobby on the fourth floor of the MegaCorp Research and Development Centre.

"Tell me about our *Pro-Retanzin* tests, I'm looking forward to some positive results," Bishop whispered.

"They are proceeding to plan, better than we forecasted actually," replied Nina in a hushed voice, "The subject that has been withdrawn from the dose has shown a steady gradual decline into a terminally depressed state. It has been rubbing its head on the bars and swaying from side to side for hours on end. Both of those are text book polar bear depression symptoms."

"And while it was on X-Ingredient?"

"The subject responded well to the drug and all signs of depression were removed. In fact the subject could have been described as *'buzzing'*."

"And....?"

"And when the X-Ingredient drug was withdrawn, it spiralled into a deeper depression showing all the signs of self-harming and suicidal tendencies."

"What about addiction?"

"Tests indicate that the X-Ingredient product is 99% addictive."

"Perfect. We'll switch the standard drug with the X-Ingredient drug this week. Stock should be in the shops by the weekend."

Six Weeks after the Power Crisis:

Monday 18:30Hrs

At the Muller and Rathbone offices, the brainstorming meeting had run on longer than planned and Max was one of the last to leave, followed by Martin Purnell. They waited outside the offices while Rachel set the alarm and locked the office doors.

"Do you need a lift anywhere, Max?" Martin Purnell offered.

"I was going to get the bus into Tiverton on the way home, my friend Pete is playing rugby this evening, the Exeter Chief's scout is supposed to be at the game."

"Okay," said Martin Purnell, "I think we could make a diversion to the game, is it at the ground opposite the sports centre?"

"That's right," said Max.

"Do you fancy coming along, Rachel, or shall I drop you home first?"

"I'll tag along, Dad," replied Rachel in a matter-of-fact tone trying to hide the fact she was quite looking forward to meeting Pete again.

They arrived at the ground ten minutes into the first half. Max spotted his mum and dad at the halfway line, standing with Pete's parents. Brian was also there. Max, Rachel and Martin Purnell joined them on the sideline.

Martin Purnell asked Max's dad why the game had stopped.

Near the twenty two yard line a circle of players stood around one of the trainers that was on the pitch applying liberal amounts of smelling salts under the nose of a player lying spread-eagle on the ground.

"Young Pete's clattered their fly-half. Knocked him clean out," said Max's dad.

Pete's dad joined in the conversation as the concussed opposition fly-half was lifted back to his feet and led to the sidelines.

"Thank heavens he's got up. Pete's already put one of them out of the game and we're only ten minutes in. I tell him to ease up but sometimes it's all we can do to stop him collecting their gum-shields as trophies."

The opposing side made an injury substitution and the game got back underway. On the far side of the pitch, the scout made notes as Pete played on, single-handedly stopping the opposition's backs from moving the ball forward. When the opposition had possession, Pete commanded an area of fifteen yards in all directions around him, effectively a no-go area for any ball-carrier. When Pete carried the ball he finished every run hitting would-be tacklers even harder than they tried to hit him. Pete could run round tacklers or through them, it made no difference.

"He's been playing first XV rugby for two years," said Joe Marshall, "The junior leagues asked us to move him up to seniors early, something about the other boys not wanting to play against him."

"I can understand why," replied Martin Purnell as he watched Peter pile-drive his way into the opposition's pack, sending opponents reeling backwards and the ball bouncing free.

"I've seen something like that before on the Discovery Channel," he said to a proud Joe Marshall, "It was a programme about anti-tank guided missiles."

Peter stepped through the floundering opposition, picked up the loose ball, ran around one tackler, ran through another and scored his second try.

Rachel had been a spectator of football most of her life and was accustomed to the petulant, spoilt unsportsmanlike attitude of professional footballers. She watched her first game of rugby and experienced the difference first hand. Despite the impact and aggression of the game, every single player abided to the rules and when corrected by the referee they addressed him as *'Sir'* and did not argue with any of his decisions, which was poles apart from football where barracking the referee had become part of the game. Rachel noticed that when Peter tackled an opponent it was strictly within the rules and he was never penalised. She also noticed that he always offered a floored opponent a hand up, before charging off in pursuit of someone else to tackle. She was soon caught up in the game and began to urge Pete's team on, not that they needed any support. The final whistle blew and they had won 28 points to 3.

"He's got talent, that's for sure," said Martin Purnell as the opposing side's trainer handed out ice-packs to his players that were limping from the field.

Rachel and the others watched as the two teams filed past each other, shaking hands. A few of the opposition hobbled past nursing injuries from the past eighty minutes. Peter jogged over to the opposition side-line and shook the hands of the two players he had put out of the game that were sitting on the bench recovering with several ice packs taped to shoulders, knees and necks. He then jogged back over to a jubilant Joe Marshall.

"Good game, son," he said patting Pete on the shoulder, "I think you made your mark, the scout's still writing notes." He ruffled his son's hair, "Get a shower and we'll meet you in the car park."

"Good game, Pete," said Max patting him on the arm of his mud-stained rugby shirt.

"Thanks, Max, glad you made it, how's the job going?"

"My new boss came along," said Max looking over his shoulder, pointing at Mr Purnell. Pete hadn't noticed a group of new faces standing next to his mum, amongst them was a face he recognised.

"Rachel came along too," Max added.

"Right….er….that's nice…." Peter stuttered as he noticed her, suddenly lost for words, "I'd better get off and get cleaned up, yeah?"

"Yeah, Pete, see you later," said Max, noticing the immediate change in his once-confident friend. He's got it bad, he thought to himself.

"Remember, don't slip up and call her Poppy, it's Rachel," Max added.

Pete nodded and jogged off to the changing rooms and the three families headed off to the car park, chatting about the game.

"Thanks for bringing Max to the game, Mr Purnell," Mrs Chambers said.

"It was no problem and besides, I enjoyed the game," he replied.

"I hope Max is doing well at work."

"Max, is doing just fine, he's helped us with some current projects, he's become quite the voice of reason and we're glad to have him on board."

Mrs Chambers was very proud of Max, although she didn't really understand what it was that Muller and Rathbone found so interesting in him, all he did was say things plain and simple. Perhaps that was something new in the world of advertising.

A cleaned-up and freshly showered Peter jogged over to join them in the car park. His bag of dirty kit was slung over his shoulder, he wore blue jeans and a deep violet coloured American Football shirt with an orange bordered white number 34 on the front and back. His parents congratulated him again for a good game.

"Cracking game, son, I reckon the Chief's scout took notice."

"Let's hope so," said Pete, "I played well, yeah?"

"Sure you did, son, we're all very proud," his father said, slapping him across the shoulders.

Rachel made a point of bumping into Pete and she caught up with him as the families dispersed in the car park to their separate cars.

"That's not a rugby shirt you're wearing is it, Pete?"

"Erm...."

"And I thought your last name was Marshall, why do you have the name Payton on the back of this shirt?" she asked trying to squeeze a response out of the word-stumbling Pete.

"Payton?" replied an embarrassed and tongue-tied Peter, "Well, er...he's sort of a sporting hero of mine."

Rachel had unwittingly hit a nerve and this was the one thing Peter could relax and talk about, he lost all his nervousness in an instant.

"Walter Payton is a legend," he said, "He was a running back for the Chicago Bears, but he didn't just run, he could pass the ball too. He was also a great receiver and blocker. He could really block."

"Block?" asked Rachel captivated by the admiration she could see in Pete's eyes.

"Yeah, block," said Peter, "He was the best, have you ever seen footage of him play?"

"Maybe you could show me someday?" Rachel offered.

Brian had joined them and took pleasure in interrupting his nervous brute of a brother.

"What you talking about, Pete?"

"Erm.....nothing," Peter replied, wishing his younger brother would disappear.

"Peter was just telling me about the shirt that he's wearing," said Rachel.

"I bet he was," said Brian, "He's got a box set of Chicago

games from the Eighties in his room that he watches all the time."

Peter mouthed the words *'shut up'* to his interfering little brother, who just ignored him.

"Anyway, tell me more about *Star Struck*, we watched a bit of it waiting for the football to start a few weeks ago, Pete got all gooey when you were in the chat room thing."

"I am going to kill you," Pete said through clenched teeth.

"That's not very nice at all, is it, Pete," Brian teased, "Your death threats aren't doing anything towards improving your already limited social skills, are they?"

"I am going to kill you later."

Brian ignored his brother again, "What did you think of the game, Rachel?"

"Well, it was the first game of rugby I've seen," she said, "Do you play, Brian?"

"Me? No. When they are picking teams, I'm usually the last one to get picked on the team that picks last," he said, "Unless there's a kid with a bad limp."

"That's a shame, Brian," she said trying not to laugh, not knowing if he was joking or not.

"It's okay, I can handle rejection," he replied with a smile, "Anyway, I can manage to string sentences together of more than a few words in front of girls. Unlike some people I could mention, eh Pete?"

Pete went to clip his brother round the ear but Brian knew what was coming and he was already heading back to the safety of his parent's car.

"You love him really, Pete," said Rachel, laughing.

Seven Weeks after the Power Crisis:

Thursday 17:00Hrs

Bishop and Nina Sharp walked through the lower laboratories in the basement of the Research and Development building. It was one of their regular weekly tours of the facility and Bishop was keen to hear Nina's report and he especially wanted an update on sales.

"It's all good news," she said, "Sales have recovered as quickly as they dropped. Market research indicates that this new honesty-campaign has been the key."

"Across all our brands?" asked Bishop.

"Yes, right across all product ranges. In fact, on some product lines we are up ten to twenty percent. We are taking market share from competitors that have continued with traditional advertising."

"Impressive."

"Yes. Since we directed Muller and Rathbone to change advertising styles, we've uncovered new markets for our products, plus we have increased on existing sales. It's quite remarkable."

She handed Bishop a folder containing the definite sales figures for all MegaCorp brands in all market sectors over the past six weeks. Bishop thumbed through the report, spending particular time assessing the graphs. It was clear that the period after Muller and Rathbone's switch to truthful advertising showed a steep increase in the trend line, twenty percent over existing sales patterns.

Bishop tapped the report and nodded his head in approval.

"This is all very good news, Nina, but we have to maintain these increased sales."

"Yes, we do."

"That brings us nicely to your report on X-Ingredient. This should keep us as market leaders. How is that going?"

"Exactly to plan, sir," she said with a wicked smile, "Would you care to take a look?"

She swiped her security key card through the access panel beside the lift and tapped in the security code. The lift arrived and Nina Sharp gestured for Bishop to go first.

"Show me where X-Ingredient will continue to make us rich," said Bishop.

Nina smiled, leaned forward and pressed the button marked B3.

Eight Weeks after the Power Crisis:

Friday 19:00Hrs

Due to the success of the new honesty-based campaign, Muller and Rathbone's advertising department had been invited to a social event at the Exeter offices of MegaCorp. Max was still somewhat in awe of the attention he was drawing and he was quick to point out to people that all he did was tell the truth. However, Muller and Rathbone were keen to promote their new truth policy and Max had been the spark that ignited it.

"You be careful," Mrs Chambers said, adjusting Max's tie.

Max reluctantly let his mum adjust his tie for the seventh or was it the eighth time. She brushed tiny imaginary specks of dust from the lapels of his jacket with a wooden clothes brush.

"There," she said in very proud voice, "Very smart, if I do say so myself."

Max wasn't happy wearing a suit, it was his first suit and he felt awkward. He looked down at his new shoes. Too new, he thought.

"Don't fidget, Max, you've got to look your best."

The doorbell rang and Mrs Chambers opened the door. It was Martin Purnell.

"Good evening, Mrs Chambers, hello, Max."

"Look after him, won't you?" Mrs Chambers said to Martin Purnell.

"Of course, Mrs Chambers," he replied, "Max has been a godsend these past weeks. This evening is MegaCorp's way of saying thank you for all our hard work."

"I'll be fine, Mum," said Max, "Don't worry."

"Back by eleven thirty, okay?"

Max walked down the garden path to the road outside his house where Martin Purnell's BMW was parked. Sitting in the front passenger seat was Rachel.

"Hi, Max," she said as he got into the back seat. Max pulled on the seatbelt and strapped himself in.

"Hi, how are you?"

"Fine," Rachel replied, "How are Brian and Pete?"

Rachel tried to hide it but it was clear she was more interested to know about Peter, "How did the Exeter Chief's trial go? Has he heard anything?"

Max told her he'd been made an offer but not accepted anything yet. Martin Purnell joined in the conversation from the driver's seat.

"Rugby's a proper man's game, isn't it, Max?" he said as he glanced across at his daughter, "Not like these namby pamby, overpaid footballers that fall over crying at the slightest little tap on their ankles."

"If they got into a tangle with Pete, I reckon that by the time they woke up, their clothes would be out of fashion," Max added.

"You're not wrong there. That boy finishes tackles like he's on some sort of one-man mission to drive all fifteen opponents into the ground, one by one."

This made Max laugh out loud, he had watched Peter play against senior players who were quick to give up the ball when he got within tackling distance.

"He can certainly hit, can't he?"

"I've never seen him take a cheap shot, though, he's always well within the rules, isn't he?" added Mr Purnell, who glanced to his left again and noticed his daughter's cheeks had turned a little red, "It's a proper gentleman's sport, isn't it, Max?"

The conversation switched from Pete to business and they spent the rest of the journey to Exeter with Martin Purnell talking about sales figures, growth patterns and new products. Max half-listened, it was still a little above his head.

It wasn't long before they were coming off the M5 motorway at Junction 29, heading for the airport and MegaCorp's modern Research and Development Centre where they parked and then walked towards the main entrance. Max glanced in the mirrored glass and decided he definitely hated wearing suits. He loosened his tie a little and caught up with Martin Purnell and Rachel.

They walked through the main entrance doors and underwent the statutory security process through the air-lock style hallway to where a MegaCorp receptionist issued them with ESCORTED VISITOR access cards.

"If you would follow me I will take you to the fourth floor," the receptionist said, as she headed to the lift lobby in the centre of the reception area.

She swiped her access card and entered her code into the keypad next to the lift. The lift doors opened and she gestured that they should all swipe their access cards and follow her.

The lift arrived at the fourth floor and the receptionist lead the way through the lift lobby along a short corridor to a glass-walled meeting room.

"Here we are," she said as she opened the door, "Please go in."

Inside the meeting room, several members of the Muller and Rathbone advertising team were already present and helping themselves to the complimentary buffet and drinks table. Nina Glover walked over to greet Martin Purnell and he introduced Max.

"Ah, young Mr Chambers, a pleasure to meet you, I've heard such good things about you," she said as she held out her hand. Max politely shook her hand and thought it felt unnaturally cold.

"Pleased to meet you, too," replied Max.

"Are you hungry, Max?" she said as she led them towards the buffet table, "I am sure we will have something here that you will like."

As they walked, she and Martin Purnell continued to talk about sales and marketing strategies. Max drifted away from this conversation and went over to the far end of the buffet table. He picked up a silver rimmed plate and a set of silver cutlery but he had no idea where to start or what to choose from the wide array of food, most of which he did not recognise. Rows of exquisitely prepared canapés, sushi dishes and mysterious food that Max had never imagined existed were presented on large glass platters. In the middle of the table was an ice sculpture of a swan with several cygnets surrounded by a selection of wines and champagne. It was a fantastic array of gourmet delicacies which the business people appeared to enjoy immensely but was somewhat wasted on Max.

Rachel appeared by his side and gently nudged him in the ribs.

"I guess you're doing the same as me, looking for the sausage rolls," she whispered.

"Yeah, I've never tried anything like this before. What is that?"

He pointed at a plate of what looked to be uncooked cubes of salmon.

"That's sushi."

"Er, I think I'll give that a miss. And what's that, a mini scotch egg?"

"No, I tried one. It's definitely not a scotch egg!"

"And these?"

"No idea. I think it might be a prawn Dim Sum. Try one, go on!"

Rachel and Max laughed together as they worked their way along the buffet daring each other to try the wide array of exotic dishes displayed in the buffet. Max ran out of food that he could safely identify.

"I could really do with the kid's menu and a coke," he sighed.

"Me too," Rachel replied, "Although I can't even find a coke on the drinks table."

"I'll tell you what," said Max, "I'll find us a couple of cokes, and you find the sausage rolls and cheese on a stick, deal?"

"It's a deal!"

"There's bound to be a vending machine somewhere, I'll take a look, do you want Diet or Full Fat?"

"Diet, please, Max."

Rachel smiled. He may be a couple of years younger than her and a tiny bit geeky but he was much better company than the advertising execs who were always trying to impress with boastful bragging and pathetic one-line pickups.

Max left the meeting room unnoticed and checked up and down the long corridor. He didn't remember passing a vending machine on the way from the lift so he turned left, heading further along the corridor. After about twenty metres, he came to a T junction, with a similar indistinct corridor heading to his left and right. He looked up and down the corridors but still there was no sign of a vending machine.

"Lucky left or risky right?" he said to himself, "Let's go lucky left."

He turned left and walked along the corridor, passing more plain white walls and plain white doors until he came to another lift at the other end of the corridor to where he had first come in from. On the wall to the left of the lift was an access card swipe and keypad.

"That's not going to work without the code," he sighed.

He turned round and headed back the way he had come

but he had only walked about ten metres when he heard a voice.

"Late, late, late," the voice said, "I can't be late again."

Max turned around to see a lab technician in a white doctor-style coat running towards the lift, carrying a large leather briefcase. Max watched as he swiped a key card through the lock and entered a code into the keypad.

"Hello," said Max, but the man was too pre-occupied to notice him.

After a second or two, the lift doors opened and the lab technician stepped hurriedly inside. He turned around and pressed a button and the doors started to close.

Max watched him pat his lab coat pockets, then the man reached out with one hand to stop the doors from closing. The doors started to reopen and he squeezed through placing his large briefcase against the lift doors to stop them closing fully.

Max called out again but the man was too preoccupied as he ran back the way he had come, muttering something about his glasses. Thanks a lot, thought Max. I'll just wait for him to come back and then ask him what floor the vending machines are on.

Max walked over to the half-open lift doors, stepped over the man's case and squeezed through into the lift. He stood there for a while waiting for the man to return. The lights on the button pad showed that the man had pressed B3. Max waited a while longer then the doors started to close so he reached out and pressed the door-hold button but the doors kept closing. The doors forced the briefcase to one side and the lift doors closed shut.

Oh, well, thought Max, we'll see where this goes.

The lift started to descend so Max pressed G for ground, then 1, 2, 3. There was bound to be a vending machine on one of those floors, he thought. The lift travelled downwards past several floors. The indicator panel above the doors showed the lift had passed the Ground floor and was still going down. This must be going to the basement first, thought Max. The indicator illuminated floor B3 and the lift started to slow and then came to a stop. With a ding, the lift doors opened and Max peered out into the lift lobby.

In front of him were two signs on the wall opposite. Test Lab A to the left and Test Lab B to the right but there were no vending machines. Max stepped out of the lift and the doors closed behind him.

"Risky right this time," he said to himself and he turned right in the direction of Test Lab B.

He went around a corner and came to a door on his left where he looked through the door's glass panel window. Inside he saw what appeared to be a very modern equivalent of his college science lab. There were two very long stainless steel benches with lab stools arranged neatly in a row and Bunsen burners, PC terminals and test equipment were spaced at regular intervals along the benches. There's a sink, thought Max, I can at least get a drink of water.

He pushed open the door and headed for the nearest sink and turned on the tap. The water seemed to be drinkable so he turned his head as if to drink from a water fountain. Out of the corner of his eye he noticed something move. In fact, he noticed several things moving so he walked cautiously over to have a closer look. At the end of the bench was an array of glass fronted cages with white mice in them. The cages were labelled either *Control, Test* or *Withdraw*.

Max noticed that a few of the mice that were labelled *Control* appeared to be perfectly happy and healthy, they were running around quite normally and playing in their wheels. A few of the mice were more lethargic, they didn't move around so much and they appeared to be a lot plumper. Max checked the mice in the cages to the far right that were labelled *Withdraw* and in these cages the mice were much more plump, bordering on being very overweight. One of them was so overweight it was almost at the point of being so bulky it was unable to move.

Max noticed the water bottles in every cage contained a pink milkshake type of liquid that was very familiar. He turned and looked at the bench and saw several tins that he instantly recognised as *'KwiknSlim'*. Next to the tins, were little teat pipettes and measuring jars. It dawned on Max this was a test lab for MegaCorp's leading-brand slimming drink. He explored further along the desk, his natural curiosity getting the better of him and he saw a PC terminal that was still on. It won't hurt to take a quick peek, he thought.

Max viewed the screen and saw a spreadsheet of dates, doses and food that were cross referenced against the test subjects. The right hand table had a summary of changes in weight.

It didn't take Max long to figure out the data: The *Control* subjects were fed only water and fruit and showed no change in weight. Other *Control* subjects were fed cheese and chocolate and gained over 10% body weight in five weeks.

Test subjects had been fed *'KwiknSlim'* and these showed absolutely no difference to the *Control* subjects. Evidently, *'KwiknSlim'* had no effect at all. The results were clear and conclusive.

Further down the table, some of the mice had been given a type of *'KwiknSlim'* that contained something called X-Ingredient. *'KwiknSlim'* with this added ingredient *did* keep weight off. That's strange thought Max. The bottom two rows of the table had data from subjects where X-Ingredient had been withdrawn. Max double-checked the results. When X-Ingredient was removed, these mice ballooned in weight to nearly 20% more in just two weeks.

Max studied the tables again. What on earth is this X-Ingredient they are testing? If a human being started to use *'KwiknSlim'* with this added X-Ingredient it would keep their weight down but the moment they stopped using it, their weight would increase and increase.

"Brian will never believe this," he said to himself.

Test Subject	Food	Liquid	Week1 Weight (g)	Week2 Weight (g)	Week3 Weight (g)		Week4 Weight (g)	Week5 Weight (g)	WEIGHT Increase
CONTROL	Fruit and Seeds Mix	Water	20.00	20.00	20.00		20.00	20.00	0.00%
CONTROL	Cheese and Chocolate Mix	Water	20.00	20.54	21.22		21.66	22.10	10.50%
TEST	Fruit and Seeds Mix	Regular 'KwiknSlim'	20.00	20.00	20.00		20.00	20.00	0.00%
TEST	Cheese and Chocolate	Regular 'KwiknSlim'	20.00	20.22	20.55		20.99	22.10	10.50%

X - Ingredient DOSE	Fruit and Seeds Mix	'KwiknSlim' X Ingredient	20.00	19.66	19.00	Continue X Dose	20.00	20.00	0.00%
X - Ingredient DOSE	Cheese and Chocolate Mix	'KwiknSlim' X Ingredient	20.00	19.99	19.44	Continue X Dose	19.22	20.01	0.05%
WITHDRAW	Fruit and Seeds Mix	'KwiknSlim' X Ingredient	20.00	19.66	19.00	Withdraw X	20.88	22.20	11.00%
WITHDRAW	Cheese and Chocolate Mix	'KwiknSlim' X Ingredient	20.00	19.99	19.44	Withdraw X	21.55	23.99	19.95%

He looked down at the keyboard and mouse, that's the only 'normal' rodent in this lab, he thought. He held down the Ctrl key on the keyboard and pressed print screen. He then opened up the PC's web browser, logged into his Hotmail account and cut and paste the print-screen into an email that he sent to himself. He closed down the web browser and turned towards the laboratory doors.

Back in the corridor, he stopped at the next door and peered through the glass panel window, it was the same layout as before, a test laboratory with animal cages in the far corner. He knew he shouldn't go in but he couldn't help himself. He pushed open the door and walked over to the cages.

In each cage was a rotating horizontal cylinder that turned slowly at about the speed of a roast chicken rotisserie. The cylinder was covered in a coarse, carpet-like material and Max had no idea what it was used for. As one of the carpeted cylinders slowly rotated, Max stepped back in horror because clinging tightly to the cylinder with its claws, was a tiny kitten. At the bottom of its cage, directly underneath the cylinder, was a metal chute which Max assumed any kitten that lost grip would fall into. Max did not want to imagine where this poor unfortunate kitten would ultimately end up. Clearly these kittens were clinging on for their little lives.

Max dared himself to check the other cages, fearing some sort of large scale kitten massacre. He saw more kittens, some of them were fixed firmly to the carpeted cylinders but some were hanging on for dear life by just a few of their tiny claws. As each kitten rotated upside down it let out a desperate meow which filled the cages with a sound like badly played out-of-tune bagpipes.

In other cages there were no kittens clinging to the cylinders. All there was were traces of fur and spots of blood on the edges of the chute where the kitten had fallen. Max shuddered when he turned to see what product was on the test benches, there were lines of little bottles with the instantly recognisable logo of MegaCorp's leading brand of nail polish *'Manicure 247'*, the one that was advertised with added strengthening agent, the one that guaranteed for nails never to break.

Max didn't wait to check the PC for results, the last thing he wanted to see was a detailed database of kitten nail strength due to X-Ingredient plus it would probably have blanks in the table where there were kitten deaths due to weakened claws.

He had seen enough of the rotating kitten tests so he quietly pushed open the laboratory doors and headed back into the corridor. Opposite was another doorway and when he peered inside he could see more cages at the far end of the laboratory which meant more test animals. He didn't want to take a closer look, but he had to.

There were larger cages this time, again labelled *Control, Test* and *Withdraw*, and in them he saw dogs of differing sizes, or rather differing waistlines. Max checked on the bench and he already knew the answer. MegaCorp's leading brand of diet dog-food, *'Activity-Dog'*, evidently using the same X-Ingredient as the mice if the poor overweight specimens in the cages marked *Withdraw* were anything to go by.

Max continued to check the laboratories along the corridor, one by one. As he progressed, he noticed that the animals became alarmingly rarer. Some of them were on the World Wildlife Fund's Threatened and Endangered Species list.

He was shocked to find rare Giant Sloths on speeding motorised treadmills that were being used to test MegaCorp's energy boost drink.

He witnessed rare Mountain Gorillas with curlers in their normally tufty, coarse hair being used to test MegaCorp softening conditioner shampoos, the ones that contained Regeneratis Reinforcium.

He saw a pair of endangered Komodo Dragons being used to test MegaCorp's brand of halitosis breath mints. It had never dawned on Max that Komodo Dragons had bad breath and he did not plan to get close enough to find out.

Max explored even further along the corridor and every laboratory was the same. Test benches, caged animals and MegaCorp X-Ingredient experiments. He peered through the glass panel of one lab and saw what appeared to be leopards. He remembered seeing a natural history programme about an endangered species of Snow Leopard that lived a hard existence in the rugged mountains of Tibet, bordering the Himalayas and could not believe there were two of them in cages in this laboratory.

He went inside another laboratory and was shocked to find a dozen rare orang-utans that stared sadly back at him through the bars. These gentle primates, arguably the closest relative to man, had lost their natural habitat in the forests of Borneo and their numbers had dwindled to an all time low, they were amongst the top three of the world's endangered species. Max shook his head, this is not good, he thought.

To his relief, several of the orang-utans seemed to be perfectly normal but as he got a little closer he noticed some of them had rubber verruca socks taped permanently to their feet. The ones without rubber socks were holding their bare feet and were rubbing vigorously in between their toes.

Max scanned to the right of the cages where he saw the test subject labelled *Withdraw.* This orang-utan had a mad distracted look in his eye and he rubbed and rubbed and rubbed and rubbed at his feet until he had rubbed off all of the loose skin between his toes. The poor animal's feet had been rubbed red-raw.

Max knew what he was going to see on the bench even before he turned around. There were tubes of *'Itchbegone',* MegaCorp's leading brand of athlete's foot cream, the one guaranteed to clear up the itching, as long as you used it regularly.

Inside his shoes and socks, Max's toes started to itch.

"Damn," he said to himself, "I use that cream."

Max decided he had seen enough and also realised he was in deep, deep trouble if he was caught. He wanted nothing more to do with MegaCorp and his mind raced as he tried to figure out how he would tell Mr Purnell about what he had seen. Perhaps Mr Purnell already knew. Max decided to keep quiet, at least until he was out of MegaCorp's building. He suddenly, and quite rightly, felt a little scared.

Max trod quietly over towards the laboratory door and opened it a few centimetres, cautiously checking up and down the corridor because now was not the time to get caught down here. It was clear so he stepped out and headed back towards the lift. He hadn't got far when he heard the tell-tale ding of the lift arriving. He doubled back and darted into the first laboratory on his right, searching for a place to hide. He saw a gap large enough below one of the test benches and dived underneath, squeezing in between a stack of cardboard boxes and some metal bars at the end of the bench. The labels on the boxes read '*Pro-Retanzin: X*'. He recognised the name. It was the over-the-counter, non-prescription anti-depressant.

Footsteps came closer along the corridor and stopped outside the laboratory door. Through the glass panel, he could see the silhouette of a man in a peaked cap. Max tried to make himself as small as possible as he sat huddled under the bench. His arms pulled his knees in tight to his chest and he held his breath.

"All clear on corridor B, awaiting further instructions, over," the security guard said.

After an agonising few seconds, a petrified Max heard the security guard speak again.

"Roger that, I'll check corridor A. Over and out."

Max waited another few tense seconds until the footsteps in the corridor gradually faded away. With a huge sigh of relief, he slowly breathed out.

So did something else dangerously close behind him. The

blast of warm air made the hairs on the back of his neck stand on end and he didn't dare turn his head to look behind. Whatever the creature was, it breathed on him again. Then it sniffed.

Max was rooted to the spot and could not move.

He then felt something cold and wet touch his neck just above the collar of his shirt. Max froze as the creature sniffed again. He tried to move but his arms, legs and body remained firmly rooted. In the eerie silence of the empty laboratory, he could hear and feel the creature softly breathing behind him. Max was about to pluck up the courage to turn his head to see what on earth it was when something that felt like a soggy piece of sandpaper ran along his collar, up his neck and across his ear.

Max spun around and in the dim light underneath the test bench, he stared directly at a huge blue-grey tongue and above that huge tongue there was a pair of large nostrils that were part of a glossy black, wet nose. He peered over the large black nose and along the ridge of a long white furry snout until he saw a pair of big dark brown eyes which were staring right back at him.

In an instant, Max's motor functions returned and he launched himself through the laboratory and out the door with the speed and agility of a scalded cat. No, he was much faster and more agile than a scalded cat because he burst through the laboratory and out through the door with the speed and agility of someone that had just been intimately nose-to-nose with a polar bear.

Max no longer cared about being caught by the security guard. He hurtled down the corridor, the soles of his new shoes squeaked, struggling for grip, as he launched himself at a rocket-propelled pace back towards the junction of Test Lab A and Test Lab B, where he knew the lift was.

If this was Test Lab B, what the hell was going on in Test Lab A, Max thought to himself, but he didn't have to wait long to find out.

As he turned the corner he could not believe what he saw because running towards him at full speed from the direction of Test Lab A, was what appeared to be a dwarf. The dwarf saw Max at the same time as Max saw him and they both slowed down to a walking pace as they drew closer to each other, until they stopped just a few metres apart. Neither of them spoke.

Max looked the dwarf up and down. Admittedly, not all that far up because the dwarf was a dwarf after all. Neither of them moved or said a word. Max couldn't help but notice that the dwarf was barefoot and was wearing a blue Gingham-check hospital gown, the type with a revealing split up the back.

Max stared at the dwarf and the dwarf stared back. After what seemed an age, the dwarf spoke in a low, secretive voice.

"You haven't seen me," he said "And I haven't seen you, okay?" and with that he tapped the side of his nose and winked.

"Okay," said Max who was already somewhat shocked by the events in Test Lab B and had no wish to find out what on earth sort of extreme human testing went on in Test Lab A. And he definitely had no wish to discover who or what this dwarf was trying to escape from.

The dwarf slowly and cautiously edged his way past Max, keeping his back tight against the walls of the corridor. He never took his eyes off Max as he went past. Max watched as the dwarf disappeared around the corner of the corridor heading towards Test Lab B.

"This is complete madness," he said to himself, "I've got to get out of here!"

He figured the lift was not an escape option without the correct swipe card and code number so he ran further along the corridor and found a door on his right. He pushed it open and saw it led to a stairwell. He sprinted to the foot of the stairs and started to run upwards, pulling on the banister rail, taking two, sometimes three steps at a time.

Three floors up, he thought, then it's the ground floor and I'm home-free.

The door marked B2 flashed past as he swung around the corner of the banister rail, still racing upwards. B1 flashed by, nearly there, he thought. As he raced up the final flight of stairs towards the ground floor exit his racing mind quickly considered his present situation. He couldn't just burst out into the reception area, he was bound to be seen by someone. No, he would have to get back to the party, blend in with the crowd and pretend this had never happened.

Rejecting the ground floor exit he pushed on upwards, running upstairs as fast as he could, a potent mix of fear and adrenalin powered him on even though his thigh and calf muscles screamed *stop!* He was still taking two steps at time when he passed the exit to the second floor. Two more floors, just two more floors, keep running, he said to himself.

As he approached the exit to the fourth floor he slowed down to a walking pace. He had to, he was completely out of breath and still out-of-his-mind with fear. His legs were like jelly, he was bent double, using the banister to pull him up the last few steps, while his aching lungs worked overtime trying to get oxygen back into his body. Exhausted, he gently pushed on the exit door and peered through the gap in both directions. It was clear so he pushed the door fully open and stepped out into the corridor.

The door closed behind with a loud click that made him jump. He spun around, fearing that something or someone had followed him up the stairwell but when he looked at the door, it was just a plain, unmarked white panel, like all the other panels along the corridor. No sign of a doorknob, or handle. It was only the keypad and swipe card which identified that there may have been a door there. he pushed against where the door should have been but it was shut solid and would not move.

Max did not hang around trying to figure out this mad building and its secret doors, he walked quickly back along the corridor to the meeting room where the Muller and Rathbone party was still in full swing. He glanced over his shoulder one last time to make sure he had not been followed then he swiftly pushed open the door and joined the rest of his colleagues.   Once inside, he breathed out another huge sigh of relief.

"Where have you been, did you find anything?" Rachel said as she tapped him on the shoulder.

"N..n...no, sorry," said Max, nearly jumping out of his skin for the second time in less than five minutes, "I got lost and couldn't find anything."

"Never mind, I've found some OJ. Do you want some?"

Max gratefully took a glass and drank it down in one.

"Easy, Tiger," said Rachel, "There's no rush."

But there was, he wanted out of this place and as soon as possible. He wanted to tell Rachel but he decided to say nothing, he didn't want to risk getting her involved. For the rest of the evening, he mingled awkwardly with the advertising executives making small-talk, while inside his head he tried to figure out what he had witnessed. What if everyone at Muller and Rathbone knew about the animal testing? What if only Martin Purnell was aware? What if Martin Purnell condoned it? No, that was not possible. Was it? No.

One thing was certain, he had to report this to someone, but who?

First things first, he thought, I've got to get out of here then I'll work out what to do.

Seven floors below, the polar bear reached out through the bars of its cage and pawed at the object the frightened two-leg had left behind. The bear sniffed it. It was Max's ESCORTED VISITOR access card.

Eight Weeks after the Power Crisis:

Saturday 06:30Hrs

Mr Bishop had been alerted to the security breach in the early hours of the morning and he had wasted no time in having the man responsible collected from his home and brought to his office. Bishop could hardly control himself. He thumped his fist down on his desk in a barely contained rage.

"Let me get this straight," Bishop snarled at the lab-technician, "You held the lift by jamming your case in the doors because you were in a *hurry*?"

"Yes, sir."

"You held open the doors on the lift, the doors to the *secure* lift that goes down to the *secure* basement levels because you were in a *hurry*?"

"Yes, sir, I'm sorry, sir."

"Well," said Bishop, "I suggest you bloody well *hurry* along to personnel where you will find your termination of contract. There's no need to return to your office to clear your desk. This has already been done."

Before the technician could protest, Nina Glover had taken him by the arm and was leading him out of the office. As they walked, she took the opportunity to remind him what the consequences would be if he were to mention his work in the laboratories.

"Think of your family," she softly threatened.

Bishop reigned in his anger, his mind focused on solving the problems the security breach had raised. He turned to face the security guard that had been on duty last night.

"And you saw nothing?"

"Nothing, sir, but we did find this in one of the labs on corridor B."

He produced Max's ESCORTED VISITOR access card from the breast pocket of his jacket and handed it to Bishop. Bishop looked at the card and tapped it on his glass topped desk.

"And how did he get out of the building without this?"

"We think he slipped out with the others from the Muller and Rathbone group."

"You think?!!?" screamed Bishop, "Of course he bloody did!"

Bishop drew in a deep breath, counted to ten in his head and slowly exhaled. He then handed the security guard a photo, it was a still image taken from CCTV footage of Max and the dwarf outside the lift.

To emphasise the point, Bishop summarised for the guard.

"Last night, we had a major breach of security in basement level three. From the CCTV footage it would appear that *this* Max Chambers and *this* escaped dwarf, wearing nothing more than a hospital gown I might add, were both running amok throughout the Project X test labs. And you say you saw *nothing*?!"

"We don't think they were working together, sir," offered the security guard, "We believe they were working independently of each other."

"Indeed," said Bishop, "Quite the coincidence."

"We did find something else, sir," the security guard said, "The intruder used one of the PC's in Lab B3-7. He sent an email to a Hotmail account. He copied a table of results, sir."

Behind the security guard, sitting silently at the back of the room on a black leather sofa, were two men. They had closely cropped military style crew cuts, hard chiselled features and a look that suggested they had served several tours as mercenaries in some of the world's toughest civil wars, a few of which they had probably started. They wore black suits, black shoes and black ties and even though they were indoors, they wore black sunglasses. The conspicuous bulge in their suit's tailoring beneath their left armpit suggested they were packing more than just a sunglasses case.

The two mysterious men had been listening intently to the conversation between Bishop and the security guard. Beside them, on the floor, was a large hessian sack tied at one end by a thick heavy rope. Inside the sack, the dwarf struggled.

"That will be all," Bishop said to the security guard and pointed for him to leave.

Bishop turned to the two men in black suits and looked down at the writhing sack by their feet.

"Mr Black, Mr White," he said, "I see you have successfully apprehended the missing test subject."

Mr White tapped the sack with his foot and the dwarf stopped wriggling.

"Yes, sir," Mr White said.

"Have you also located the whereabouts of the intruder?"

Mr Black answered, "Affirmative, sir, we are good-to-go."

"Good," said Bishop, "Then you know what to do."

The two black-suited men stood up and left the office. Mr White dragged the wriggling dwarf-filled sack behind him.

Shortly after they had left, Nina Sharp returned to the office. The look on Bishop's face spoke volumes. They both knew what needed to be done and it was Bishop that broke the silence.

"We will shut down Project-X for the time being, at least until this blows over. Get Mr Pink and Mr Green in here, they can oversee the laboratories. I want all trace of animals in the labs removed."

"Yes, sir," confirmed Nina.

"And encrypt the test data and put it on a removable hard drive."

Nina nodded in agreement.

"Then dispose of the test subjects," he ordered, "Get rid of all of them."

Eight Weeks after the Power Crisis:

Saturday 07:30Hrs

Max had hardly slept.

Images from the previous evening's events flashed in and out of his mind and he had spent a restless, sleepless night thinking about what he should do, whether he should keep quiet or whether he should tell someone. But tell who? He had not told Rachel in the meeting room because of the risk of MegaCorp thinking she was involved and he had not been able to say anything in the car on the way home either because he was unsure about Muller and Rathbone's involvement.

He got out of bed, showered and put on a pair of jeans and a tee shirt then he sat at his desk and racked his muddled brain for a solution.

He reached into his laptop case and took out the pager/calculator device and entered a short message for Brian asking to meet up at the skate park at nine o'clock. Within a few minutes a reply came back with a short message saying 'Ok'.

Max turned on his desktop computer. When it had booted up, he opened his web browser and Googled *'MegaCorp'*.

Page after page of search results came up.

He narrowed his search by entering *'MegaCorp animal testing'*.

The results that appeared were not what he expected. There were hundreds of search hits and he quickly scanned through the links and every single link pointed to official MegaCorp press releases where they stated they were proud *not* to use animals in their product testing.

Max scrolled down the results and checked through all the pages. There was absolutely nothing online to link MegaCorp to what was going on in their lower basement laboratories.

Max's hands hovered over the keyboard and for a split second he wondered if it had all been a bad dream. He wished it had but the stark reality of the previous night came rushing back into his head when his PC beeped, signifying he had a new email. He already knew what it was. The first email in his inbox was from himself, and it contained the print screen of the mouse weight spreadsheet which was the evidence he needed. If he showed this to the police they would……hmmm…..they would do what? They would think it was a prank or a hoax. He could hardly walk into Tiverton Police Station with just this as evidence and expect them to mount a full scale investigation into MegaCorp based upon one spreadsheet, especially considering it had been sent from his own email account.

Should he put this up online through Twitter or YouTube? He opened up the YouTube home page and logged into his account. He stopped typing and thought through this idea. Anyone seeing the spreadsheet would be able to trace it directly back to him. He looked down at his hands and for the first time noticed the left one was trembling slightly.

"Think Max, think," he said to himself.

What if he started a new Youtube account? No. He would need to use an email account and a new email account needed verification. He couldn't risk anything being linked back to him.

Brian, he thought. He should ask Brian. Brian would know how to get this up on line and make sure the sender was anonymous. That was the answer. He printed out a hard copy of the spreadsheet and as it came off the printer he checked over the figures again and again.

In his hand he held the conclusive proof of the sinister, addictive element in MegaCorp's X-Ingredient.

Eight Weeks after the Power Crisis:

Saturday 07:30Hrs

While Max was getting ready to meet his friends, Mr Black and Mr White were driving through the small village of Nomansland on the B3137 heading for Witheridge. Their black BMW M5 purred softly past the Mount Pleasant pub as the two henchman coasted through the village's crossroads at a very conservative twenty eight miles per hour. In the passenger seat, Mr White glanced down at a paper map on his lap.

"We should be there in three minutes," he said, "The road forks to the right in two miles and then we'll be in the target's village."

Mr Black acknowledged the directions with a nod and gently accelerated the BMW up to a steady fifty five when the speed limit increased outside the village. Mr White and Mr Black were seasoned, well-trained professionals. They did not use GPS satellite navigation because they knew that the satellite signal could also pinpoint *their* location, and for this job they wanted their location kept secret. They also stayed well within the speed limits to ensure they had no unwanted interest from a police patrol car or photographic evidence of their whereabouts through being caught on a speed camera. They were careful not to take any risks that could link them with this mission.

Exactly three minutes later, they entered the outskirts of Witheridge, again keeping well within the thirty miles per hour speed limit through the village.

"Turn right in one hundred metres," instructed Mr White.

Mr Black coasted through the narrow main street and turned right into Rackenford Road.

"Park there," Mr White said, directing Mr Black to a space between two parked cars on the right hand side of the road.

The two men sat in their car and observed Max's house which was less than one hundred metres further along the road, on the right hand side. They didn't say much at all to each other, they were now in a stake-out mode and their years of training had taught them vigilance was the key to executing a successful mission. Mr White kept a continuous visual observation of the house, while Mr Black checked his rear view mirrors, covering any movement behind them and also monitoring their planned emergency exit routes.

The two hired henchmen had been in position for nearly an hour when Mr White observed movement at the house. He saw the front door open and Max came into view.

"We're in business, Mr Black."

"Indeed we are, Mr White," said Mr Black as he started the engine of the car.

Mr White examined the access card that Bishop had given him and compared the photo with the person he could see walking down the garden path from the house.

He then opened the glove compartment and took out a pair of black leather gloves and put them on, flexing each finger into the tight fitting leather to ensure he had full movement. Satisfied with the flexibility of the gloves, he reached underneath his left arm and produced his 9mm Glock semi-automatic pistol. From the inside pocket of his jacket he produced a black metal cylindrical silencer which he expertly attached to the Glock's muzzle. He then pulled the slider back, loading a fresh round into the chamber and he placed the loaded, silenced weapon back into his shoulder holster.

"Just in case," said Mr White, "We can't be too careful, can we?"

Eight Weeks after the Power Crisis:

Saturday 08:45Hrs

Max walked quickly along Rackenford Road, he had other things on his mind and he didn't take any notice of the black BMW and the two dark-suited men sitting inside. As he drew level with the driver-side door window he instinctively glanced into the car and saw that both men were dressed in the same style of clothes which were not the typical casual dress code of a local person and neither was the car a local person's typical model of car. It instantly made him suspicious but it was too late.

Mr White jumped out of the passenger door and spun around the back of the car before Max had any time to think.

Mr Black calmly reached down for the electronic boot release button which flipped open the boot lid at the same time as Mr White stepped onto the pavement and grabbed Max. With one slick movement he clamped his huge leather-gloved hand over Max's mouth, while with his free hand he twisted Max around and pulled his wrists behind his back, clamping them into a pair of police-grade metal handcuffs. Before Max even had time to gasp for breath, a strip of duct tape had been firmly fixed across his mouth and he was bundled roughly into the boot of the BMW and the lid was slammed shut.

Mr White scanned around to check no one had seen him and he calmly walked to the open passenger side door and joined his partner in the front of the car. It was all expertly done in less than a few seconds, both men clearly had a lot of experience with kidnapping and abduction.

"Nicely done, Mr White."

"As always, Mr Black."

Mr Black reached down and placed the car's gear selector into Drive and he slowly pulled out from the parking space without drawing any unwanted attention.

Before long, the road narrowed down to a single car's width as they drove deeper into the countryside. After three miles, at a place called Five Crosses, not far from the village of Nomansland, Mr Black parked the car in an entrance to a cow field. For as far as the eye could see, there were grassy fields of open pasture with nothing in them but a few cows and sheep. Off in the distance, there was a solitary farmhouse but this spot was quite secluded and the BMW was hidden from view.

Mr White got out and went to the rear of the car. Inside, Max had regained some composure and was kicking the inside of the boot. Mr White tapped on the boot lid to get Max's attention.

"We can do this the easy way, or the hard way, it's up to you," he said with a certain amount of menace in his voice, "All we want to do is have a talk about what you saw last night."

"I didn't see anything," Max mumbled through the duct tape.

"You may say you didn't, but we have to make sure."

"I promise I didn't," Max mumbled.

"You'll need to be a little more convincing for us to believe you."

"I didn't see anything, I promise."

"Listen to me," said Mr White, "We are now going for a little drive. If you continue to kick the inside of the car and make a fuss my colleague Mr Black is going to get annoyed. And when he's annoyed he gets very violent. Do you understand?"

Max kept quiet. Mr White got back into the car and the car sped off down the lane, heading east.

As the car twisted and turned along the country lanes, Max

tried to keep a bearing on where they were heading. This would have been easier in a town but in the pitch black darkness inside the boot it was much more difficult, plus the winding country lanes and indistinct junctions soon had Max totally confused.

Max lay on his side and arched his back, stretching for the pager/calculator device in his back pocket. The handcuffs behind his back cut into his wrists but he fought through the pain to reach behind and get one hand in his pocket. The cuffs cut deeper the more he stretched but he forced himself to stretch a little further until he managed to grasp the pager between the tips of his fingers. He slowly and carefully pulled the pager out of his pocket.

He took a deep breath through his nose, ignored the pain and dug deeper into his pocket to find the calculator. He felt the plastic sides and rubberised buttons, gripping it as hard as he could between two outstretched fingers. He carefully pulled the calculator out of his pocket and breathed a huge sigh of relief as the pain in his wrists subsided.

Max felt the car was travelling in a straight line now and that it had picked up speed. This is either the A361 Tiverton bypass or the motorway, thought Max. He tried to remember if he had felt the car take any roundabouts recently. No, so this is the A361. After about ten minutes of straight-ahead driving, the car swung left then right on a large roundabout. This must be the M5 motorway roundabout, he thought, they are taking me to the MegaCorp building.

He held the calculator in the palm of one hand and he tried to orientate the device behind his back. It was hard trying to figure which way was up in the dark but doing it behind his back as well made it doubly difficult. He felt across the outer edges and worked out by softly touching the number keypad which was up and which way was down. He brushed his thumb across the large button on the lower right hand side. That must be the equals sign. He worked his way across to the left and found the + button. He racked his brain to visualise the number keys. 9 is bottom right?

He focused his memory and pictured the calculator in front of him.

Yes, 9 is located bottom right.

9, 6 and 3 go up. Then it is 3, 2 and 1 that go across.

The rough metal edges of the cuffs cut deep into his wrists and he struggled to keep the calculator level. He carefully pressed out the message. *'help at mc'.*

Max pressed the *equals* button to send it. He hoped they would understand *mc* meant MegaCorp. He put the pager and calculator into the back pocket of his trousers and breathed out a long sigh through the duct tape gag as the handcuffs loosened slightly and the pain in his wrists eased.

Eight Weeks after the Power Crisis:

Saturday 9:30Hrs

Peter and Brian had been waiting for Max for over thirty minutes, sitting on the wooden park bench opposite the skate park on the outskirts of Witheridge.

Brian held his pager/calculator invention in his hands and typed in *'at skate park'*. He waited for a reply but none came through.

"Let's face it, the gizmo doesn't work," Peter said as he gently tapped Brian repeatedly on the top of his head with his rugby ball.

Brian swiped at the ball that was now getting very annoying.

"It does work. He probably doesn't have it switched on."

Brian typed into his calculator's front panel, *'max p and b at skate park'*.

There was no reply.

"I suppose we'd better go and call for him. See what he's up to."

"Ok," agreed Brian, "I've got his binoculars and camera in my bag, I thought he wanted those for this weekend. We can drop them off at his house if he's in."

The two brothers walked into the village and headed for Max's house, Peter was idly spinning his ball from one hand to another, Brian checked the pager-calculator again. They hadn't gone far when their pagers beeped and a message flashed up on the calculator's screen. Brian stopped to read it. *'hlpmc'*

Brian read the message aloud to Peter.

"I told you it doesn't work, that makes no sense at all."

"It's working fine, Pete, you know it is, but I don't get what that means."

"I'll find out," Pete said. He took his device out of his pocket and typed in *'what max'.*

They then set off at a fast walking pace towards Max's house.

Brian was talking aloud to himself trying to work out what the possible problem was with the device and couldn't come up with a technical reason for it not to work.

"He's probably changed his mind and gone to work with his dad and not noticed he's sitting on it or something," he said to Pete as they crossed over the playing fields, taking the short cut to Rackenford Road.

Eight Weeks after the Power Crisis:

Saturday 12:30Hrs

But Max was not at work with his dad and he had not been sitting on the calculator. For the past three hours he had been sitting on a wooden chair in a dark empty, featureless room somewhere deep within the MegaCorp building. His legs had been bound with duct tape and the handcuffs behind his back still cut deep into his wrists. Standing by the only door to the room was Mr White and he said nothing to Max.

The door opened and Bishop entered the room.

"Thank you, Mr White," Bishop said, "You've checked him for a mobile phone, yes?"

"No phone, sir, all he's got on him is a calculator, some loose change and this piece of paper."

Mr White passed Mr Bishop the mouse-weight spreadsheet. Bishop looked at it for a second then folded it carefully and placed it in his trouser pocket. He walked over to face Max.

"Ah, Mister Chambers," he said, with a false tone of surprise, "We finally meet, my name is Mr Bishop."

Max had heard the name but this was the first time he had met Mr Bishop. He held eye contact with him for only a very short time then he let his head drop and he stared at the man's shoes.

"I understand you were having some fun last night with a dwarf and that you both were running through *my* laboratories upsetting *my* animals."

Max tried his best to talk through the duct tape which was firmly stuck across his mouth. He wanted to tell Bishop that

216

firstly, he didn't know the dwarf and he certainly hadn't been running anywhere with him and secondly, if anyone was upsetting the animals it wasn't him! All that came out of his mouth were mumbled, incoherent words, barely audible through the duct tape gag.

"So what are we going to do with you?" Bishop asked. It was a rhetorical question.

Max tried to say he hadn't seen anything and that he wouldn't tell anyone. Bishop put his finger under Max's chin and lifted Max's head up.

"Such a shame," he said, "And you had such a promising career in front of you."

A maelstrom of emotions welled up inside Max. He was afraid to the point of being petrified but his fear released a burst of adrenalin and this gave him the courage to lift both feet up as high as he could despite the duct tape round his ankles and he brought his heels down with full force on Bishop's toes.

Bishop recoiled and he went to hit Max but he stopped just short of striking him across the face. Bishop regained his composure. He smiled and turned to Mr White who was watching events from the door.

"It appears we have a little fighter on our hands."

Mr White's steely composure cracked into a slight smile, "Yes, sir, it seems we do."

"Mr White?" asked Bishop, "Are the laboratories ready to be cleared?"

"Everything is proceeding according to plan and schedule. Mr Green is overseeing the closure and clean-up operation in the laboratories and the exotic specimens will be the last ones loaded onto the transport, sir."

"And everything has been prepared at the dog food factory?"

"The factory will be clear by the time the transport arrives with the test subjects, sir. We plan to be processing the disposal of the first animals by around eight o'clock."

"Good," Bishop said as he turned and pointed at Max.

"Mr White, please add this one to the list of the specimens for disposal."

"Yes, sir."

"And don't forget to remove these handcuffs. They tend to blunt the blades of the crush-and-grind machinery."

Eight Weeks after the Power Crisis:

Saturday 16:00Hrs

Brian and Peter had called on Max earlier that morning but no one had answered at his house. They figured he was in Exeter at work with his dad so they had left a note poking out from the corner of the front doormat telling him to call round to their house when he got home.

Brian had been in his bedroom/workshop all morning and most of the afternoon where he had dismantled and reassembled his pager/calculator device three times checking for a possible cause of the problem, testing the device over and over again. He could not find a fault, at least not one that was due to technical failure. He figured it must be Max's unit but he was certain that one worked, it was the first one he had made and it was very robust.

He racked his brain for a possible solution to the meaningless messages coming from Max's pager/calculator device. All of a sudden he realised it was not a technical issue at all.

"Pete!" he shouted, "Pete, come here!"

There was no answer. He remembered Pete saying something about going to the village shop. He grabbed his satchel bag, picked up his pager/calculator and placed it inside, along with Max's binoculars and camera. He ran downstairs and out the front door, running as fast as he could towards the village square.

Peter was crossing the square when Brian came into view running around the corner of the Angel Pub, dodging a group of red-socked ramblers that were resting on one of the pub's wooden benches.

"What's up?"

"Pete," said a breathless Brian, "I've got it."

"You've got something, for sure. It's probably a heart attack."

"No, Pete, listen, that last message from Max…."

"What about it?"

"I reckon M.C.R.P means MegaCorp."

Peter nodded, "Yeah, you're probably right but so what?"

"The *hlp* could I suppose mean help, what do you think?"

"It could be, but why would he need help?"

"He was with Rachel at MegaCorp yesterday, wasn't he?" Brian was thinking aloud, "She may know something, have you got her number, Pete?"

"Yeah, but…." Peter was about to say they had no mobile phone when he noticed the number 155 bus was stopping at the village square.

"Quick, there's the bus, let's ask her ourselves," he said as he sped off in a sprint to stop the bus.

Eight Weeks after the Power Crisis:

Saturday 16:30Hrs

Meanwhile, at MegaCorp, all of the regular security guards had been replaced by more black suited henchmen that now manned all the security desks and regularly patrolled the offices and corridors. The loading of the test subjects and the clearing out of the laboratories was well underway.

Max had been left alone in the empty room, bound and gagged, for over four hours. He had sent regular messages to Brian and felt the pager vibrate as a message arrived but he had no way of reading the reply with his hands in the handcuffs behind his back.

He had one hundred and one questions racing around in his head. Was it possible this was all just a dream? This sort of thing didn't happen in real life, did it? The pain in his wrists convinced him that this was not a dream and the direct threat, or rather the direct instruction, to dispose of him in a dog food factory's crush-and-grind machine, along with several dozen rare and exotic animals, was a very real instruction indeed.

He had to focus. He was in deep trouble. Someone would surely be searching for him so he had to stall for time, he had to try to escape. He looked around the room. There was nothing he could think of to use, no tools and no windows. There was just the door which he knew was guarded on the outside so he reached into his back pocket and tried the pager again. The pain in his wrists was bordering on unbearable as he tried to remember the correct key presses to send the message *'mcorp dogfood'*.

Eight Weeks after the Power Crisis:

Saturday 17:00Hrs

Sitting on the bus, Peter and Brian had already passed through the town of Tiverton and were on the A396 which ran parallel to the River Exe. They were less than fifteen minutes from Rachel's house when the pager vibrated again. Both boys looked at the screen and knew Max was trying to get a message to them, something about MegaCorp. *'hlp mcdgfd'*

That message had come through twice, convincing Brian it was definitely not a tech-issue.

Peter and Brian stepped off the bus at the village of Stoke Canon and jogged the last few hundred metres across the old stone bridge over the River Exe towards Rachel's house. Peter had been the driving force on this trip but as they approached Rachel's house he slowed down to a walk.

"Are you, okay?" asked Brian.

"Yeah, er, I'm okay," he started to stammer, "Perhaps you'd better knock, yeah?"

"A little tongue-tied, are we?" Brian teased.

"No," Peter said firmly, "It's just that you've got the pager thing with the messages, that's all."

"Yeah, right," said Brian, "So have you, I reckon you are all nervous...."

He didn't finish his sentence. Peter quickly had him in a head-lock and was rubbing the top of Brian's head with his knuckles. Not too hard, just hard enough for Brian to know who was boss.

"Submit!" Peter ordered, "Submit or you'll be in the river!"

"Pete," protested Brian from within the head-lock, "We haven't got time for this."

Both boys had not noticed a silver Ford Fiesta that had drawn up alongside them. From the driver's seat, Rachel leaned across the passenger seat and opened the window.

"Peter Marshall," she said in a mock stern voice, "What *are* you doing to your little brother?"

From underneath Peter's armpit, Brian spoke first.

"Rachel, hi, me and Pete were just…."

Peter quickly let Brian go. *"He started it,"* he began to plead but he knew from her raised eyebrows and disbelieving eyes that she wasn't going to buy that excuse and the look on her face said don't bother trying to sweet-talk your way out of it.

"Are you ok, Brian?" she asked in a soft voice with a very slight sarcastic tone, "If you like, I can call Child-Line for you."

A red-faced Brian rearranged his jumper, adjusted his bag and tucked his shirt back in.

"It's fine," he said, "But his social skills are still rather lacking, aren't they?"

Rachel laughed. Peter stood awkwardly beside the open car window and blushed some more.

"So what are you guys doing here?" she said.

They explained about Max and that he was sending odd messages which they thought meant he was at MegaCorp.

"Well, we can easily check to see if he's at MegaCorp, I know where their offices are. They are near the airport. Jump in."

Brian and Peter got into Rachel's car, Brian strapped himself into the rear seat, Peter sat next to Rachel in the front.

"So apart from bullying your little brother into submission, Pete, what else have you been up to?" she asked as she turned her car around.

"Er….um…" He wanted to talk, he really did but somehow, when he was with her his brain felt disengaged from his mouth and his tongue felt twice the size.

From the back seat, Brian helped his brother out, "The Cornish Pirates have been in touch and want to arrange a trial."

It was all Peter could do to nod in agreement. He was aware he had a stupid nervous grin on his face.

"That's good, Pete," she replied, "You said that without moving your lips."

"Er, yeah," he stammered.

As she changed through the gears and headed into Exeter she glanced sideways out of the corner of her eye at Peter sitting next to her. She watched him nervously trying to find something to do with his hands and he finally decided it was best to sit on them. He was clearly trying to muster up the courage to speak to her.

She smiled to herself. This guy had the ability to terrorise on a rugby field through sheer strength and determination but didn't have the courage to talk to her. He could side-step tacklers with agility and finesse but in her company he was clumsy, nervous and self conscious. It was cute that he clearly liked her but what was best, she thought, was he was considerate and protective, something she had never ever experienced before.

Eight Weeks after the Power Crisis:

Saturday 17:00Hrs

The upper floor offices at MegaCorp were empty of staff but the underground car park was a hive of activity with forklift trucks working back and forth between the basement laboratories, loading cage after cage into the back of a large black articulated lorry. The forklift truck drivers were not the regular drivers, every one of them was dressed identically to Mr Black and Mr White. Even down to the black sunglasses.

Inside the cages were the test subjects; the polar bears, the orang-utans, the gorillas and komodo dragons, the dogs, sloths, leopards and even the kittens were all packed into the back of the lorry. At around five o'clock the last of the animals were loaded and the men in black suits that had been forklift truck drivers switched roles to become laboratory cleaners and they started to remove all trace that the animals had ever been there. When they had vacuumed from top to bottom using industrial-size hoovers, they started the job of disinfecting each laboratory with eye-wateringly strong disinfectant.

Bishop, Nina Glover and their hired team of henchman would make sure not a single piece of evidence remained to prove the existence of Project-X. If the boy had blabbed and the police or animal rights activists turned up, they would find nothing. However, the test results and chemical data had been encrypted onto portable computer hard-drives and stored safely off-site, ready for when X could once more be implemented.

Max was contemplating what appeared to be his very short future when Mr White opened the door to the room and walked quickly towards him. He did not say a word as he lifted Max onto his shoulder in a fireman's carry and left the room. Max could only see the floor and the back of Mr White's black shoes as he was taken through the offices and down several flights of stairs to the underground car park beneath the MegaCorp offices.

Mr White dumped Max roughly beside the rear wheel of his BMW and went over to speak to Mr Black, who was busy overseeing the last of the cages being loaded onboard the lorry. Max reached down into his back pocket, feeling for the pager/calculator device. Once again, he fought the pain in his wrists to orientate the device. He felt across the buttons. It took him less than a minute to send another brief message. *'help mc dog food'*

"Check his pockets and dispose of anything to link him with being here," ordered Mr White.

Mr Black smiled a wicked smile as he walked over to Max who was propped up against the rear wheel.

Mr Black picked Max up from the floor and balanced him awkwardly on his feet against the rear of the BMW, he rummaged around in Max's pockets and tipped the contents on the concrete floor. The calculator and pager came apart as they hit the ground.

Mr Black looked down at the broken pieces and stamped on them until they were completely destroyed.

Mr Black opened the boot of the BMW and took out a dustpan and brush and a black bin liner. He swept Max's belongings into the bag and placed the bag into a large refuse-bin with the words INDUSTRIAL WASTE printed on the side. He whistled to get the attention of another black-suited operative, who acknowledged the order and wheeled the refuse-bin away.

Mr Black then took out a fresh roll of duct tape from the boot of the car. He unlocked the handcuffs from behind Max's back and removed them from his wrists. Max let out a sigh of relief as the pain in his wrists eased but it was a short respite because Mr Black pulled Max's wrists from behind his back and held them together in front of him. Mr White then taped his wrists with duct tape from his thumbs almost up to elbows, looping the tough silver-coloured tape over and over. When he was finished, Mr Black held the handcuffs up for Mr White to see. Mr Black also knew about not blunting the blades in the crush-and-grind machine.

Max desperately tried to move but being professionally bound hand and foot made his attempts to escape futile. Mr Black picked him up and threw him over his right shoulder, carrying him towards one of the empty three metre square metal cages that had previously been used for polar bears. Mr Black opened the cage door and pushed Max inside, slamming the heavy metal door behind him. He then closed the bolt on the door and secured it with the anti-tamper mechanism, designed to stop animals from opening the bolt themselves.

Max lay on the floor of the cage in a foetus position and gave up any idea of escape, it was all he could do to move his securely taped wrists to scratch his nose with his thumb. He stared in despair out through the bars of the cage and saw Mr White appear at the controls of one of the forklift trucks which lifted his cage up and then placed it beside the other cages in the rear of the lorry.

Mr White parked the forklift and jumped up into the rear of the articulated lorry. Max lay on his side on the floor of the cage and he stared at Mr White, eyes wide open in terror, as he reached up and took a small leather bag down from a shelf on the inside of the lorry. He placed the bag on the floor and reached inside. He took out a small glass bottle of clear liquid which he placed on the floor beside the bag. Then he reached into the bag again and took out a large syringe which had an extremely long hypodermic needle.

He stabbed the syringe's needle into the thin metal cap of the bottle and slowly drew liquid out of the bottle until the syringe's chamber was full. He checked the contents through the clear sides and applied a little pressure to the handle, forcing a small jet of liquid to squirt out in an arc.

Satisfied the syringe was working correctly, he then reached up on the shelf and took down a long metal pole with a handle at one end and a green coloured dart at the other. He used the syringe to inject the liquid into a small opening on the side of the dart. The dart was now primed to administer the tranquiliser.

Max had not taken his eyes off Mr White as he assembled the tranquiliser pole fearing that he was going to be on the sharp end of the dart. Mr White saw Max looking at him and he smiled. It was not a friendly smile, it was a grimace of pure wickedness and cruelty. Max had been so totally focused on Mr White and the tranquiliser pole that he had not noticed that in the cage next to him was a polar bear and on the cage was a sign that read *'Control'*.

Max shut his eyes for a few seconds. This is all a bad a dream he said to himself, any minute now I am going to wake up and all this will be a dream. Max didn't get the chance to wake up of his own accord, he was snapped out of his daydream by the polar bear roaring and throwing itself around in the cage. The cage reverberated as the bear lashed out with both front paws swiping through the metal bars with snapping, snarling teeth that threatened to remove Mr White's arm if he came any closer.

Mr White stepped back a few steps from the cage and laughed.

Mr Black appeared next to the cage.

"Did you double dose the tranquiliser, Mr White?"

"Yes, Mr Black, It's a double dose. It's time for this one to go to sleep. For good."

Mr Black had a metal pole of his own except this one had two electrodes on one end, it was a tazer style cattle prod, designed to apply a short but very sharp electric shock to move stubborn cows, except here it was going to be used on the polar bears.

Mr Black ran the electrode end up and down the cage, clattering across the bars, teasing the bear. The bear knew exactly what the cattle prod was and immediately responded by lashing out, launching its full body mass towards Mr Black. Even though this adolescent bear was not fully grown the metal bars resonated as if the cage had been hit at thirty miles per hour by a medium sized family car.

Mr Black was tactically distracting the bear while Mr White outflanked it.

The tranquiliser pole was quickly poked through the bars and struck the bear in its upper left forearm and the dart fixed itself deep into the bear's thick skin. The tranquiliser steadily flowed into the bear's bloodstream and the bear retreated.

Max watched in horror as the bear slumped against the bars closest to his own cage.

Mr White and Mr Black were pleased with themselves. They moved along the cages to the next bear which had 'Withdrawn' written on its cage. Max was an unwilling spectator in a one-sided bear baiting massacre. He wanted to kick, scream, shout and punch Mr Black and Mr White, but he was unable to do anything.

The second bear was already slumped down on the floor of the cage. Mr White walked up and poked the bear through the bars with his foot. The bear hardly moved.

"This one's already had it, Mr Black."

"X-Ingredient has seen to that, there's no need to tranquilise it."

Mr White packed up the tranquiliser kit and jumped down from the lorry. Mr Black followed him and slammed the doors shut.

Inside the lorry a cacophony of different animals started to whimper and call to each other. Max wriggled on the floor over to the rear of his cage. He jammed his back against the bars and swung his legs around until he managed to lever himself up onto his backside. His legs and arms were still tightly bound but he was able to shuffle around on his backside to get more comfortable. He leant back on the cold metal bars and looked at the tranquilised bear in the cage opposite.

With every breath, its huge muscular body was starting to relax under the effect of the tranquiliser drug. Its powerful forearms were splayed out and its head rested between them as it drifted into a deep terminal sleep. Its breathing became softer and with every long slow breath out, its eyelids closed a little further. Compared to the determined bear that had defended itself against Mr White and Mr Black this bear was now letting life slip slowly away. The shine in the bear's brown eyes was dimming. Max had to do something.

He shuffled across the cage floor on his bottom using the heels of his shoes for grip and he made his way cautiously towards the bear and the two of them made eye contact. He kept moving forward as they stared at each other. Max wasn't stupid, he was bound and gagged, shuffling awkwardly towards the world's largest predator, albeit a very doped one. He knew the danger but moved forward anyway.

As he got closer, the bear rolled over slightly onto one side, its huge powerful forearm fell through the bars and its heavy paw flopped gently onto the floor of Max's cage. Its paw was huge, the size of a dinner plate and on the end of each pad there was a jet black claw, the size of Max's thumb.

Max looked at the bear's powerful forearm and saw the tranquiliser dart nestled firmly between the dense white fur. He shuffled closer and rolled over from his backside to his knees, balancing awkwardly against the side of his cage. Max positioned himself so that he could reach the dart with his bound hands and although his movement was restricted by the duct tape, he managed to hold the dart in between his fingers and he pulled it free. The dart fell to the floor of Max's cage where the rest of the tranquiliser liquid spilt harmlessly onto the floor.

The bear's eyes followed the dart and then it looked back at Max.

Max struggled for breath through the duct tape across his mouth and his heart pounded. He twisted over and leant back against the bars of his cage where the bear's huge forearm lay alongside Max's leg. One swipe of its massive paw would have easily knocked Max out, or much worse.

Outside the lorry, Max now heard voices and he noticed the bear's ears prick up. Mr White was giving instructions to several other men directing them to take different routes to the factory. Max heard the group of men move off and soon the lorry's large diesel engine fired into life and revved. Max felt the wheels of the lorry go over a set of speed bumps and then it picked up speed.

Inside the lorry, the animals started to stir and call out to each other. Max looked past the bear closest to him and saw the other polar bear start to get up onto all fours. It shook its huge white head and slowly opened its eyes then it let out a low, deep growl that was exactly how Max imagined a bad-tempered, sore-headed, depressed bear would growl like.

Eight Weeks after the Power Crisis:

Saturday 18:00Hrs

Rachel had driven through the busy traffic in Exeter City Centre, heading for the motorway, she had left the A30 slip road at Junction 29 and was en route to the airport's business district. She slowed down at the first roundabout to give way to a black BMW M5 that was already on the roundabout. The BMW took the first exit heading towards Exeter. A second M5 followed but took the second exit towards Sowton. A third M5 appeared and then doubled back on itself taking the third exit, heading east on the A30.

"That's odd," Peter said as he pointed at the M5's, "Three cars all the same."

"I've seen those outside the MegaCorp building, I think they are company cars," Rachel said as she crossed over the roundabout into Airport Way, heading towards MegaCorp. Approaching their car from the opposite direction was a large black lorry. All three of them followed it with their eyes as it went past.

"That looks like it's from the same place," said Brian, "The same metallic black and the driver was wearing the same clothes as the drivers in the other cars."

"It doesn't seem right to me at all, something's up, for sure."

"It's *not* right," said Peter, "Can you get Max on the pager?"

"No, I've not heard anything for ages."

Rachel slowed down and turned her car into the driveway towards the MegaCorp building. She stopped at the automatic barrier and pressed the intercom button. Above it was a CCTV camera that pointed down at the car and the driver's window. After a short while a man's voice came through the intercom speaker.

"Can I help you, Miss?"

"Yes," said Rachel, "I'm from Muller and Rathbone, I was here yesterday evening and I think one of my colleagues may be with you now, his name is Max Chambers. Would you check for me, please?"

"Give me a moment," the voice said and the intercom clicked. The voice returned after a short while.

"I have checked with security and a Max Chambers was here yesterday evening. He left with the rest of the Muller and Rathbone representatives."

"Could you check again, please?"

"There's no need for me to check again, Miss. Our security records show he used his access card to swipe out of the building yesterday evening. He has not been back since. May I ask your name, Miss?"

Rachel did not answer, she put the car into reverse and backed away from the barrier. She turned the car around and headed back out to Airport Way.

"He's lying," she said, "Max had lost his access card. We used my card to get both of us out."

Brian thought out loud, "So we know Max was in MegaCorp yesterday and the security guard is lying about him signing out. The dodgy security guard is covering something up and we've had messages from Max about MegaCorp. It figures the *'hlp'* means help but I'm clueless on what *dgfd* means."

"D.G.F.D", Peter said, "I don't get it either."

"Maybe it's another MegaCorp building, but I still don't get it. D.G.F.D," said Peter, "D.G.F.D," he said it again and shook his head. "We should have followed those cars, or the lorry."

Rachel was by now heading back to the roundabout and the A30 to take them into Exeter. "We'll never catch them, all I can think is we check the locations of all MegaCorp buildings, you never know we may find something."

"How can we do that?"

"I can check where our executives have visited MegaCorp. I can get into the company diary if we go to the Muller and Rathbone offices and we can be there in ten minutes."

Eight Weeks after the Power Crisis:

Saturday 18:15Hrs

In the back of the lorry, Max was in shock. He was in double shock to be precise. If being kidnapped and shut in a cage wasn't surreal enough, he was also sitting in a cage next to two polar bears that appeared to be coming back to their senses and they were now all too animated. The effects of the tranquiliser were wearing off and Control's head began to clear. Next to Control, Withdraw was, for the first time, shaking off the effects of being force fed double doses of X-Ingredient *Pro-Retanzin* anti-depressants.

Max bit his lip just to make sure for the twelfth time that he wasn't dreaming. He snapped out of his shock and shuffled across his cage to where the tranquiliser dart had rolled. He positioned his feet on either sides of the dart and slowly, millimetre by millimetre he used the edge of his shoes to work it into a vertical position. It took him several attempts but after a determined effort he managed to manoeuvre the dart upright and it stood proud of his shoes by about five centimetres. He carefully positioned his wrists so the duct tape underneath them was in contact with the pointed end of the dart, then he carefully started to lift his wrists up and down to make holes in the duct tape. He was extra careful because one false move and he could end up tranquilising himself.

Max got into a rhythm and he had soon made dozens of tiny perforations in the duct tape.

Control watched Max with a bear's natural curiosity. He sniffed between the bars of the cage and he instantly recognised Max's smell. He could also smell that Max was afraid. The other two-legs had hurt this smaller one and they treated him as if he was a bear, just like him and his brother. Control watched Max intently, this was a new experience and the small two-leg fascinated him.

Next to Control, Withdraw was shrugging off the worst of the addiction pains in his head and body, he had arrived at MegaCorp already showing signs of extreme depression and was an ideal test subject for X-Ingredient *Pro-Retanzin*. Excessive testing of the drug had made Withdraw an anti-depressant junkie and when they stopped the dosing, he spiralled into an ever deepening depression, exactly what the drug was designed to do. Addiction meant repeat business for MegaCorp but for Withdraw it meant accepting he would end his days locked in a cage drifting into a terminal mental illness. But now he had a new focus and a desire to get even with a taste for revenge and this spark elevated his spirits more than any drug could. Withdraw was now a bear with a grudge. To be precise, it was considerably more than a grudge. He was a bad-tempered, vengeful, two hundred and fifty kilogram, arctic polar bear with a bite that could crush a man's skull and a set of claws that could cut a man in two. Withdraw was on a mission to get even with every two-leg that crossed his path, especially the ones that dressed like penguins[*].

"The first two-leg I find is going to get it," he said to his brother.

"Glad to see you are back to your usual grumpy self. But we're not going to harm this one, this one is different, he is not like the other two-legs."

Max stopped making the perforations because he was aware both bears were now watching him. He was aware because their heavy breathing was not only audible, but because he also felt it on his cheeks and in his hair. He had read somewhere it was best not to look dangerous animals in the eye but he couldn't help himself and he stared into

---

[*]*It is a common misconception that polar bears do not know what penguins are because penguins come from the Antarctic whereas polar bears live in the Arctic. It's not true, polar bears do know what penguins are. You go ask one.*

their big dark brown eyes and a wave of fear washed over him.

Both bears sniffed. Max could see their huge nostrils moving as they smelt the air.

"Do you smell that, Brother?" said Control, "He's afraid."

"Sure, and so he should be," answered Withdraw.

A glare from Control reiterated to his brother that this two-leg was not to be harmed.

Max snapped back to the job in hand and stabbed more perforations in the duct tape between his wrists. Control sniffed the air again. A wave of adrenalin crossed the front of his nose.

"He's got some fighting spirit, Brother, can you smell that?"

Withdraw begrudgingly acknowledged it with a grunt.

Max stared ahead, focused totally on the duct tape, as he continued to make more tiny perforations. One thing at a time, he thought, one thing at a time. Cut through the tape. Escape from the cage and then get away from these bears as quick as I can.

He quickened the up and down movements of his wrists. Control watched intently as Max worked away at the duct tape. Max caught the bear in his peripheral vision and he took his eye off the ball and slipped. The dart grazed the side of his skin and he instinctively flinched and lifted his wrists up sharply. The dart was stuck in the tape and Max's quick jerk upwards sent the dart flying across his cage and it ricocheted off one of the bars then rolled over towards the back doors of the lorry.

Max was angry with himself, he tried to pull his wrists apart but the layers of duct tape were still too intact. He tried again but the duct tape would not separate, there were not enough perforations and for the first time he felt like giving in. He stared out through the bars and watched the dart as it rolled back and forth with the movement of the lorry, far out of his reach. He had thought he was making good progress but now his hopes were dashed and he was back to square one. He was in a cage, next to two polar bears and he gave up any idea of getting away from this mess. He leaned back on the bars and started to bang the back of his head against them. He kept on banging his head for several minutes. After a while he took a deep breath again and shut his eyes.

Control watched him intently.

"He even bangs his head like you do when you've had enough, Brother, he's definitely got more in common with us than other two-legs."

After a while, Max stopped banging his head and he glanced at the bear to his left.

"I am dreaming," he said aloud, "I must be, because that's not really happening, is it?"

He followed the bear's eyes as it looked down at its upturned paw. Control had put his huge paw through the cage and turned it palm-side up. One of his huge black claws was standing proud through the dense white fur.

Max and the bear stared at each other. He tried to swallow but his mouth was too dry. After what seemed an eternity, the bear snorted and looked down at its paw again. I have got to be dreaming, thought Max as he bit his lip hard enough to make certain he wasn't.

Eight Weeks after the Power Crisis:

Saturday 19:00Hrs

Rachel had parked her car on double yellow lines beside Exeter Cathedral because there was no time to waste finding a parking space on a busy Saturday evening. She locked the car and joined Peter and Brian who had already vaulted over the cathedral's low perimeter wall and the three of them ran across the grass courtyard towards the Muller and Rathbone offices.

Rachel unlocked the glass office doors and opened them wide for the two brothers to follow. Once inside, she disabled the alarm system and the three of them were soon walking at a jogging pace through the offices as Rachel headed for her desk. Rachel pulled her swivel chair out and switched her computer on. Brian and Peter found two spare chairs and wheeled them next to Rachel's. She tapped her fingers impatiently on her desk while they waited for her computer to boot up.

After a short while, her monitor came to life and she logged on. In a few seconds she had opened up the office calendar and in the search bar she typed in *MegaCorp* which would narrow down the search to only the appointments that contained that word.

"This is what we're looking for," she said pointing to an appointment on the screen:

Roger Pearson at MegaCorp, Product Development Meeting

"Check the location," offered Brian but Rachel was already doing that.

Location: MegaCorp Central Office, 112 Fenchurch Street, EC1 2GH

Rachel scrolled down to the next appointment.

239

Martin Turner at MegaCorp, Advertising Meeting. Location:
MegaCorp Pharmaceuticals, Unit 3, Bowman Road, Guildford,
GU1 3DR

"Do you recognise anything? Anything at all like DGFD?"

Both boys shook their heads.

"What about the postcodes?" Brian suggested, "It could be a postcode like GU something-something DR."

Rachel scrolled further down through the calendar appointments. "What about this one?"

Evans at MegaCorp, Regional Sales Meeting. Location:
MegaCorp Investments, Lancet Street, Basingstoke, RG24 3XT

"Here are some more, what about these?"

Michael Brown and Roger Pearson, at MegaCorp. KwiknSlim
Production Shoot. Location: Elstree Studios, London NW2 4FR

Andrew Peterson at MegaCorp, Branding Meeting. Location:
MegaCorp Canine Nutrition Processing Plant, North Tawton,
Devon EX18 3RF

Martin Purnell at MegaCorp, Contracts Meeting. Location:
MegaCorp Research and Development, Airport Way, Exeter,
EX2 4GF

Alan Harrison at MegaCorp, Retail Stores Monthly Meeting.
Location: MegaCorp Pharmaceuticals, Unit 3, Bowman Road,
Guildford, GU1 3DR

"Whoa!" shouted Brian, "Go back!"

"Where?" asked Rachel, "Which one, the one with my dad?"

"No, up one more," he said and pointed at Peterson's meeting, "Canine Nutrition? That's got to be dog food, right? DGFD, that has to mean dog food."

In an instant they were on the same wavelength, Peter was already up and heading out of the office, Brian followed close behind. Rachel stopped to scribble down the address on a post-it note and then ran after the two brothers.

The three of them raced through the offices and downstairs and out through the main entrance doors. Outside in the street, Peter and Brian waited while Rachel reset the alarm and locked up. Rachel shook the doors to make sure they were secure and then the three of them ran at full speed through the narrow alleyway and across the cathedral's courtyard, back towards Rachel's car.

Peter leapt over the low courtyard wall in a single bound, Brian was close behind and vaulted over the wall using his hands, his satchel bag swinging wildly by his side. Peter stopped and turned round to hold out a hand to help Rachel down from the wall.

"You're always the gentleman, Pete," she said as he helped her down, "But you're still too slow!" she shouted as she sped off to her car at a full sprint.

"She got you again there, Pete," Brian teased, "But look on the bright side, at least you're managing to string more than just a couple of words together now!"

There was no time for Peter to teach Brian another lesson in respecting his elders and they sped off after Rachel who was not far from her car. As she got closer, she blipped her key fob and unlocked the doors ready to make a quick entry and departure.

Standing on the pavement, next to the car was a traffic warden with a parking ticket poised a few inches from the car's windscreen. The warden saw them running towards him and instantly recognised Rachel.

"You....You're Poppy Purnell, aren't you?" he said as Rachel slid to a stop and then nimbly side-stepped him to open the driver's door.

"I used to be," she said with a disarming smile.

This confused the traffic warden even more.

"You used to be?"

Peter and Brian were already beside the car, opening the passenger doors. A second later they were inside and three doors slammed shut.

"Yeah, I used to be," she said through the car's window as she turned the ignition key and put the car into gear, "But not anymore though!"

The traffic warden was totally confused. He was sure it really was Poppy Purnell and he tried to take a closer look but it was too late, Rachel had already pulled away with tyres screeching, leaving the bewildered traffic warden on the pavement still holding the parking ticket.

Rachel weaved her little car through the city centre traffic, heading for the St Thomas roundabout and the exit to the A377, towards North Tawton.

"There's an OS map in the glove box, Pete," she said, "We should be there in about thirty minutes."

Eight Weeks after the Power Crisis:

Saturday 19:15Hrs

Meanwhile, Max was doing his best to reassess his current situation. If he did nothing, he faced being crushed and turned into dog food along with the rest of the animals. If he escaped from the cage, he still had to get past Bishop's black-suited henchmen. And where would he hide? He didn't like to think what other creatures lurked elsewhere in the lorry. His last and most difficult decision was the one that he faced now.

He looked again at the bear's upturned paw and then back to the bear's eyes. If it is possible for a polar bear to be anywhere near '*safe*', then this one definitely had an expression of '*safeness*'. Its paw had been outstretched for a while now and every time he looked at the bear, the bear looked down at its paw and then back up at Max.

Max weighed up the options:

Accept death in a crush-and-grind machine and being turned into dog food or trust a quarter ton, carnivorous bear not to cut him in half with a paw the size of a baseball glove and claws as sharp as steak knives.

Max made up his mind.

He edged slowly towards the bear's outstretched, upturned paw never losing eye contact with the bear. The bear breathed gently out not moving a muscle. Max gingerly outstretched his wrists until they were above the bear's paw. Max glanced down and adjusted his wrists so that the underside of the duct tape came into contact with the razor-sharp claw. He stared into the bear's eyes and he gently applied downward pressure and felt a reassuring pop as

243

the duct tape split. He made another careful movement and popped the tape again and again and again.

Max made very good progress, the bear's claw easily cut through the duct tape, much quicker than the dart and soon he was able to split apart most of the perforations. He forced with all his might to get his wrists apart and with one final effort he broke through the duct tape and his arms swung wide open. The first thing he did was rip the duct tape gag from his mouth and gulp in a huge lungful of air.

The bear let out a low growl, slowly turned its massive paw over and placed it gently back inside its own cage.

EIGHT WEEKS AFTER THE POWER CRISIS:

SATURDAY 20:00HRS

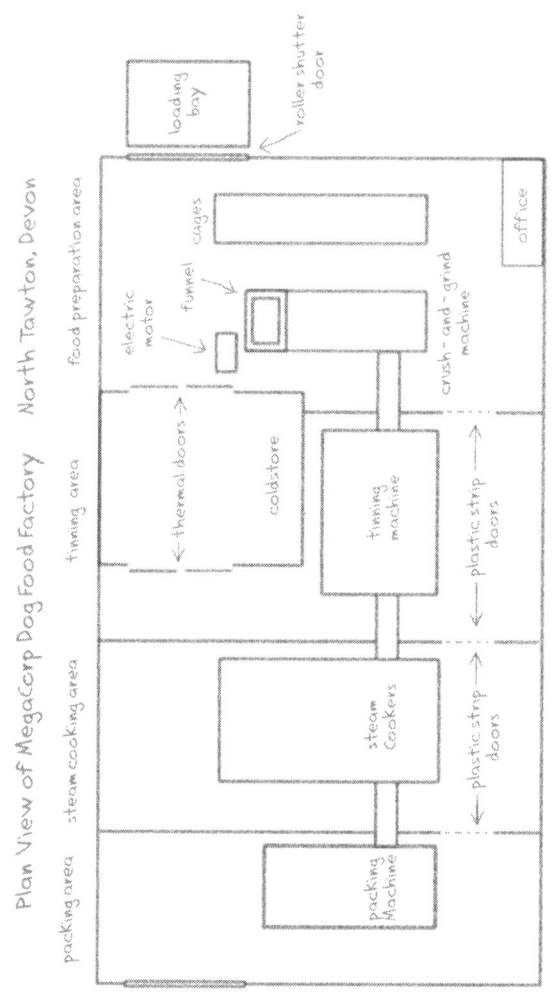

The dog food factory was a metal fabricated unit, like any industrial unit found in a regular town or city, except this factory nestled deep within the green patchwork quilt of fields in Mid Devon, just a few miles from the small town of North Tawton. At one end of the factory was a loading bay with a roller shutter door that led into the interior. The factory was split by low partition walls into four separate areas, and each area was a specific part of the dog food production process. Just inside the roller shutter door was the food preparation area which housed the specialised machinery that crushed and ground up solid blocks of frozen processed meat into tiny chunks of uncooked dog food. The second section of the factory was the tinning area, where a machine added the uncooked dog food to tin cans on a conveyor belt system, adding a gravy mix into every tin.

Linking the food preparation and tinning area was a vast coldstore where the frozen blocks of meat were stored.

The third section of the factory housed large, steam-pressurised cooking ovens where the tins of dog food were sealed and then steam-pressure cooked. The fourth and final section of the factory was where the tins were labelled and packed ready for despatch. It was a streamlined operation where lorry loads of processed frozen blocks of meat went in at one end of the factory and thousands upon thousands of tins of dog food came out of the other.

The factory was three stories high and occupied an area as big as a football pitch. The corrugated roof had vents spaced evenly along its length where wispy clouds of steam billowed out. Along the windowless metal walls were pipes which hissed more hot steam from a variety of valves and outlets. The factory was surrounded on all sides by fields of sweetcorn and the only road access to the factory was by a two hundred metre long driveway. Halfway along the driveway was a security checkpoint with a heavy steel barrier. It was in here that the regular security guard had been dismissed for the weekend, replaced by one of Bishop's black-suited henchmen.

Max felt the lorry slow down to a gradual stop and he heard some people have a short conversation before the lorry moved off again a short distance. Then the engine stopped.

The rear doors swung open and Mr White appeared at the back of the lorry. He raised his arm and signalled to someone that was out of Max's view. Almost immediately, Mr Black arrived at the controls of a forklift truck and started to unload the cages from the rear of the lorry. At the same time, the lorry's fabric sides were drawn back and Mr Green started to unload the cages from the side using a second forklift. Max watched as cages full of mice, kittens and dogs were offloaded. Then they unloaded the exotic animals: sloths, snow leopards and komodo dragons followed by the orang-utans and gorillas.

All of the exotics were unwanted rejects from wealthy private collections, sold for a bargain to be test subjects in the drug industry. Now they were about to be disposed of by being processed into tinned dog meat.

Last to be unloaded into the factory were the polar bears, and then Max.

Eight Weeks after the Power Crisis:

Peter checked the Ordnance Survey map and checked the road ahead.

"The factory entrance should be coming up on our left."

Rachel slowed down as she drew level with the end of the factory's driveway. In the back seat, Brian had rested Max's binoculars on the edge of the car's window to steady them. He scanned the area, reporting to the others what he could see.

"It seems to be closed but I can see a large black lorry at the rear of the factory," he paused as he refocused the binoculars slightly, "It's the lorry we saw near the airport. There is a gatehouse with a barrier across the drive and one of those black-suited security guards inside."

"Well, we aren't going to get in that way," said Rachel, "Pete, can you find another way in?"

Peter checked the map again as Rachel drove slowly away from the end of the driveway.

"I reckon there could be a footpath across the fields at the back. We could check that out."

Rachel drove a few hundred metres further down the lane and took the next left into another narrow country lane and over a humpback bridge. She then took another left turn, effectively doing a large U-turn to get to the rear of the factory.

"Up here, about another two hundred metres," Peter said.

Out of the car's left side windows they could see the factory in the distance, partly hidden behind a wide field of sweetcorn. Rachel slowed down and stopped at the entrance to the footpath where a five bar metal farm gate crossed the path.

Rachel parked the car a little further up the lane and pulled on the bonnet release catch under the dashboard. The bonnet popped open a few inches.

"That should make any passers-by think we've broken down," she said.

The two brothers were already out of the car and running towards the gate. Rachel caught up with them as they were climbing over the gate into the field of sweetcorn and the three of them were soon hidden amongst the tall green stalks.

The setting sun had almost totally disappeared behind the horizon and it was getting dark as they made their way stealthily through the field, the only sign of their approach was a gentle rustling of the upper stalks of the sweetcorn. Brian and Rachel could walk upright and remain hidden, Peter stooped a little to remain out of view.

Halfway through the field, Brian took the binoculars out of his bag and stood on tiptoe to see over the stalks. He reported back to the others what he could see.

"There is a wire fence all the way around this side of the factory."

"How high is it?" asked Peter.

"Two metres at least, with no barbed wire. At the edge of this field there's a gate, and a black car."

"Is there anyone in it?"

"Yeah, a man in a black suit, just like in the gatehouse at the front."

Brian handed Peter the binoculars. Peter focused in on Mr Orange, who was sitting in his company-issued BMW M5, with the door open. The car was parked about twenty metres from the gate on the other side of the fence. Peter scanned a little to the left and he focused on a yellow plastic tag on the fence.

"And the fence is electrified, Brains," he said handing Brian the binoculars, "Do you recognise the manufacturer's tag?"

Brian gave him a thumbs-up sign and handed back the binoculars.

Peter focused on the black lorry. He saw a pair of forklift trucks unloading what appeared to be animals in cages but he just couldn't make out what they were. He twisted the focusing dial to get a sharper image. He blinked, lowered the binoculars and rubbed his eyes because he could not believe what he saw the first time. He looked through the binoculars again to check he had not been imagining it. That was an orang-utan. There were lots of orang-utans. And they were in cages.

"You are not going to believe this," he said as he handed the binoculars to Rachel, "The things in those cages are orang-utans."

Rachel scanned the lorry and cages with the binoculars.

"Pete," she gasped.

"I know," he said, "That doesn't look good at all."

"No, it's not just orang-utans," she whispered, "That's Max in there!"

"Max?"

She handed the binoculars back to Peter. He focused on Max in one of the cages that had been unloaded along with the other animals. He passed the binoculars to Brian so he could see it was Max.

Peter turned to Rachel, both of them had a worried look in their eyes. Rachel spoke first.

"We should call the police, this is way more than serious."

"Have you got a signal?" Pete asked.

She felt in her pocket and took out her phone. The display showed one bar of signal.

"Not much of one, but it will do," she said.

She dialled 999.

"Have you got any other ideas?" she asked as she waited for the operator to answer.

"We're thinking you get the police, we're going after Max."

"But how?"

"Leave that to us. Take the binoculars and wait for our signal then walk up to the gate. Can you distract the guard?"

"I reckon so, but what are you planning?"

The two brothers had already disappeared into the sweetcorn. A slight rustle of stalks indicated they were zigzagging towards the fence.

The operator on the emergency service line answered the call and listened to Rachel tell them that at MegaCorp's dog food factory they were unloading cages full of animals and in one cage was a seventeen year old boy. The operator warned Rachel that it was a serious offence to waste police time by making prank calls to the emergency services. Rachel had assured the operator that she was deadly serious.

The operator was trained to filter out hoax calls so she asked Rachel to confirm her name and where she was calling from. Rachel replied with her name and said she was standing in a field of sweetcorn behind the factory and that her friend was being unloaded in a cage. Rachel was talking as calmly as she could and the operator sensed a genuine sound of urgency in her voice. Despite the call sounding totally improbable, the operator passed it over immediately to the Duty Inspector. He listened to the recording and decided to despatch a patrol car to see what was happening, if anything, at the dog food factory.

The nearest patrol car in the area was in Okehampton, ten to fifteen minutes away and it was PC Burrows and PC Martin that confirmed they could respond. They looked at each other in disbelief when the despatcher replayed the call. It was probably a hoax but it had to be checked out.

PC Burrows turned the patrol car around and headed towards North Tawton.

"Shall we put the blue lights on?"

"We'd better do I suppose, it may be a hoax but we've got to check it out, the caller sounded distressed so something may be up."

They sped off towards North Tawton, blue lights and siren on.

Back at the police station, Superintendent Todd had overheard the call on the police network. Normally, on a routine shout to a probable hoax call he would not have taken any notice but he was a member of Exeter Quay Golf Club and Bishop was someone he often shared a round of golf with. He took his non-police issue mobile phone out of his pocket and called Bishop.

"Is there a disturbance at your North Tawton factory, Bishop? I am only asking because we've had the strangest of calls come through the emergency call centre. A girl has reported seeing some odd goings on."

Bishop went silent.

"We have despatched a patrol car which should be there in about five minutes. Maybe you want to make a call to your Head of Security?"

Bishop regained his usual steely nerve.

"I doubt it's anything serious, Superintendent, but I will make a call to check, would you mind holding for a moment?"

Bishop placed the Superintendent on hold while he called Mr White for a situation report.

"Mr White, are things going to plan?"

"We're unloading the last of them now, sir."

"Good," replied Bishop, "But you may want to shut up shop and get the lorry moved as soon as possible, someone has tipped off the police and a patrol car is due at your location in less than five."

"Understood, sir, leave it to me."

Bishop hung up on Mr White and returned to the call with Superintendent Todd.

"There's nothing to report, there is a technical crew there undertaking regular maintenance," Bishop lied.

"That would make sense," replied the Superintendent.

"Although one of our security guards did report seeing some youths on bikes that were up to no good but they've moved off now, heading for North Tawton. Maybe your patrol car will be able to intercept?"

"Thank you, Bishop, are we still on for this weekend?"

"Yes, let's hope you fair better on the back nine this time," Bishop replied, "I hate taking money from you, you know."

Bishop and the Superintendent chatted about golfing for a short while. As soon as the called ended, Superintendent Todd put his mobile back in his pocket and used the police phone on his desk to dial through to the despatch room.

Max's cage was jostled onto the forklift truck and was taken into the factory through the roller shutter door where he saw Mr White on the phone. Mr White finished the call and shouted to the team to get them moving faster. One of his team of henchmen switched off the factory's exterior lighting and Mr White pressed the button that closed the shutter door.

Standing alone in the sweetcorn, Rachel heard the police car before she saw it coming through the country lanes. Its siren drifted in and out as it passed behind hedgerows and fields of corn and its blue flashing lights lit up the evening sky like streaks of lightning.

"Jeez!" Rachel said aloud, "They didn't waste their time getting here."

She watched with a growing sense of relief as the police car drew closer. It was only a mile or so away and it would be here in less than a minute, she thought.

Her heart sank when the siren stopped and the blue lights faded out. The police car slowed down and turned around, heading back to the town of North Tawton.

"What?" she said to herself, "What are they doing?"

She dialled 999 again but she had no signal.

She checked her watch. Peter and Brian had been gone for over ten minutes so she used the binoculars and looked over towards where the BMW was parked but with the factory's exterior lights off she couldn't see much at all. She could just make out the shiny bonnet of the BMW with its driver's door open and the metal gate. She scanned left and picked up some movement in the shadows. She twisted the focus dial and saw it was Brian. He was signalling for her to make her move.

Eight Weeks after the Power Crisis:

Saturday 20:30Hrs

The loading bay roller shutter door slammed down with a loud bang that echoed through the silent factory. Lined up side by side, were two dozen three metre square cages that contained the exotics. Max was at one end, and the polar bears were in the cages to his left. Directly in front of Max was the crusher he had heard Bishop and the others talking about. Max sat in his cage and stared in terror through the bars at the monstrous machinery. Now that he could see it, he was able to imagine in gruesome high detail exactly how it worked and what was in store.

The crush-and-grind machine was constructed entirely from stainless steel and it was so huge it almost filled one half of the food preparation area of the factory. The main section was a rectangular tower, four metres high, that flared out at the top in the shape of a funnel. At the base of this funnel was the crushing-and-grinding section.

Inside this section, a pair of solid metal shafts, over two metres long and thirty centimetres in diameter, spanned the width of the machine. On each of these shafts there were over one hundred hardened-steel blades that meshed together as they counter-rotated inwards. The blades were hooked, like an eagle's claw, perfectly designed to grab, grind, slice and dice anything that was placed into the funnel.

Below the first pair of rotating shafts, a second pair with slightly finer blades sliced through the chunks that the first pair had broken off and a third pair of even finer blades sliced these chunks into even smaller pieces. This array of precision-engineered, interlocking blades was capable of turning a three hundred kilo solid block of frozen meat into pea-sized pieces in under ten seconds.

The shafts were driven by a high torque near-indestructible gearbox attached to a huge electric motor located on a ground level platform beside the base of the tower.

Underneath the tower a deep stainless steel trough collected the material which had passed through the blades and transferred it by conveyor belt to a large rectangular section, about the size of a shipping container, which had massive hydraulic pistons on the outside. The conveyor belt continued out of the other side of this section and disappeared through a hole in the partition wall to where Max assumed the next part of the dog food production process took place.

Max managed to stop staring at the horrendous machinery and he looked around the rest of the food preparation area.

To the right of the crush-and-grind machine, was a pair of sliding doors with a sign above them that read COLDSTORE. A sign on the wall beside the doors read CAUTION FORKLIFTS IN OPERATION and next to that was a sign which read EXTREME COLD – PROTECTIVE CLOTHING MUST BE WORN.

To the left of the machine, there was a wide doorway which didn't have solid doors, it had opaque plastic strips hanging down from the top of the doorframe to the floor and next to this was a small, one windowed, concrete office with the words SHIFT MANAGER above the door. Hard hats and fluorescent safety jackets hung on hooks outside the office.

Max heard a whooshing sound and the insulated coldstore doors opened and a swirling mist of frozen air swept through the doorway. The coldstore was a vast freezer, larger than the size of a tennis court and it was kept at a constant minus seventeen degrees centigrade. The coldstore had automatic, thermally-insulated sliding doors on both sides to allow the through traffic of forklift trucks travelling from the tinning area to the food preparation area.

Two bright spotlights loomed out of the semi-dark interior, cutting through the cold frosty mist. The spotlights were from a yellow forklift truck that appeared through the doors with Mr Black at the controls and he expertly manoeuvred it around the electric motor and into place, facing the funnel. On the forks were three blocks of frozen processed meat which gave off a cloud of frozen steamy vapour, like dry ice in a chemistry lab. The insulated doors automatically closed behind the forklift truck to maintain the temperature inside.

Mr Black skilfully operated the truck's lifting gear controls and raised the blocks of meat to the top of the funnel, he tilted the forks forward and then reversed. The heavy blocks slipped off the forks and banged against the sides of the funnel as they fell down the chute and into the crush-and-grind machine, which made a sound like distant, rolling thunder that echoed off the metal walls of the factory.

Mr Black parked the forklift truck, switched off the spotlights and joined Mr White, Mr Pink and Mr Green beside the crush-and-grind machine. Mr White took command of this evening's operations.

"No need for me to ask who will operate this machinery, I take it that will be you, Mr Black?"

Mr Black nodded.

Mr White continued, "Mr Pink, you will manage the tinning machine. Mr Green, you take the steam cooking plant. I will operate packing, so let's get to it, I want to be done and out of here by midnight, we may still have the police snooping about."

Mr White, Pink and Green left through the plastic strip doorway heading to their positions in the other areas of the factory. Mr Black was the only one that remained with Max and the animals. He walked over to the funnel end of the machinery and picked up a crowbar that was lying on the back of the forklift. He spoke in a loud voice so Max could hear his every word.

"It's just you, me and these dumb animals."

There was a mean purpose in his stride as he walked over to a palette load of empty dog food tins. He picked one up and examined it closely.

"Oh, and of course, it's you, me, some dumb animals *and* an industrial meat processing and tinning plant."

Mr Black looked over to see a frightened Max, sitting awkwardly in his cage, bound and gagged. Max stared back at Mr Black as he walked back to the funnel end of the machinery. Mr Black stopped beside a stainless steel control panel, reached into his jacket pocket and took out a key. He inserted the key and turned it clockwise. A dozen amber and red lights came on. On top of the funnel, an orange warning light started to flash. Mr Black started to tell Max all about the inner workings of the crush-and-grind machine.

"This is a state of the art, twenty first century, fully automated, dog food processing plant," he paused for dramatic effect, "The first stage of the process is the crushing-and-grinding machine."

He pressed a green button on the panel and a siren sounded two warning blasts, then the electric motor started to hum loudly as it built up to its maximum power output. Mr Black then pressed a second green button which engaged the gearbox and Max could hear a high-pitched whirring sound coming from deep inside the machine as the intermeshed cutting blades picked up speed, making the stainless steel panels shake and vibrate.

"I thought we'd start with a little test run on some frozen meat, just to get the blades warmed up," said Mr Black, "Then we'll move onto some more exotic, fresh ingredients that are on tonight's menu."

He stopped and pointed at Max, "If you hadn't guessed already, that will be you and your fuzzy friends."

Mr Black pressed a third button, the electric motor reached its maximum operating output and the rollers inside the machine spun so fast that they became a blur. He then pushed a lever and the frozen blocks were released onto the first pair of rotating shafts. Instantly, the machine started to shake and the sides reverberated as large chunks of meat were broken off, flung against the sides of the funnel and were dragged back down again by the spinning blades.

Mr Black had to raise his voice so he could be heard over the increasing noise of the machinery.

"Inside this crush-and-grind machine there are three pairs of interlocking tungsten carbide tipped cutting blades on stainless steel shafts rotating at five hundred revolutions per minute."

Mr Black pointed just below the funnel with his crowbar, as if he was giving a university lecture on mechanical engineering.

"The first pair of shafts have broad, hooked blades, more suited to grinding large objects, such as bone. The second pair of blades are a little more fine, they dice up the chunks that the first pair have broken off. By the time you are through the third pair, you will be cut down into little tasty bite-size morsels."

He paused as he pointed his crowbar at the bottom of the crush-and-grind section.

"I expect by the time you get here, they will have you cut up into a teenager-flavoured pâté in less than three seconds."

Max's eyes opened wide.

"It's really quite simple," said Mr Black laughing out loud, "A week ago, we were making Quarter Pandas!"

Max visualised panda bears being shoved into the crusher and winced at the thought.

Mr Black was still laughing at his clever play on words when he moved along the machine to the conveyor belt where tiny pieces of processed meat fell out of the chute and travelled to the next stage. He then pointed with his crowbar at two huge pistons which flexed and contracted at a steady rhythm.

"Once you are through the blades, the machine filters out all the bits we couldn't crush into a paste, like your clothes, hair and the fillings in your teeth. Then you will be passed further through the machine towards these hydraulic pistons. These have two tons per square centimetre of pressure, more than enough to squeeze you into shape so we can slice and dice you into little tasty chunks of meat, the ones that all dogs know and love."

Max watched in horror as compressed meat was ejected like modelling clay onto the conveyor where rows of metal rollers were stretching it out into a long sausage shape. As it passed into the next section, a sharp blade went up and down, slicing the meaty sausage at regular intervals into tiny cylindrical chunks of processed meat.

"But this is only the first part of the process."

Mr Black paused for a moment and picked up one of the chunks as it went by on the conveyor. He held it up so Max could see it.

"Once you've been turned into these little meaty morsels, you will travel on this conveyer belt through to the tinning room where you'll be squeezed into tins like this one."

He held the tin up so Max could see exactly what was in store for him.

"We then add a little hot gravy with some added X-Ingredient zing to make it irresistible to dogs and totally addictive. The conveyor belt will then take you, in your gravy-goodness, to the steam room where a machine fits a lid on the tin, to keep the freshness in, and then you'll be pressure boiled in a steam oven at one hundred degrees centigrade to seal in the flavour."

He stopped walking beside the machinery and turned to look at Max again.

"You *don't mind* being turned into dog food do you?" he said with a sarcastic tone and false expression of concern.

He continued walking along the front of the crush-and-grind machine.

"When you are steamed to perfection, the conveyor belt will then take you, in your tin of meaty goodness, to the packing room where the machinery sticks on an outer label. You'll then be packed into crates of twenty four tins and then you are off to the binding machine."

Max watched him do a very bad impression of a magician waving a wand, except he waved the crowbar in a wide circle.

"Hey Presto!" he shouted with barely suppressed glee, "You will be on the supermarket shelves before anyone even reports you missing!"

Mr Black was still laughing as he walked from the conveyor belt to the small office and for the first time in Max's presence, he removed his dark sunglasses and placed them carefully inside his jacket pocket. He picked up a white hard hat and placed it firmly on his head and then he put on a pair of plastic safety glasses. Through the clear lenses Max saw his evil, dark, emotionless eyes.

He turned to face Max and tapped the side of the glasses.

"One must always wear these, you know," he said with a sinister tone, "The last thing I want is bits of you flying about all over the place and hitting me in the eye."

Given the chance Max would have punched him repeatedly in his piggy little eyes but instead he sat motionless, watching Mr Black as he walked from the office to the far end of the cages.

"I suppose," Mr Black continued, switching to a very matter-of-fact tone, "All we really need to discuss is whether you would prefer to go in head first or feet first?"

Max gulped.

Mr Black's manic, psychopathic laughter rose above the deafening hum of the machinery, "Should we toss a coin? What will it be, Heads or Tails?"

Max watched Mr Black flip the crowbar in his hand like a juggler as he started to walk back towards him, dragging the pointed end across the bars of the cages. The clanging sound resonated through the factory and drove the animals wild. Max saw a cruel, wicked grin spread across Mr Black's mean pointed face when he drew level with the bears. He loved tormenting all the animals but he particularly liked baiting the bears and took great pleasure in prodding them for a response. He poked the crowbar through the bars of Control's cage and swung it from side to side hitting the bars making a sound like a deafening alarm bell.

"Wakey, wakey, Mr Bear!" he shouted.

The bear did not stir, it slowly turned its head and looked at Max then stared back at Mr Black.

Mr Black reached further into the cage, close enough to prod the bear but then he realised something was not right. He glanced down at the safety bolt that held the cage door locked shut and in half-a-heartbeat the grin faded from his face. Running from the end of the bolt was a length of silver coloured cord that Max had created from some of the duct tape he had removed from his wrists. Mr Black followed the cord along to where it ended in Max's hands that were clearly not securely taped anymore.

With a sharp movement, Max pulled the cord releasing the tamperproof safety latch and the bolt on Control's cage door lifted up and moved back in its slider. Mr Black instinctively reached out to stop the bolt but it was too late, Max pulled again and the bolt unlocked. At the same time Control moved forward and pushed the cage door hard enough to open it a few centimetres. Mr Black backpedalled and his crowbar fell uselessly to the floor. The bear sensed freedom and launched head first into the cage door with a force that caught Mr Black off balance, sending him sprawling backwards. In less than half a second, two hundred and fifty kilograms of bad-tempered adolescent polar bear was loose and on the warpath.

As fast as the bear was running forward, Mr Black was running backwards, desperately trying to avoid its snapping jaws that were dangerously close to the end of his nose. The bear's hot breath steamed up Mr Black's safety glasses and a pair of ice-white incisors sliced down across the surface of the plastic lenses.

Mr Black jerked backwards and twisted round in one movement so he could run forwards to get clear of the razor-edged teeth and slashing claws. Control gave chase and one of his massive paws swiped at Mr Black's jacket leaving four huge rips in the black fabric. Mr Black's leather soled, city-shoes struggled for grip on the smooth concrete as much as the bear's paws did, and the two of them clattered into crates and boxes in a wild chase around the crush-and-grind machine, sending empty tin cans crashing to the floor and rolling under feet and paws, adding to the total confusion. Mr Black ripped off the hard hat and glasses and threw them at the bear, Control swatted them away sending them flying across the room. Mr Black was running for his life and the bear was gaining on him. Mr Black vaulted over the metal roller conveyor belt, the bear leapt over it in one huge easy bound, nearly landing on Mr Black. In the remaining cages, the orang-utans and gorillas shook the bars and whooped as the bear closed in on their common enemy. The dogs howled and barked encouragement and the cacophony of animal sounds drove Control to run faster and faster. Another swipe of his paw left the back of Mr Black's jacket in tatters and his white shirt shredded, millimetres from his skin.

Mr Black had run around the crush-and-grind machine twice with the bear gaining ground on each circuit. He swerved right, changing direction to run along the front of the cages. When he drew level with the last cage containing a large, angry, hissing komodo dragon, he nimbly dodged its snapping jaws, grabbed hold of the bars and swung himself around, causing Control to overshoot. The bear skidded to a stop, turned and continued the chaotic chase around the back of the cages. Mr Black had managed to open up a gap between him and the bear's snapping jaws when he looked along the line of cages and saw that Max was free and standing next to the other bear's cage. Max opened the bolt and the second bear fired out of its cage like a pumped-up pedigree greyhound and joined his brother in the chase. Max quickly got back into his own cage, taking cover.

Mr Black now had two revenge-focused polar bears closing in on him from different directions. He swerved again and slid under the conveyor belt with Control and Withdraw in hot pursuit, crashing into each other as they skidded underneath, sending metal rollers and meaty morsels flying through the air.

Mr Black was up and running instantly, his legs and arms pumped as fast as they could. He could feel his heart pounding like a jackhammer inside his ribcage but he felt the bear's hot breath not far behind so he ran on, ignoring the pain in his chest and legs. He reached underneath his armpit through what was left of his ripped jacket, trying to find the handle of his 9mm Glock pistol. He just needed to get ten to twelve metres between him and the bears and then he could turn around and fire off a few well aimed shots. He dodged and darted between packing crates to get some more distance between him and the bears. He ran around the funnel end of the machinery and back along the front of the cages, passing Max who was by now urging the bears on as much as the other animals were.

Mr Black managed to get his pistol out of its shoulder holster. Just a few more metres between him and the bears was all he needed to get off two shots which would be enough to slow them down, allowing him to finish them off. Then he would do the kid.

He sprinted on, glancing down as he pulled the cocking-slider back on the pistol. He checked a fresh round had entered the chamber and the pistol was cocked, ready to fire. He prepared himself to spin around and take aim but when he looked up he ran head-first into an orange metal pipe. Dazed and seeing stars, he was sure it was an orange metal pipe that he had run into. The pain across the bridge of his nose and the smell of blood in his nostrils confirmed he had run into something very hard, like a metal pipe, except this metal pipe appeared to be covered in wispy orange hair. By the time he realised it had been the outstretched arm of a male orang-utan, it was too late, he had dropped his gun which slid harmlessly under the heavy machinery. The bears were now upon him and he felt a tug at the back of his trousers that felt like an anchor dragging him backwards, the material ripped and he felt four sharp, well aimed teeth sink down into his bare buttocks. He was not waiting around for a bear to take a second chunk out of his backside so he ran with a renewed sense of his own impending demise towards the tinning area, through the plastic strip doors, screaming and running faster than he had ever run before, with the remains of his trouser legs flapping around his ankles.

Withdraw skidded to halt just short of the plastic strip doorway. He had a large amount of blood-stained boxer short material in his mouth that he shook from side to side. It was a well-earned trophy. Control ran on and continued the chase, barrelling through the plastic strips in hot pursuit. Withdraw spat out the shreds of boxer shorts and sped off after his brother, hungry for more trophies.

Max gingerly opened the door to his cage. The gorillas were going wild and the dogs were spinning around and around in their cages, barking and howling like a crazed pack of wolves that had scented a kill. In a rash moment of euphoria at being free, Max ran to the far end of the cages, turned around and ran back opening every bolt as he went by. He then took cover again in his own cage which had become a personal safe-room separating him from the chaos that was happening around him.

The orang-utans burst out of their cages and formed into a large group, hugging each other. The huge male that had incapacitated Mr Black took charge and the group nimbly climbed into the upper reaches of the factory roof, swinging between the pipes and air ducts, crossing over the factory's inner partition walls to the tinning room in the same smooth way they would have crossed from tree to tree back home.

The two snow leopards adapted quickly to the inner factory, leaping from crate to crate upwards into the walkways and pipework that criss-crossed the factory's roof. They quickly found perfect ambush positions high above the machinery and conveyer belts and they had one thing on their mind, it was payback time for their months of being subjected to X-Ingredient testing. Mr Black and his colleagues were about to find out that testing spot cream on snow leopards had been a very bad idea.

The gorillas huddled together into a formidable band of brothers, bonded by their determination to get even for a humiliating six months being subjected to relentless shampoo trials. Despite their over-shampooed, soft, shiny, tufty hair, they had a look of uncontrollable, all-out retribution about them. They beat their chests and whooped themselves up into a frenzy as the entire troop stormed en masse into the dog food plant, searching for more men like Mr Black.

Behind the marauding gorillas, the dogs had formed up into a swirling pack of fur and flashing white teeth. An alpha male was instantly and unanimously elected, a large Doberman aptly named Razor became pack leader. He was a natural born leader, he had a wild glint in his eye brought on by a desire to also sink his teeth into Mr Black's behind, plus like the other dogs he had an insatiable addiction. The pack of crazed dogs set off at speed in search of more of Mr Black's companions and an open tin of X-Ingredient-gravy flavoured dog food.

Max watched the animals disappear into the depths of the factory and he breathed a deep sigh of relief. If this dream was a nightmare, it had definitely just taken a rather entertaining turn for the better.

He had watched Mr Pink lock the shutter doors so knew he would have to find another way out but for now, ironically, the safest place to stay was in his cage.

Eight Weeks after the Power Crisis:

Saturday 20:30Hrs

The last thing Mr Orange expected to see at that time of night was a pretty girl walking towards him from out of a cornfield. He didn't suspect anything so he didn't bother to report it by walkie-talkie to Mr White. He stepped out of his car to take a closer look.

He shone his torch into her face so he could see more clearly. The girl shielded her eyes by holding her hand across her eyebrows and stared down at the ground.

"You can't come in here, Miss," he said, with an unusual politeness, considering he was a hired killer.

Rachel put on her best damsel in distress voice.

"My car's broken down and I can't get a phone signal. Can I use a phone, please?"

"There are no phones here and I would step away from the gate, Miss. The fence is electrified."

Rachel kept walking forward until she was less than a few metres from the gate.

"Please, I'll only be a minute, I need to call my dad."

Mr Orange stood roughly the same distance away, on his side of the fence, "Sorry, Luv, I can't let you in, it's the rules. The factory is shut for the weekend. It's for routine maintenance."

"Please, I'm desperate," Rachel said as she took her hand away from her eyes and looked straight into the torchlight.

"Wait a moment," said a surprised Mr Orange, "Aren't you Poppy Pur……"

Before he could finish his sentence, he was struck from

behind by Peter, hitting him like a pile driver squarely in the middle of his back. The force knocked Mr Orange forward, his knees dragged on the rough concrete and he skidded along the ground, falling forward onto the electric fence. Instinctively he put his hands out and grabbed the metal chain links. Immediately, the shock hit him and he shook violently as pulses of stored energy passed through the electric fence, down his arms, through his shoulders, down his back and earthed through his scuffed bare knees. He tried to get to his feet which would have given him some form of insulation through his shoes and a respite from the charges that were pulsing through his body, but it was no use, Brian was already there. This had been a two pronged attack, Peter's first blow was followed up by Brian who had removed one of the large insulated crocodile clips from the fence's power pack terminals, lifted up Mr Orange's trouser leg, and reattached the clip, clamping it directly onto his Achilles' tendon. The fence's power pack had enough electrical charge to electrify a fence twenty kilometres long. Rerouting it directly through Mr Orange's body made it a very short circuit indeed and Mr Orange convulsed as the full charge of the fence's power sent huge pulses of electricity surging through his body.

"T....T...T...Turn it o...o....o...off!" Mr Orange pleaded.

"Wow. There's enough juice there to stop an elephant let alone a dozen dairy cows," remarked Brian as Mr Orange flapped and floundered, kneeling on the ground, unable to let go of the fence. "Don't touch him, Pete, he's still live."

"Give him a few more minutes and he'll not be *a-live* anymore," said Peter, "He's starting to smoke." Peter and Brian stood back a safe distance.

"T....t...t...turn it o...o....o...off!" Mr Orange begged through his chattering teeth.

"We're not going to turn it off unless you ask nicely," said Peter, who was enjoying this. Anyone messing with Max deserved a bit of pain. In fact, they deserved a lot of pain.

Mr Orange lowered his tone. "P….p…p….p…please turn it off."

"Belt," said Peter.

Brian whipped off his belt and handed it to Peter.

"Books and bag," Peter instructed.

Brian obediently opened his satchel bag. He knew what to do. He placed one of his thick college text books next to the jiggling feet of Mr Orange. On the other side, he placed his satchel. Peter stepped on the book and satchel, straddling the heels of Mr Orange. More importantly, he was earthed and could safely touch Mr Orange without getting a shock himself. He looped the belt around Mr Orange's ankles and pulled it tight and secured it with a knot through the buckle. Peter moved the satchel and book up to the fence and wrapped his own belt around one of Mr Orange's wrists. Mr Orange's eyes were rolling around in their sockets as his whole body shook and convulsed out of control. Peter signalled for Brian to cut the power. Brian squeezed the insulated handles of the crocodile clip and loosened the clip's grip on Mr Orange's ankle. He held the clip poised, ready to reapply if necessary.

While he was rather effectively stunned, Peter spun Mr Orange over so he was sitting on the ground. He quickly lifted Mr Orange's free hand off the fence and tied it securely to the other hand with the rest of his belt, he then looped the belt back on itself securely fixing both of Mr Orange's hands to the electric fence above his head.

"Have you had enough, or should we connect you up again?" Peter asked, standing clear.

"Go to hell, you little…"

Brian reapplied the crocodile clip to Mr Orange's bare leg. Mr Orange shook violently. He started to dribble and he uncontrollably wet his pants.

"Are you sure you want more?" asked Peter who noticed the puddle of pee forming underneath Mr Orange, "Oh, dear, that's not going to help matters, is it?"

The sarcasm was wasted on Mr Orange who tried to shake his head but as his whole body was convulsing it made little difference.

Peter held up his hand and Brian removed the clip. Mr Orange gasped taking in deep lungfuls of air and was unable to say anything without his teeth chattering. On the other side of the fence, Rachel watched for signs of movement at the factory while the two brothers worked together to incapacitate one of the people responsible for kidnapping their friend. Under normal circumstances she would have told them to stop, but these people had their friend inside the factory, doing heaven knows what to him.

"What now?" she said, "Can I come through?"

Peter reached inside Mr Orange's jacket and searched his trouser pockets. He found some keys and threw them over the fence to Rachel.

"Is the gate still live?" she asked.

"Oh, it's ok, you can touch the gate. It's quite safe. Brains has rerouted the current from the fence and it's all going into Mister Electric here. He got the full current load, and he will be getting it again if he starts to struggle."

Rachel opened the padlock on the gate and came through to join them. These boys were quite amazing but what was even more amazing was that Peter had strung a complete sentence together. Under pressure, he obviously forgot about being shy.

Mr Orange glared at Brian who was poised, ready to reapply the crocodile clip to complete the circuit if he moved.

"We don't want him getting free, do we?" said Rachel.

"No, we need to keep him here," replied Peter who was trying to think of a solution.

"We could lock him in the boot of the car?"

"We could, but I've got a better idea," said Peter with a grin. He was even more determined to get even for Max, "Have you got something like a bank card on you?"

"Yes," Rachel said as she took a small leather wallet out of her jacket pocket. "Will this do?" she handed him her AA membership card.

Peter reached out and took the card from her. He then pulled off Mr Orange's shoes and stripped out the laces. He pulled off Mr Orange's socks and rolled them into a ball, stuffing it into Mr Orange's mouth. He wrapped one end of the lace around the AA membership card and tied the other to Mr Orange's big toe. He then placed the plastic card between the spring loaded terminals on the fence's power pack and he pulled the lace tight with a slip knot.

Mr Orange had a look of sheer terror in his eyes. He had served in warzones from Iraq to Central America and he had never experienced such ruthless professionalism like this before. But then he had never kidnapped Max Chambers before.

"Brian, attach the clip to his other big toe!"

Mr Orange winced as the sharp teeth of the clip closed on the sides of his big toe and he anticipated the electric shock, but nothing came. The plastic card that Peter had fitted at the spring terminal isolated the circuit. Mr Orange realised that if he moved so much as a centimetre he would pull the card out, the terminal would reconnect and he would be shocked again.

Peter walked up to him and patted him condescendingly on the cheek, "I think you've already figured out what happens if you move, so I suggest you stay still because we won't be here to turn it off."

Peter gave the belt a tug to make sure Mr Orange was secure. The belt was so tight it had already turned his hands blue.

Mr Orange nodded. Peter reached inside Mr Orange's jacket again and felt for the pistol in his shoulder holster. He took it out, flipped out the magazine and threw it over the fence. He then threw the pistol in the opposite direction into the sweetcorn.

"Not bad for a pair of farm boys," Rachel said approvingly as she patted Peter on the arm.

"Yeah, we may be simple country folk to you city girls, but we know a thing or two about electric fences."

Peter suddenly realised he had been having a proper conversation with Rachel for the past five minutes and she was also touching his arm. He went shy in an instant.

"We...we...had better go and get M..M..Max."

Brian nudged Peter, laughed and shook his head, "When you've stopped blushing, perhaps we should find a way into the factory."

"Wait up," said Rachel, "I'll call the police again."

She dialled 999 and after two rings the same emergency operator answered.

"I recognise this mobile number, if this is another joke, young lady....."

Rachel cut her short, "It's not a joke!"

She quickly lowered her tone, shouting was not going to win the operator over and she did not want to attract any unwanted attention from anyone in the factory. In a calm voice, she explained for a second time what was happening at the factory. The operator passed it up to her Inspector who in turn despatched it to PC Burrows and PC Martin.

"Here we go again," PC Martin said, "No blues and twos this time, if it's a hoax, I want to catch the little beggars."

PC Burrows turned the car around and headed back towards the factory. Superintendent Todd had heard the re-despatch and he called Bishop.

"Bishop, another call has come in regarding suspicious events at your factory. I'm pretty sure it's a hoax but I must insist on re-deploying...."

Bishop interrupted, "I'm on my way there myself, I was planning on checking the maintenance team's progress so I can kill two birds with one stone and check out this hoax call at the same time. I'll give you a call in a few minutes to assure you that there's nothing for you and your officers to be concerned about."

"Ok, Bishop, I'll wait for your call."

"Thank you, Superintendent."

Bishop ended the call and accelerated through the country lanes towards North Tawton. Maybe not two birds, he thought to himself, but I can definitely kill two polar bears.

Eight Weeks after the Power Crisis:

Saturday 20:50hrs

Meanwhile, back inside the factory, Mr Pink was preparing the tinning section of the process. He stood beside the conveyor belt and checked the rollercoaster style chute that force fed a continual supply of empty tin cans into the side of the tinning machine, twelve tins at a time. The tinning machine itself was a room-sized metal rectangular box which covered the conveyor belt that brought the diced and sliced meaty chunks from the crusher section. The conveyor passed through a small hatch on the front of the tinning machine, where the tins were automatically filled. Midway through the machine, twelve pressurised jets fired piping hot X-Ingredient gravy into the meat-filled tins. They exited the other side of the machinery as semi-cooked tins of dog food. The tins then passed further along the conveyor, through another hole in the partition wall to the steam room where the tins were sealed with a tin lid and steam-cooked.

Mr Pink was priming the compressors on the steam powered gravy jets when he saw Mr Black running towards him at full speed. Over the noise of the compressors he could not hear what Mr Black was shouting although it was clear he was shouting something very important. Mr Black was sprinting, knees high and arms pumping, in his eyes was the look of a very scared man. Mr Pink had served three tours in the French Foreign Legion with Mr Black and he had never seen him run from anything or anyone. What he was running from, he could not see.

Mr Black never stopped looking ahead, he ran with a fixed stare, eyes wide open, focused somewhere off in the middle distance. He passed Mr Pink and the tinning machine and headed at full speed into the steam cooking process room. Mr Pink turned and watched the fleeing Mr Black. The entire back half of his suit was missing, blood poured from four holes in the left cheek of his backside and his shirt was in tatters. Mr Pink spun round to check the direction he had come from and he saw for the first time what it was that was chasing Mr Black.

He instinctively drew his pistol which was already loaded. He pulled back the hammer and clicked off the safety. He pointed it at one bear, then the other, then back and forth between them. Both bears stopped in their tracks less than fifteen metres from Mr Pink.

Polar bears, like all predators, have not risen to the top of the food chain by being rash or impulsive. They know when to hunt and they know when not to hunt, they know when to stand their ground and when to flee. Control and Withdraw had no idea what a pistol was but their natural instincts warned them that Mr Pink had a confidence about him that meant he did not fear them. To stand his ground he must have an advantage and although they didn't know what it was exactly, they just knew he had one, and that made them very cautious.

Mr Pink's mind was also weighing up the situation. Was a 9mm round enough to stop a polar bear? Would it need two, maybe three? If it needed three, would he get six aimed shots off in time?

The bears started to circle, one going one way, one going the other, opening the gap between them. Mr Pink assessed and recalculated the ever widening angle. Could he get all his shots on target? He pointed the pistol at Control and he took up the first pressure on the trigger. Six shots, all he needed were six aimed shots. Did he have the time?

He took a step backwards which closed the angle in his favour. He took another step. He took a third but the back of his heel hit something hard and he lost his footing. Whatever he had walked backwards into suddenly had a grip like a vice on his ankle. He twisted around and looked down. Around his left lower leg were the drooling jaws of the komodo dragon. The two metre long lizard opened its jaws wider for a bigger bite but Mr Pink was too agile, he put his weight hard down on his right leg and lifted his left leg clear as the lizard's jaws slammed shut. He jumped up onto the conveyor kicking wildly at the monstrous lizard that now hissed and snapped at him. Jumping up onto the conveyor belt had been a good move but he soon regretted it because he could not get grip on the rubber belt and metal rollers that slipped under his feet. He slammed face first onto the rubber belt which propelled him feet first into the tinning machine. The komodo dragon tasted the air with its tongue. It picked up the scent of Mr Pink's X-Ingredient breath mints and launched itself up onto the conveyor eager to find the mints that it craved.

As its huge scaly tail whipped around, the tip struck a green button on the machine's control panel. A yellow beacon started to flash, a siren sounded two blasts and the machine began to feed tins onto the conveyor whilst the compressors fed boiling hot gravy into the jets. The dragon turned to face Mr Pink, cornering him against the entrance to the tinning machine. He tried to get up onto his elbows but the back of his head struck the top edge of the entrance hatch as he slipped backwards, deeper into the machine. He slumped, semi-conscious down onto the belt, dropping the pistol which fell to the floor, out of his reach. Where Mr Pink had struggled on the conveyor, the dragon's long pointed claws had a much better grip and it quickly closed the gap on Mr Pink and his breath mints. Mr Pink struggled to get up again but he came face to face with the septic mouth of the lizard that dripped venomous saliva between rows of needle-sharp teeth. Its long tongue poked out and flicked side to side as it tasted the air again, millimetres from Mr Pink's face. His reaction was to grab the sides of the rollers and push away from the approaching lizard, launching himself backwards, deeper into the tinning machine, anything was preferable to having his face bitten off by a lizard that was the size of a man.

In an instant, he changed his mind. The searing hot gravy from a dozen pressurised jets hit the back of his legs, scalding him through his trousers and the worse thing was that he knew more pain was to come. Twelve more tins were forced into the machine and a second burst of red-hot gravy scalded the backs of his knees. He tried to reach around to protect himself with his hands but the third blast blistered his hands red-raw and he squealed in pain. He tried to wriggle backwards to get through the machine as quickly as possible but he was restricted by three dozen empty tin cans that had been forced into the rapidly overloading tinning mechanism and they jammed the screaming Mr Pink in solid. The gravy jets fired again and the scalding hot liquid burnt through his clothes and scalded his delicate skin. He was stuck halfway through a machine that was designed to process a dozen tin cans at a time, not a man and six dozen cans.

Twenty more blasts of searing hot gravy later and he was still no further through the machine. More tins were pushed into the mechanism, jamming him in tight. His ears suffered the worst, his head was stuck fast between the top of the machine, six dozen tin cans and several layers of piping hot gravy. The jets repeatedly fired at point blank range into his ears, boiling, tenderising and flavouring them until they resembled juicy little mini-steaks, braised to perfection in X-Ingredient gravy.

He thought he was about to die a slow death being boiled alive when he felt a tug at his trouser leg, pulling him through the machine. More piping hot gravy squirted into his eyes, ears and nose. Thankfully his colleagues had arrived to save him. They were tugging at his trouser legs and soon he was free of the machine. He sat up on the conveyor and wiped the steaming gravy from his puffed-up swollen eyes with his third-degree burned hands. He had expected to see Mr White or Mr Green pulling at his legs but instead he saw that attached to his trousers legs were two Jack Russells, a Beagle and a Labrador, all of them tugging and pulling, ripping his trousers and nipping at his gravy soaked ankles. In his ear was the unmistakable rumbling growl of a hungry dog. Not just any dog, it was Razor and he smelt X-Ingredient all over Mr Pink and his mini-steak shaped ears on the side of his head smelt irresistible. It was double-bubble, Christmas-come-early with two birthdays rolled into one.

Razor hesitated, he didn't know whether to lick the ear or bite it first. He chose the latter and his jaws snapped shut. Mr Pink screamed and pushed the Doberman off, leaving the tip of his ear lobe in the dog's mouth. Mr Pink wasted no time, he was on his feet and running but the little Jack Russells remained firmly attached to the bottom of his trousers, determined not to give up the taste of X-Ingredient gravy again. Razor and the Labrador gave chase, biting at the meaty parts of his gravy-flavoured backside. The Jack Russells were still attached to his trousers and they swung around his trouser legs like a pair of oversized flares making Mr Pink waddle more than run.

Out of the corner of his eye, he saw the remainder of the pack closing in on his left and he headed for a fire exit not far off on his right. As he scrambled to the door he pushed down on the handle and dived out into the cool night air that soothed his scalded skin. But the respite was short-lived because twelve dogs, with Razor at the lead, powered after him.

Peter, Rachel and Brian spun round as the door burst open. They watched in surprise as Mr Pink hopped and skipped past them trying to beat the two manic Jack Russells away from his gravy-tastic tasting legs. He eventually managed to break the Jack Russells free and he sprinted, screaming across the compound, chased by an increasingly large pack of dogs. Razor wanted more than an ear lobe so he put on a sprint and dived at the man's leg, taking a huge amount of material away in one bite. The man yelped and ran faster into the darkness, heading for the gate where he hoped and prayed Mr Orange would be able to help him.

Peter and Brian stood together and watched in amazement as the crazed canine manhunt disappeared into the night.

"I hope he doesn't trip over the other guy's shoelace," Brian said, with a genuine concern in his voice. The words were not long out of Brian's mouth when the night sky over by the fence was illuminated by a brilliant, electric blue flash. It was very quiet for a few seconds then an unearthly muffled scream punctuated the silence.

"Too late," said Peter, imagining what was happening to Mr Orange, "But it serves him right."

"Over here!" Rachel called in a half shout, half whispered voice, "This is our way in."

She was already over by the door, holding it open, stopping it from swinging shut.

"Top work, Rachel," said Brian.

The two brothers jogged over to the open door and the three of them peered cautiously inside. They were not sure what to expect.

What was surprising was that there was nothing going on inside. The conveyor had jammed solid and the protective thermal overload system had switched the machinery off. There was no one about on the factory floor so Peter took a tentative step inside, searching left and right for any sign of people or animals in cages but there was nothing in this part of the factory.

Brian and Rachel followed him inside, checking the length and breadth of the tinning area, but if they had looked up they would have noticed a mixed bunch of very determined apes, sloths, large cats, small cats and even smaller mice looking down at them.

"Can you hear the noise in the other room?" Peter whispered.

"Yeah, it's coming from through those large doors," said Rachel as she pointed towards the coldstore, "Max may be in there, let's check it out."

Peter led the way, crouching almost bent double as he walked towards the large insulated doors. Rachel followed close behind with Brian walking backwards, checking for any sign of movement on the factory floor behind them. The three of them approached the automatic sensors and the coldstore doors opened in front of them and they walked into the dimly lit interior, surrounded by the swirling cold misty air.

On the other side of the coldstore, in the food preparation area, Max pushed open the door to his cage. He had decided it had been quiet for long enough and he had to check for a way out in case Mr Black and the other henchman came back. The cage door was only open a few centimetres when through the plastic door strips burst Control, followed soon after by Withdraw. Max slammed the door shut and bolted it. He retreated to the middle of his cage.

The larger of the two bears lumbered over to Max's cage and poked its white muzzle through the bars and snorted. Max instinctively backed away. The bear moved back as well. It then turned around in a tight circle and sat down in front of the cage. It twisted its head slightly to one side and it put its huge paw through the bars. Max had seen this expression on the bear's face before. It snorted again, then the bear lifted itself up into a seated position and mouthed at the bolt as if to open it. Not to get in, but to let Max out.

The other bear barked and the bigger one stopped what it was doing and got back to its four feet. Both bears moved off towards the other end of the crush-and-grind machine, towards the coldstore. The automatic sensor detected them and they walked purposefully into the darkness of the huge freezer.

Max was aware he had been holding his breath and he let out a gasp and drew in another breath which did something to clear his fuzzy head. He contemplated whether the bear would be the same towards him if he was out of the cage but he decided it was too risky to try. I'm staying put, he thought.

With a whoosh the insulated doors opened and Max prepared himself for another polar bear close encounter.

Out of the darkness, a cloud of steamy mist came through the coldstore doors as the sub-zero air mixed with the warmer air of the crush-and-grind room. Out of the mist came Peter. Then Brian followed by Rachel.

Max could not believe his friends had found him and he breathed out a huge sigh of relief. It did not register with him that somehow, in the darkness, the bears and his friends must have crossed paths. It had been ages since Max had spoken a word, his mouth and lips were bone dry and he tried to speak but he could only manage a croaked, "Over here!"

Rachel saw him first.

"There!" she shouted, "There he is!" Before the words were out of her mouth she was at the cage door.

"Max!" Peter and Brian shouted, "Max!"

Rachel was already opening the bolt on the cage, Peter had hold of the bars of the cage door and was poised to swing the heavy door open to rescue his friend.

"Are you ok, Max?" asked Rachel.

Max pushed the door open.

"Get in," he said softly but with a firm tone in his voice.

"What?"

"Get in!" he said as he pushed the door open a little wider.

"Are you mad, Max? We're here to get you out."

"Don't argue, please get in the cage. Don't turn around, just get in the cage," he whispered.

"Alright," said Rachel, "but I don't see why I can't turn around....."

Peter and Brian had already turned around to see the bears coming through the coldstore's automatic doors.

"Get in the cage, Rachel!" Peter shouted, pushing Brian, who knocked Rachel forward through the open door. Peter scrambled in behind them and slammed the cage door shut. Max reached through and closed the safety bolt.

The four of them sat huddled together, back to back in the three metre square cage. All four tucked their legs up tight to their chests, feet held away from the edge of the cage, staring through the bars at the two bears. Max was a little more relaxed than his friends as he had become more accustomed to the bears in the past twenty four hours.

Control and Withdraw circled outside the cage. It was Control that came forward and sat in front of the cage door again. He squeezed his long white muzzle through the bars and gave out a gentle snort through his jet black nose.

Rachel was watching this, speechless in a mix of awe and terror from behind Pete's shoulder, not wanting to look, but unable not to look as the bear passed his front paw through the cage and placed it flat on the floor of the cage. This time, Max responded and edged forward.

"No, Max!" Brian whispered, "What are you doing?"

"I'm sure it's ok," replied Max as he carefully stretched out his hand, "This bear's done this before."

Max placed a very careful hand on top of the bear's paw and the bear snorted, gently lifted its snout to stare directly into Max's eyes. Max fought the urge to pull away, he kept his hand on the bear's massive paw and he gently rubbed the dense white fur. He could feel the powerful muscles and rock hard tendons underneath.

"I pulled a tranquiliser dart out of this one's shoulder," whispered Max.

"You did what?"

"They were trying to overdose him with sedatives and they nearly killed him but I got the dart out in time. That's what I used to get free of the duct tape."

"The dart?"

"Yes, but also this," Max gently lifted the bear's paw up.

It was so heavy he had to move slightly closer to the bear to use a little leverage from his elbows. He raised the paw up slightly and slowly turned it over until it was almost completely pad-side up. The huge bear gave no resistance, it just breathed ever so softly through its jet black nose. Max now cupped the huge white paw in his hand.

"Look at this," Max whispered.

He ran his forefinger along the rippled pad of soft black skin that stretched the width of the paw, moving down to where there were five smaller pads.

"Careful, Max," whispered Pete.

"It's okay," Max said as he gently separated two of the bear's pads. In between the dense white fur at the point of its pad was a razor-sharp jet-black claw.

"That's how I was able to get free to release the bears."

"What?"

"The duct tape, they tied me up with loads of duct tape. I cut through the last of it with this claw."

"No way."

"Yes way," said Max, "Look up there," he nodded in the direction of the bolt on the cage opposite where a line of the cord he had made from duct tape was still attached.

"That's how I opened the cage from the inside, you should have seen the buggers run when I let the bears out."

"Max?" whispered Brian, "What about the other one?" He pointed at Withdraw who was standing a short distance away, facing towards the plastic strip doorway.

"He's not so friendly in coming forward, it's this one that's been doing the paw thing."

Withdraw had stood on guard not far from his brother all this time, occasionally turning to check on the two-legs but he remained focused on the plastic strip doorway. His ears pricked up and he gave a low growl. Control looked Max directly in the eye, never breaking his gaze as he slowly withdrew his up-turned paw, placing it down on the outside of the cage. As the bear applied pressure, its paw splayed out and its claws projected from the soft white fur like tiny black daggers.

Withdraw had definitely heard something and alerted his brother. Both bears turned to face the door and sniffed the air.

"Jeez, Max. Are you telling me they've been like this all night?" whispered Pete.

"Shhhh, something's up, they've sensed it."

Both bears positioned themselves in front of the cage, facing whatever it was that was approaching from the other side of the plastic strip doorway.

"Are they p..p.pp..protecting us?" stuttered a near speech-less Rachel.

Eight Weeks after the Power Crisis:

Saturday 21:20Hrs

At the far end of the factory in the packing area, Mr White looked back along the conveyor towards the square hatch in the wall that led to the steam room. Tins of exotic dog meat should have been making their way down to him by now. Impatiently, he tapped on the metal rollers of the conveyor and he checked his watch. Where are they? What's the hold up? He reached down to the walkie-talkie on his belt and unclipped it. He pressed the talk button.

"White to Green, what's the hold up, over?" he released the button but all he heard was static. He pressed the talk button again.

"White to Pink, status report, over," he released the button and heard nothing except more static.

He pressed the talk button again, "White to Black, status report, over."

More static.

It must be a problem with the machinery he thought, so he strode through the packing area and pushed through the plastic strips hanging down in the doorway that led through to the steam cooking area. Mr Green should have been in here managing the ovens but he was nowhere to be seen. Mr White strode on with even more purpose through the factory, heading to the tinning area. He pushed the doorway's plastic strips apart and walked at a fast pace over to the tinning machinery. It was a complete mess. Empty tin cans and blobs of spilt gravy covered the floor around the machine and Mr White could see several warning lights were flashing on the machinery's control panel indicating a jam in the system. Mr White turned off the mains power and peered inside the rear hatch on the machine. It was splattered in gravy, with crushed tin cans stuck to the roof with more tins wedged into the rubber belt and metal rollers of the conveyor.

Mr Pink had better have a bloody good explanation for this machine, he thought.

He did not stop to clear the jammed tins, he was more interested in finding Mr Pink and hearing his explanation. With his patience running dangerously thin, he headed to the crush-and-grind section, determined to find out what the problem was and why the others had not already fixed it.

He pushed forcefully through the plastic strips in the doorway leading to the crush-and-grind machine and quite quickly wished he hadn't. He froze. All the cages were empty and the two polar bears were out in the open, staring right back at him with their black lips drawn over their ice white teeth in a low, menacing growl.

Mr White was frozen to the spot with the plastic doorway strips draped over him like thin see-through curtains. When he spun around to flee, the plastic strips wrapped around him like tentacles and held him tight, he twisted and struggled, making the plastic strips hold him even tighter and it took him a few valuable seconds to break free. He did not look back, he ran at full speed through the tinning area, slipping and sliding on the scattered tins and pools of gravy while behind him he heard the plastic strips slap apart as the bears burst through.

Inside the cage, Max was the first to speak. Strictly speaking, he was the first capable of speaking. The others were still wide-eyed after their first polar bear encounter, struck dumb by the closeness of the bears and in awe of their power as they launched themselves after Mr White.

"It's been like this all night," said Max calmly, "The bears have been chasing those evil sods all over the place. In here is the safest place to be right now."

"P..p...p...polar   b..b...b..bears?!!!!" stammered   Rachel, getting to grip with the situation at last.

"Yeah, polar bears," Max answered, "You've seen that one of them is quite friendly."

"Friendly?!" shouted Rachel who had regained the power of speech.

"Yeah, friendly, we've sort of bonded."

"Bonded?!"

Peter placed a reassuring hand on Rachel's arm, "It's ok, Rachel, we're safe in here."

He then turned around in the cage to face Max.

"I'm guessing that machinery is part of the food prep and you let the bears out to take care of those guards?"

"That's right, although those buggers are not your average security guards, they are more like MegaCorp's hired hitmen who do Bishop's dirty work."

"Bishop?"

"He's head of research and development, he's in charge of all this," Max explained, "I let the bears out and they've been chasing them around the place all night. If the bears don't get them, the other animals will. Somewhere out there in the factory is a komodo dragon."

"A *what* dragon?!" screamed Rachel, grabbing Pete's arms in shock.

Brian helped explain.

"It's a large lizard, native to Indonesia, it can grow to a length of two metres..."

"Two metres?!" Rachel's face was ashen grey and she was shaking. Pete tried to calm her down.

"It's ok, Rachel, this cage is solid enough," he said in a soft voice and shook one of the bars to prove the point, "We will be ok in here."

Max took a deep breath and started to explain to his friends about the test labs, the caged animals and the X-Ingredient testing. He told them about the kidnapping and the crush-and-grind machine and how he had removed the duct tape using the bear's claw and that was how he got free and was able to let the other animals out.

"Exactly what *other* animals?" asked an incredulous Rachel, hoping to god he wasn't about to say a pride of lions were on the loose. Or worse still, spiders.

"There's a pair of snow leopards, a group of gorillas, a family of orang-utans…."

Rachel shook her head.

"I don't mean to be picky," said Brian, "But it's a troop of gorillas and I think it's a buffoonery of orang-utans."

The others looked at him in amazement.

"Now's not the time to be splitting hairs over collective nouns," Peter said, giving him a gentle cuff around the ear.

"Okay, point taken but what is important is that a komodo dragon could easily squeeze through these bars and I'd rather not be in here when it does. We need to move somewhere else."

"He's right, and we need to get to a phone, mine's dead," said Rachel.

"That office looks safer, who's up for going first?"

Mr White cowered behind the packing machine. He had given the bears the slip and was crouched down in between two large wooden cable drums of blue nylon binding tape. He hardly dared to breathe but he was out of breath so he sucked air into his burning lungs as quietly as he possibly could.

His eyes darted frantically around the factory searching for the bears. He very carefully reached down to his belt for his walkie-talkie but his fingers felt only the sharp plastic of the broken clip. Damn, he thought, I've lost the radio. He reached inside his jacket for his pistol and shut his eyes in blissful relief when he felt the reassuring plastic grip of the pistol. He opened his eyes and scanned around the packing area again. To his left, he saw the unmistakable shape of a bear's back and huge shoulders moving towards him, or perhaps more accurately, stalking him. The bear disappeared from view as it passed between the packing machine's conveyor belt and a row of wooden crates.

Mr White's military training kicked in, that bear was the scout, and the other bear was undoubtedly flanking him. He scanned right and drew his 9mm pistol. He was not wrong because less than ten metres away was Control. In a flash, Mr White drew his pistol and aimed at Control. He fired but the pouncing bear was quicker on the draw and the bullet whistled harmlessly between two huge outstretched paws. The gun's loud crack and blinding muzzle flash made the bear flinch and instinctively jerk sideways in mid-air, crashing with full force into the side of one of the wooden cable drums. Mr White tried to get his aim back on target for a second shot but the cable drum had started to roll, blocking his view. The drum gathered momentum leaving Mr White exposed as it rolled towards the packing machinery. Control scrambled to his feet trying to close the gap on Mr White, to get within striking distance.

The charging bear knocked over a large metal packing desk that flipped upside down on the concrete floor, sending piles of paperwork into the air that rained down like oversized wedding confetti. The bear slipped as it tried to get grip through the paper that was now strewn across the concrete floor. Mr White twisted to face the bear and took aim. He fired but the bear's slipping, sliding erratic movements meant he missed a second time. The bear found grip and dived after him, growling, mouth wide open, white teeth flashing.

Mr White did not try for a third shot, the bear was too close. He vaulted over the upturned packing desk as the bear clattered into the metal doors of a full-height cupboard which shook under the impact and toppled over onto the side of the packing machine.

On top of the cupboard were the test lab kittens.

Seven startled kittens were catapulted forward, gliding in a wide arc, paws outstretched. In mid-air they adjusted themselves perfectly for a soft, perfect, cat-like landing onto the concrete floor. However, the panicked Mr White crossed their flight path and the first of the spiralling kittens was on a collision course with his close-cropped head. Seconds from landing, the kitten extended its claws.

Mr White felt the soft pad of the kitten's paws on his head and thought it was just more of the packing paper falling around him. Then sixteen X-Ingredient hardened claws dug deep into his scalp.

Months spent on the test lab cylinders had taught this kitten how to hold on for its little life and it now clung on like a demented limpet to the top of Mr White's head as sixteen tiny trails of blood spread out from under its tiny but lethally-equipped paws. A second kitten landed on his shoulder, digging another set of hardened claws deep into his skin, making him wince and twist in excruciating pain. With claws as hard as steel and as sharp as hospital needles, two more kittens fixed themselves permanently to the delicate soft areas of his groin making him scream in a soprano-esque yodel, as he leapt from one foot to another in a futile attempt to dislodge the life-or-death grip of the kittens.

He reached down and grabbed them by the back of their necks, trying to pull them free but they simply would not budge. The more he pulled, the more the pain increased, especially around his now red-raw privates. He dropped his gun and tried to prise the kittens off with both hands. He was in so much pain, he had completely dismissed thoughts of the bear.

"Oh my god!" he panicked, "The bear, where was the bear?"

He need not have worried. The bear's natural curiosity had got the better of him and it now stood back and watched intently as the pincer-pawed kittens incapacitated Mr White. For a bear that had spent the majority of its life locked in a cage doing nothing but go slowly mad, this day was without doubt the most entertaining day of its life, full of new experiences that were to be savoured. Withdraw skidded to a stop beside his brother and the two bears watched in sheer pleasure as a sixth kitten applied itself across Mr White's forehead, front paws digging into his cheeks, back paws piercing the tender parts of his ears. He spun around wildly, trying to lift one set of claws off at a time, but each time he freed one and moved onto another, the first one clamped down again even harder.

Mr White could not see much more than the kitten's furry belly spread across his eyes but he knew he had to keep moving towards the packing machinery where he could make an exit through one of the emergency doors. He anticipated that at any moment, one or both of the bears would be upon him so he pulled and tugged at the kittens, disregarding the pain as their claws took away large strips of his skin.

"Get off me you little bastards," he shouted, "Get off!"

One by one, he dragged the kittens off and he threw their little bodies to the ground where they all expertly landed paw-side down. One little tabby cat kitten looked up at Mr White and its big round kitten eyes saw only the hard leather sole of Mr White's shoe. Mr White was about to commence on some well deserved kitten-stamping, starting with this one, right under his left foot.

The defenceless kitten let out a little meow and raised a delicate paw.

Mr White lifted his foot a little higher, getting into the perfect kitten-stamping position.

"Now you're gonna get it!" he snarled.

The hapless kitten let out another meow, except the high-pitched meow that came out of its little mouth was drowned out by a deafening unearthly roar, evidently not from the little kitten, this came from above. Mr White instinctively looked upwards, searching left and right, peering into the shadows of the factory's roof for the source of the stomach-turning, menacing growl. The ill-fated hitman recognised the sound but it was too late, he was already doomed because high above him, hidden in the rafters, crouching in a perfect position to strike, was one of the snow leopards. The exact same snow leopard he had baited with an electric cattle prod for the last six months.

The leopard pounced, eager to protect its much smaller cousin and determined to get some payback for all the cattle prodding. Mr White, still standing on one leg in kitten-stamping position, was unable to dodge out of the way in time. Delicate little kittens landing on your head are one thing, ferocious thirty kilogram leopards with claws designed to grip onto sheer-sided, mountainous rocks are a completely different matter all together.

The bears were captivated onlookers, watching intently as Mr White twisted and turned, gyrated and spun in ever tighter circles in an attempt to dislodge the ferocious leopard that was firmly attached to his blood-stained, claw-shredded head and shoulders. Mr White spun round and round, round and round like a giant gyroscope and the leopard clung on as if it was on a wild-waltzer fairground ride. Eventually, the centrifugal force from Mr White's crazed spinning was so great that even the leopard's claws lost grip and it was flung through the air taking most of Mr White's crew-cut scalp with it. Mr White stumbled left and right, half-blinded by the blood pouring into his eyes and dizzy from all the spinning. He crashed awkwardly into metal tables and packing crates, sending empty tin cans bouncing across the floor in all directions. He spun around and collided with the sharp metal sides of the conveyor which flipped him head over heels, depositing him heavily on the rubber belt. Before he had time to clear his dizziness, he was already in the packing machine.

The bears had been willing spectators in Mr White's demise and they were satisfied with their feline friend's handling of the senior henchman. They got back up on all fours and walked together towards the coldstore in search of more black-suited tormentors and hopefully another trophy for Withdraw.

Peter was the first out of the cage. Max held the door slightly ajar, ready in case he needed to get back in a hurry. Peter crept over to the plastic strip doors and peered through. It was clear so he turned around and gave a thumbs-up signal, then turned back to scan for any animals or hired killers approaching. Max pushed the cage door fully open, he stepped out and walked over to the crush-and-grind machine's control panel which had a large red plastic button that was marked EMERGENCY STOP. He was about to press it when Peter called him over to the plastic strip doorway.

"Max, come look at this!"

Brian and Rachel headed for the small concrete office, on the way Brian picked up Mr White's walkie-talkie while Rachel peered through the wire mesh that covered the window. She did not want to open the door and come face to face with something that had big teeth and big claws. It was clear so she opened the door and Brian followed her into the office. She found a phone on the desk and started to dial 999 as Brian held the door open for the others.

"Pete! Max!" Brian shouted, "In here!"

"Wait up," said Pete, "I can see something."

Max was now standing next to Peter, peering through the plastic strips. Max had become accustomed to the events of the evening but Peter stared with disbelieving eyes at what he saw coming towards them.

Eight Weeks after the Power Crisis:

Saturday 22:00Hrs

Mr Black had made it as far as the steam-cooking area where he had found a small cupboard under a packing table that was big enough for him to hide in. He climbed inside and pulled the door closed, trying to catch his breath, not daring to make a sound.

He sat huddled in the corner of the cupboard and shivered with fear. His clothes were in tatters, he had blood pouring from the bite wound in his left bum cheek plus he had lost his gun and phone and he had dropped his walkie-talkie. He was on his own and he was scared but he figured the cupboard's metal door was strong enough, so he decided he would wait until help arrived.

It had been quite some time since he had made his escape and he was concerned about the throbbing pain in his backside so he reached around and gingerly felt the wound. It was sore to touch and still bleeding. He looked at the blood on his hand and wiped it off using the lapel of his shredded jacket. He tried to recollect when he had last been for a tetanus jab, he could not remember so it must have been ages ago. Ever since he was a little boy, he had hated having an injection but after having a polar bear clamp its teeth down on his rump, he would never complain again.

There was not much room in the cupboard and he did his best to make himself comfortable. It was cramped but he was safe so he rested his head and tried not to think of his bleeding buttocks.

He wasn't sure how long he had dozed off for when a noise from outside rudely startled him back to his senses. He awoke stiff, sore, cold and wondering where he was. It all came back to him in a flash. Alone in the cupboard, paranoia crept up on him and his mind started to play tricks. He heard what he thought were gunshots but he wasn't sure. Was that someone screaming? What are the first symptoms of tetanus poisoning? What if the police came? What if no one came? Did he leave a trail of blood? What if his bum cheek gets gangrene? When had he last seen his mum?

Paranoia turned to panic.

Would polar bears follow a trail of blood? How was he going to get out of this mess? Would he bleed to death? Where was Mr Green? Is lockjaw the first symptom? What if the others had left him behind? Is drowsiness a sign of hypothermia? Why had he not told his mum that he missed her? Do they amputate bum cheeks? Where is Mr Pink? Was his jaw getting stiff? When was his last confession? When was Mother's Day? Why couldn't he move his legs? Is it cramp? Could it be blood-poisoning? Did he just hear some footsteps?

He was hyper-ventilating and his heart was racing as fast as his troubled mind.

He tried to settle himself down by assessing his situation:

Mr White should be in the packing area to his left, he thought. Mr Green should have been in this section, manning the cookers but he hadn't seen him when he came through. He figured Green must be out there somewhere. If those bears had got past Mr Pink, they would be in the steam cooking room by now. Perhaps Mr Pink had shot them, perhaps those were the gunshots but he could not remember if he had definitely heard gunshots. If the bears had taken out Mr Pink then they would surely be in this section of the factory by now and Mr Green would be dealing with them. All these assumptions and permutations twisted around and around in his head. The one question he could not answer was why it was so quiet.

He opened the cupboard door slightly and peered through the crack. Outside, he could see the steam from the cooking machinery. Mr Green must be out there somewhere. His best bet was to regroup with the rest of the team so he opened the cupboard door a tiny amount more and peered out. No sign of polar bears. Good. He opened it a little wider to get a better view around the cooking and steam processing area. He waited and listened. He opened the door a little wider still.

A huge hand reached into the cupboard and pulled him out by his shoulder, a second huge hand grabbed his wrist and he felt himself being dragged at high speed out of the cupboard and then thrown upwards. He was passed from hand to hand by things he couldn't quite make out because they were moving so fast, he just felt huge hands grab his wrists and throw him to other waiting hands above. His head smacked hard against the factory's pipework and ducting, blurring his vision, as he was tossed higher and higher into the roof space.

One of the huge hands let go of his ankle and he fell in a heap onto the metal chequer plate decking of one of the upper walkways, high above the machinery in the rafters of the factory roof. It took a while for his vision to fully return but when it did he found himself surrounded on all sides by orang-utans.

He glanced over to the opposite side of the walkway where a troop of gorillas had Mr Green pinned down and they were taking it in turns to pluck single hairs from his head. Each strand they held between their finger and thumbs, holding it up to the light to check for softness and sheen. Mr Green mouthed the words *'help me'* but Mr Black had problems of his own. Four huge male orang-utans closed in on him, one grabbed his leg and dragged him upward again. The powerful animal easily carried Mr Black in one hand while climbing with the other. More orang-utans joined the large male and Mr Black was passed from orang-utan to orang-utan, first by his ankles then by his wrists, flipping him head over heels through the factory roof.

It was as if Mr Black was doing star-shaped cartwheels through the air.

Peter and Max looked through the plastic strip doorway as Mr Black was spun through the factory's rafters by a gang of trapeze artist orang-utans heading towards the crush-and-grind machine. The swooping, swinging apes covered the length of the factory with graceful ease, tossing the luckless Mr Black from one giant orange hand to another.

Peter and Max craned their necks upwards as they watched the screaming Mr Black get thrown ankle over wrist, head over heels, through the trusses and girders of the factory roof. As he spun overhead, Mr Black caught Max's eye, on his next revolution he saw Max reach into his pocket and on his next revolution he saw Max flipping a coin.

"Heads!" shouted Max as Mr Black was swung towards the funnel end of the crush-and-grind machine.

"Heads?" asked a puzzled Pete.

"It's a private joke, Pete, between me and Monkey-Boy up there."

Max ran over to the funnel end of the machine and watched with amazement the whimpering Mr Black and the mob of orang-utans who clearly wanted payback for their incessantly itching feet.

There was a clear leader among this well organised pack of foot-sore primates, it was the large male and he positioned himself, hanging from a metal roof truss high above the funnel. He whooped and one of his long-armed colleagues threw the helpless Mr Black spinning through the air towards him. The large male caught Mr Black by his wrist and positioned the swinging henchman perilously close to the top of the funnel. A second orang-utan joined the large male and the two of them linked arms and formed a monkey-chain, dangling Mr Black even further inside the funnel, closer and closer to the spinning, tungsten-carbide blades. Max stood at the base of the funnel and with a sinister tone delivered his killer punchline.

"Oh dear, Mr Black, it looks like it's going to be tails!"

Mr Black did not see the funny side of the joke, the orang-utans held him directly above the blades and he was all set to be going in feet first.

"Turn the machine off!" he shouted.

"Sorry," said Max, cupping his ear, "What did you say?"

"I said turn the….!"

His words were cut short as the two orang-utans lowered him a little further into the funnel, dangerously close to the claw-shaped spinning blades which wanted to drag him further into the grinding, thrashing and crushing machinery below. Mr Black tried to save himself by jamming his feet into the sides of the funnel but as he was lowered further in, he was forced into doing the splits and it was now his backside that was even closer to the rotating blades. His splits widened until both legs were at ninety degrees to his body and he squealed in pain as his muscles and tendons stretched close to breaking point.

Max rejoined Pete by the plastic strip doorway and they both watched Mr Black gymnastically fight for his life while half a dozen orang-utans egged on their comrades to drop him further in. Mr Black's spread-eagled legs could not hold the splits for very long and his right leg buckled underneath him. The fabric of his tattered trouser leg caught in the first of the blades and wrapped at high speed around the spinning shaft. The outside edge of his right shoe bounced and skipped on the whirring blades as the material of his trouser leg was dragged down into the machine. With his free hand, Mr Black fumbled for the belt buckle around his waist which he desperately tried to release so the remains of his trousers would not pull him into the crush-and-grind machine. Seconds from losing his right foot, his belt came free and his trousers were whipped off and dragged down into the blades, shredded into thousands of tiny black pieces. The orang-utans whooped even louder, clearly entertained by seeing Mr Black so brutally and efficiently undressed down to what was left of his already blood-splattered boxers.

The large male orang-utan caught the eye of the other

member of the monkey-chain below him and gave a simple command. The lower ape let go of Mr Black's wrist.

Mr Black fell into the funnel. As he slid inside, he jammed himself into the stainless steel shaft scrabbling for grip on its smooth sides just a few millimetres from the flashing blur of two hundred tungsten carbide tipped, case-hardened blades.

From within the office, Rachel gasped. She may have hated these men for wanting to dispose of Max in the crush-and-grind machine but she certainly did not want to see them go the same way. Neither, truth be told did Pete or Brian.

Max had a slightly different view. He had experienced the extreme cruelty of Mr Black and part of him was not sorry to see Mr Black's head disappear below the top of the funnel.

Max braced himself for the scream.

Eight Weeks after the Power Crisis:

Saturday 22:30Hrs

But it was not a scream that Max heard, it was the high pitched sound of the machine's siren that filled the factory and the crush-and-grind machine came to a very abrupt stop. Standing by the control panel, with the palm of his hand on the red emergency stop button was the unmistakable figure of Bishop. In his other hand he had a 9mm semi-automatic pistol which he pointed up towards the rafters and took pot-shots at the orang-utans who scattered in all directions. Peter and Max wasted no time and they slipped quickly through the plastic door strips as bullets ricocheted off the roof trusses and whistled dangerously around their heads. Brian and Rachel ducked down in the office and took cover underneath the office desk.

"Mr Black!" Bishop shouted, "Get out of that machinery and get down here now!"

Bishop ejected the spent magazine from his pistol letting it fall with a clatter to the concrete floor. He took a fresh magazine from his jacket pocket and reloaded the weapon then replaced it into his shoulder holster.

A shocked but very thankful Mr Black tentatively put all his weight on the stationary blades. He could feel their sharp points through the soles of his shoes as he scrambled out of the top of the funnel and collapsed on the cold metal decking of the walkway above the machine. He did not have time to catch his breath before Bishop barked more orders.

"Get down here now, Mr Black, we don't have all night!"

Mr Black dutifully got to his feet and wobbled down the stairs to join Bishop who was still standing by the control panel. Next to Bishop was a canvas bag. Mr Black staggered towards Bishop who looked him up and down with disgust. His trousers were missing, his jacket was in tatters and blood poured down his bare legs through the back of his boxer shorts. Mr Black was a broken man.

"Where's Mr White?" demanded Bishop.

"Er….Colin…" said Mr Black, who in his dazed state forgot to use their special codenames, "I mean, Mr White, I haven't seen him."

"Really," said an incredulous Bishop who by now had come to the conclusion that if you wanted a job done properly, you had to do it yourself.

"I did see Mr Pink, but I don't know what happened to him," Mr Black added, "The animals are loose and the p….p….p… polar…"

"Pull yourself together, Black," barked Bishop who had no time for his feeble explanations, "Get some kit from my bag, we're going to have to tidy this mess up ourselves."

Mr Black hesitated because he wanted nothing more to do with this mess and wished he was somewhere safer, somewhere like the streets of Helmand Province or downtown Mogadishu.

"Did you not hear me, Mr Black?" screamed Bishop, "Open my bag, get yourself a weapon and start hunting down these animals!"

Mr Black snapped to attention.

"Yes, Sir!" he shouted.

"And, Mr Black," said Bishop, "Put some bloody clothes on!"

Within a few minutes, Mr Black had found some fluorescent yellow workman's trousers and armed himself with a double-barrelled shotgun. He had also picked up the crowbar he had dropped earlier which he tucked into the waistband of his high-visibility trousers.

Bishop took control of the situation and barked more orders at Mr Black.

"You search through the factory and drop any animals you see. I will then load them into the crusher by forklift, is that clear, Mr Black?"

"Yes, Sir!" replied Mr Black, heading through the plastic strip doors to the tinning area, shotgun in his hand. Bishop took out his mobile and dialled the Superintendent's number.

"Hello, Superintendent," he said in a calm voice, "I'm pleased to report there's nothing untoward happening at the factory, except routine maintenance. I think it's perfectly safe for you to have your officers stand down."

From inside the office, Rachel and Brian poked their heads up from behind the desk that they were hiding under, just enough to see what was going on. They watched as Bishop started the crush-and-grind machine up again.

"Where's Pete and Max?" Rachel dared to whisper.

"Getting as far away as possible, I hope," said Brian.

"The police should be here by now, I'll call them to check."

She dialled 999 again and this time was put straight through to the patrol car.

Parked in a side road next to the hump back bridge not far from the factory, PC Burrows and PC Martin listened to Rachel as she described what was happening *inside* the factory. Superintendent Todd had just been on the phone and advised them that this was yet another hoax call.

"You have been made aware of the consequences of making hoax calls, haven't you, Miss?" PC Martin said, "And yet you still continue with this made up story of polar bears and meat grinders and men being chased by dogs through electric fences?"

"Yes!" shouted Rachel as loud as she dared shout, "I'm not joking and if you don't come now, something terrible is going to happen, you have to believe me!"

"Ok, Miss, we're going to let you off this time with a caution but if you call again we will trace the call and you will be prosecuted."

The line went dead.

"No luck?" whispered Brian.

"No, they're still bloody threatening to prosecute me for hoax calls," she said despondently.

"Here, let me try," said Brian, "I've got an idea."

Bishop remained at the control panel and made sure the crush-and-grind machine was up to operational speed. He then walked over to the forklift truck, climbed into the driver's seat and checked the dashboard. Damn, he thought, the key is missing. He cursed Mr Black who probably had the key to the forklift in his jacket pocket.

"The man's become a liability," he said to himself.

Bishop knew there was another forklift he could use on the other side of the coldstore so he jumped down and walked over to the coldstore doors. They automatically opened with a whoosh and he stepped into the dark misty interior, wishing he had picked up a thermal jacket as he shivered in the damp, freezing atmosphere that filled the huge coldstore.

He was halfway through the coldstore when he heard a noise to his left and instinctively turned to see what it was. In the swirling frosty air he made out a shape hiding in the shadows and so he calmly took his pistol out of its shoulder holster. Bishop was old-school and he liked his personal sidearm to pack more of a punch than the modern Glocks which his men carried, he preferred his well-used, ex-military issue Browning Hi-Power. He pulled the pistol's hammer fully to the rear and let off the safety catch.

"If that's you, boy, I am going to shoot first and then come and get you."

In the damp, cold, semi-darkness of the shadows, Max tried his best to stop shivering and he felt around for something he could use to defend himself.

"I don't have time for games, boy!"

Bishop fired in the general direction of the sound. The bullet whistled past Max, just millimetres from his left ear and embedded itself in a stack of processed meat that split in two with a loud crack as the red hot round sizzled through the frozen blocks. The flash from the muzzle illuminated the inside of the deepfreeze for a split second then it was plunged back into semi-darkness. Bishop's heavy handgun recoiled, the slider came back and the loading mechanism picked up a fresh round from the magazine and smoothly fed it into the chamber. Locked and loaded in a fraction of a second, ready for Bishop to fire again.

Max reached inside an open plastic tub and pulled out something hard and cold that felt axe-like. Max was in the mood to use it on Bishop, he did not care if he was armed or not, he drew back the axe and realised it was nothing more dangerous than a frozen cod-fish. In a rare act of temper, brought on by desperation, Max still threw it at Bishop.

Bishop ducked as the frozen fish flew over his head, shattering into tiny frozen chunks as it hit the wall behind.

"You've got spirit, boy, I'll give you that. Now come out, you really don't want me to come in there after you."

Max reluctantly took a few paces forward and so did something else beside him. Max reached out with his right hand into the gloomy mist and felt the hard, furry, muscular shoulder of one of the bears. The bear breathed out, the frosty air parted in front of them and in the dim half-light inside the coldstore, Max came face to face with Bishop again.

Bishop also came face to face with a snarling, growling, over-protective polar bear, the very same bear he had bought for next to nothing, drugged senseless and discarded as dog meat.

Bishop reacted in an instant and took aim.

The cold frosty air around Bishop's neck suddenly felt warmer and he knew, even before he looked, that he had been outflanked by the second bear. Control roared into his ear causing Bishop to flinch as he squeezed the trigger. His shot missed its target and the bullet slammed into the inner wall of the coldstore, bursting a coolant pipe, sending a fine spray of frosty water arcing through the freezing-cold misty air.

Bishop's pistol recoiled and reloaded again.   He saw a glimpse of Max through the mist, aimed and fired a third shot. This time his bullet struck home but it was Withdraw that roared in pain as the heavy 9mm round struck his forearm. The bear had deliberately jumped between Bishop and Max and it limped off into the darker corners of the coldstore, blood pouring from the wound. Bishop stepped back and lined up a fourth shot but the pistol did not fire. He pulled the trigger again but the loading mechanism was frozen in the open position. He would have unjammed it with his free hand but the second bear was closing fast and he had to act fast. He reached inside his jacket and drew out another of his favourite weapons.

Control had been closing in on Bishop when he recognised what was in Bishop's hand. It was a telescopic cattle prod, a high voltage stun-gun on a stick.   Control had been subjected to these all his life and knew what they were only too well. Bishop waved the cattle prod in the bear's face and the bear backed slowly away, baring its teeth in defiance, growling and snapping at Bishop who waved the electric prod back and forth in front of him.

Bishop shook the pistol but the loading mechanism would not free itself. Undeterred, he kept the pistol pointed directly at Max who could do nothing but raise his hands and stare down the muzzle. In the misty semi-darkness, Max had no idea it was unloaded and that it was effectively useless in the extreme damp, cold conditions. Bishop gained the upper hand in this three way stand-off. He pointed his jammed 9mm pistol at Max and waved the cattle-prod at the bear forcing them both to step backwards. The hind quarters of the bear tripped the infra-red beam that triggered the automatic doors and they slid open with a whoosh as Max and Control retreated through the doorway.

Bishop pulled the trigger on the cattle prod and a high voltage arc of electricity flashed through the terminals making Control snarl in defiance. Beside the bear's huge shoulder, Max was forced up against the cold metal side of the funnel end of the crush-and-grind machine. The cattle prod stopped Control from launching at Bishop and tearing him to shreds. Max would have gladly taken care of Bishop himself but the gun in his face was a meaningful deterrent.

"I suppose you're banking on someone coming to save you, boy?" sneered Bishop, "Well that's not going to happen, I can assure you!"

Bishop pointed the pistol at Max with a menacing look that said he meant business.

"Move back, you little runt," he spat the words at Max, "No one's coming to save you!"

Bishop moved forward and jabbed at the bear, the high-voltage charge struck home on the side of its muzzle and it recoiled as the current shocked through its body.

Bishop forced them to retreat around the side of the crush-and-grind machine's large electric motor, he wanted them clear of the coldstore and as close to the funnel as possible so that when he shot them, they would be easier to lift with the forklift, and of course, there would be less mess to clear up. The hot fan of the electric motor blasted across Max's face and made the bear's white fur ruffle all along its back as they slowly stepped backwards. Bishop advanced level with the motor and held his pistol in the flow of hot air, defrosting the loading mechanism's jammed spring. Almost in an instant, the slider freed itself and shot forward, loading a fresh round in the chamber. When it clicked home, Bishop smiled, his bluff with the unloaded gun had worked and Max knew he had been outsmarted.

"You bastard!"

"Now, now, young man," said Bishop in a condescending voice, "Mind your language."

Bishop pressed on with a renewed confidence, Control protected Max by shielding him with his huge body, the bond between them instilled in him a natural instinct to protect his two-legged little brother. The bear lashed out with one of its huge paws and snarled at Bishop who retaliated with well-aimed jabs with the prod. One caught the soft underside of Control's paw making him hobble awkwardly backwards pinning Max against the vibrating sides of the machinery.

"'*Polar Bear Chunks in Teenager Gravy*' has a certain ring to it," Bishop mused to himself but loud enough for Max to hear, "Or perhaps we'll call your special blend something more exotic like, hmmmmm, how about '*Aromatic Bear Cutlets Seasoned in a Braised Know-it-all Sauce?*"

Max didn't get a chance to reply. Two shotgun blasts echoed through the factory, coming from the steam cooking area.

Mr Black wished he had not fired both barrels at once.

He had underestimated the agility of the gorillas above him in the roof, they had dodged his badly aimed shots and he fumbled in his pockets for two more cartridges. Behind him, another more human-like gorilla was tracking him at high speed. Mr Black heard the footsteps at the last moment but it was too late, he turned to face Peter who was a split second from impact, travelling at a pace bordering on that of an Olympic sprinter. Peter struck with a perfectly-aimed, bone-shattering, head-first torpedo-tackle straight to the rib cage, lifting the hired henchman cleanly off his feet, knocking every ounce of breath from his lungs.

Even before he hit the ground, Mr Black had given up the fight. Polar bears, orang-utans, gorillas and now an eighty five kilo, muscle-packed guided missile had beaten the very life out of him. He was a gibbering, half-conscious wreck who gave up little resistance as Peter dragged him by his ankle through the factory, heading back to the crush-and-grind food preparation area.

Bishop just about heard the shots over the sound of the ear-deafening crush-and-grind machine. Finally, he thought, Mr Black was doing his job of cleaning up the escaped animals. Bishop wanted to get the bear a little closer to the funnel, so he pushed forward, edging Max and the bear backwards. Max could feel the vibrations of the spinning cylinders through the sides of the funnel and he imagined the hundreds of hardened cutting blades spinning on the other side of the stainless steel panels. Being shot or ground to death? Neither option appealed to Max and he prayed that the police would arrive in time. Bishop must have read his mind.

"Don't think the police will come and dig you out of this one, I've seen to that. They are off chasing hoax callers in North Tawton."

Bishop relished the thought of making Max suffer before he killed him.

"It's the crusher for you, boy. The police are not going to help you now!"

Eight Weeks after the Power Crisis:

Saturday 23:00Hrs

PC Burrows was looking out of his driver's side window as a pair of car headlights on full beam snaked their way through the country lanes, travelling at high speed towards their position. He mouthed the words *'Joyriders'* to his colleague and started up the engine of their patrol car in readiness of a fast pursuit.

Despite the warnings, Rachel had repeatedly called 999 and had been put through to the patrol car for a third time.

"Urgent police business is taking priority now, Miss," said PC Martin, "I suggest you stop making these hoax calls, the penalty will be severe and you have been warned."

Before Rachel could protest, he ended the call and pulled his seatbelt tighter, strapping himself securely into the passenger seat.

The headlights drew ever closer, beams like searchlights snaked across the fields and hedgerows, dipping and rising, following the contours of the road. Whoever it was that was driving, they were definitely driving at a break neck speed towards the factory. PC Burrows and PC Martin were perfectly positioned in a side road to intercept.

Through the open driver's door window, they could hear tyres screeching and engines screaming at full revs, getting closer and closer.

"We've got a right one here," said PC Martin, tightening his seatbelt even more, "He must be doing ninety at least."

The words were not long out of his mouth when the blinding flash of car headlights illuminated the road in front of them. A white sign-written Vauxhall Astra van came over the humpback bridge at high speed and flew past the startled policemen, millimetres in front of their patrol car's bonnet. Sparks flew up where the van bottomed out on the tarmac and it sprayed dust and stones in all directions, peppering the two policemen through the open passenger window.

PC Burrows gunned the engine and started to pull out of the side road when a second Astra van flew past, missing the patrol car's bumper by a hair's width. When it landed, a second shower of dust and road grit sprayed through the window again making the two policemen duck as tiny stones scattered like buckshot inside their car.

"D..d....d...did that say what I thought it said on the side?" PC Martin stuttered.

"Was that the RSPCA?" his amazed colleague replied.

"I think so!"

"Well, what are we waiting for, let's get after them!"

PC Burrows floored the throttle and lifted the clutch making the tyres spin and screech as they pulled away. They had not gone two metres when PC Burrows jammed on the brakes and stared wide-eyed through the car's windscreen as a near-naked man running at full speed collided with the patrol car's front left wing and somersaulted over the bonnet.

"What the hell!" PC Martin shouted, "What the hell is that?"

With his clothes in tatters, a bruised and badly bitten Mr Pink slid across the patrol car's bonnet on his bare backside. His bum cheeks squeaked on the shiny metal as he flashed past.

The policemen watched in total disbelief as Mr Pink glided off the other side of their patrol car, got to his feet and continued running at a phenomenal pace away from the factory.

"Bloody hell! Whatever next!" PC Martin shouted.

They didn't have to wait long to find out as Razor, the

Project-X crazed Doberman, crossed the bonnet in a single leap, followed by a black Labrador that landed midway across, skittering, slipping and sliding along the rest of the bonnet before leaping off the right-hand wing and giving chase.

Both policemen looked at each other in amazement.

Then they felt two solid bumps on the left side of their car, there was some scurrying underneath the floor of the car followed by two more bumps on the right hand side.

PC Burrows looked out of his window and saw a pair of oil-streaked Jack Russells appear from under the car and disappear off at full speed after the other dogs in the chase to get some more of Mr Pink.

"Get to the dog food factory, pronto!"

"Roger that!" said his colleague, stamping on the throttle.

Eight Weeks after the Power Crisis:

Saturday 23:00Hrs

Bishop had the upper hand, he kept his pistol pointed at Max while he jabbed and shocked the bear with the tazer-tipped cattle prod. He was determined to see both of them in the crusher, just a few more paces and he would have them in the perfect spot.

"Back up!" ordered Bishop.

Max stood still and so did Control.

"Back up!"

From behind the huge bulky shoulder of the bear, Max shouted over the noise of the machinery with a renewed confidence that brimmed in his voice.

"*You* back up!"

"What?" shouted a bemused Bishop.

"Oh, maybe you can't back up, can you?"

Max moved forward and stood defiantly beside Control's massive shoulder and pointed behind Bishop. Bishop spun around to see the overpowering muscles, teeth and claws of Withdraw just a few paces away.

The huge bear stood on its hind legs almost filling the coldstore doorway with its immense size, towering over Bishop, poised to strike.

Bishop froze, rooted to the spot like a statue. The bear's forearms were wide open, black pads and huge slicing claws were contrasted against solid white fur that covered forearms the size of tree trunks. One forearm was stained red but the bullet had merely grazed the bear's skin, the wound had done little more than make the bear even angrier and more bad tempered than ever.

Bishop unfroze but he was uncoordinated and off-balance, he tried to strike with the prod and fire his pistol at the same time but the bear was much, much quicker. It swung both monstrous paws forward, knocking the prod and pistol out of Bishop's hands and its steak-knife sharp claws slashed close to Bishop's exposed neck. The pistol fell spinning barrel over handle to the concrete floor and it bounced and tumbled, coming to rest beside the wheels of the forklift truck.

Bishop was now trapped between both bears and they roared above the sound of the machinery making the metal sides of the crusher reverberate and shake even more than the spinning blades inside. This was their long awaited moment of revenge.

Both bears lunged forward but Bishop regained some of his quick reflexes, he ducked and rolled like a paratrooper, then he sprung back to his feet and started running towards the roller shutter doors. He desperately pulled and pulled at the padlock but it was locked. With fear in his eyes he spun around to face his worst nightmare.

Withdraw and Control were methodically hunting down their prey, they carefully closed in on Bishop, making sure he had no gap in which to make a break for freedom. He had narrowly escaped being the meat in a polar bear sandwich but he was now cornered against the cold metal of the roller shutter door. He would have run but he had nowhere to run to as the bears approached, their mouths open, baring their huge, razor-sharp teeth, snarling, finally facing their nemesis.

Just as Mr Orange had done earlier in the evening, Bishop uncontrollably wet his pants.

Brian watched in awe from the safety of the office while Rachel made more and more desperate calls to the police. Rachel only stopped calling when the emergency operator assured here that help was on its way.

Rachel opened the office door and gingerly stepped out, followed by Brian. They stood beside the nearest cage with its door open ready to dart inside because they did not have the same trust that Max had in the bears. From behind, they saw the soft white furry hindquarters of two polar bears but Bishop had a totally different view. He faced the business-end, their black lips were drawn high over their polar-white teeth threatening to tear him to shreds if he so much as moved a muscle.

Max ran over to join his friends. On the way past the crush-and-grind machine's control panel he hit the EMERGENCY STOP button and the machinery stopped instantly. The food preparation area fell silent, except the silence was punctuated by the deep guttural growls of two bears as they prepared to pounce.

Max stood next to Rachel and he could feel she was shaking with fear.

"I can't watch," she said, "Can't you do something, Max?"

"What can I do?" he replied.

Brian knew he was about to witness something truly horrific. On one hand, he realised Bishop had no qualms about gruesomely disposing of his best friend and he had accepted this was justified retribution but he still didn't fancy witnessing the final act. He wished there was something else that could be done.

So did Max. He definitely wanted revenge but he did not want it to happen in such a macabre way. He had faced the worst of Bishop and his henchmen and despite all of their cruelty he still showed them compassion.

Instinctively, Max put his fingers into his mouth and wolf-whistled.

The piercing two-tone blast made both bears stop and immediately look in his direction, postponing their final, bloody execution of Bishop. Brian and Rachel looked at Max in utter amazement. Max was even more amazed at himself. Control stared at Max, clearly hanging on his next command. For Bishop, the next few seconds felt like an eternity; Max held his life in his hands and Bishop knew it.

Max made a softer, single-toned whistle and nodded towards the coldstore as if he was guiding a working gundog. Control's facial expression acknowledged the command and he slowly backed away, followed by his brother.

Rachel breathed out a deep, deep sigh. All three of them watched in astonishment as the bears turned and headed for the coldstore doors, which opened as they tripped the sensors. A final snort from Control puffed a ring of cold misty air through the insulated doors as they closed.

"Bloody hell, Max...."

But Brian didn't manage to finish his sentence.

All three friends instinctively ducked as the roller shutter door burst inwards with a loud bang that made the metal sections shake and vibrate. A car's headlights shone though a slight gap that formed under the door, its tyres screeched and smoked as it reversed, revved its engine and drove forward into the shutter doors a second time. Bishop had been hit hard by the impacts which sent him sprawling across the hard concrete floor.

Brian, Max and Rachel had instinctively ducked down behind the cage and they peered through the bars to see the car hit the door a third time, buckling the metal inwards and lifting it completely out of its runners, widening the gap underneath. They could hear people shouting outside then the unmistakable uniform of a policeman slid under the door, followed by another policeman and two RSPCA Animal Welfare Officers.

Bishop shook his dazed head and got gingerly up onto his knees.

"Stop right there!" PC Burrows shouted as he spotted Bishop, but Bishop had a different plan. He crawled towards the forklift truck where he knew his pistol was. He was prepared to shoot his way out if he had to.

"Stop!" shouted PC Martin, "Stop there!"

But Bishop never made it to the pistol, the policeman was too quick and he wrestled Bishop roughly to the floor, PC

Burrows kicked the gun away and assisted with the arrest by applying a liberal amount of knee-pressure to the side of Bishop's head.

More policemen arrived and soon the crush-and-grind food preparation area was filled with men in uniform. Some of them were from the armed tactical response unit but these trained marksmen were not required. Bishop and his team of hired killers had already been beaten, scalded, electrocuted and bitten into submission by Max, his friends and a few dozen vengeful MegaCorp test subjects.

Peter appeared through the plastic strip doors, dragging the semi-conscious Mr Black behind him. Two armed policemen quickly handcuffed Mr Black who made no resistance, he was trying to shake off the worst of a concussion. Mr Black figured that being arrested was his way out of this nightmare and he pleaded with the police officers.

"Get that bloody human battering ram away from me!" he screamed, "Get me out of here, put me in prison, I'll go quietly, I promise, just get me out of here, please just get me out of here!"

Peter reluctantly let go of Mr Black's ankle, he had wanted to deal out some more punishment on the men who had kidnapped Max but he need not have worried. The two armed policemen dragged the screaming Mr Black out of the factory and threw him unceremoniously and with a high degree of velocity, into the back of a police transit van. They slammed the doors shut, locking them from the outside. Despite the pain from the handcuffs and the ringing in his ears, Mr Black was relieved to be in the safety of a locked van. One of the armed officers remained on guard at the van's rear doors.

In the van's dimly lit interior, Mr Black noticed the silhouette of another police officer sitting in the driver's seat.

"Get a move on, Officer, take me away and lock me up, just get me away from this bloody factory, okay?" pleaded Mr Black.

The police officer in the driver's seat said nothing.

"I'm begging you, let's get moving! Lock me up in the cells!"

The police officer turned to one side, his face silhouetted in the moonlight.

As his eyes adjusted to the dim lighting inside the back of the van, Mr Black noticed that the police officer appeared to be sporting a very unkempt beard with some outlandishly overgrown sideburns. He was also wearing his helmet at a rather jaunty angle.

When the officer turned around, Mr Black revisited his worst nightmare.

The large male orang-utan flipped off the police helmet he had picked up when he had slipped out of the factory and he jumped over the front seats into the back of the van, closely followed by the dwarf who had picked up the discarded cattle prod during his escape. Both of them were more than pleased to meet up with Mr Black again.

Despite being dressed in a pretty floral-printed hospital gown, the dwarf had the appearance of a psychotic killer, albeit in pint-sized proportions. As he closed in on Mr Black, he pulled the prod's trigger and a bright blue flash of high-voltage electricity sparked and crackled at the tip.

Mr Black banged loudly on the back door and screamed to be let out.

"Quieten down in there, you scumbag!" shouted the policeman standing guard outside.

One of the orang-utan's huge hands clamped over Mr Black's mouth which made sure his cries for help went unheard.

The van rocked violently back and forth as the orang-utan dealt out some long overdue revenge for the indignity of being subjected to a rather infectious fungal foot disease in the X-laboratories. He grabbed Mr Black by the legs and started to swing him from side to side, banging his already concussed head on the insides of the van.

"Stop kicking the van, or I'll come in there and bloody kick you, got it?" threatened the police officer, "You're staying there, and that's that!"

Inside the van, Mr Black passed out.

Then he was rudely shocked back to full consciousness by the cattle prod equipped dwarf, just so he could fully appreciate a second bout of swinging-head-banging retribution.

"Quieten down, or we'll send in the riot police and they'll bloody quieten you down, got it?" threatened the police officer, thumping on the back doors of the van.

The orang-utan had hold of his ankles and was starting to swing him around again. Mr Black begged the officer to send the riot police in but his feeble pleas went unheard. After several more high-speed revolutions, he passed out for a second time.

The dwarf took great delight in liberally applying the prod until Mr Black jerked and convulsed his way back to full consciousness.

The police officer thumped louder on the doors, "Keep making that racket, it's all the same to me, you won't be getting out for some time!" he shouted.

Inside, Mr Black was finding out the hard way that there *was* in fact more than enough room to swing not only a cat but it was possible to swing a full-size human around and around inside the back of a Ford Transit. He passed out for the third time. Not wanting to be short-changed on revenge, the dwarf shocked him fully conscious again with the tazer-tipped cattle prod which crackled and sparked, filling the van's interior with electric blue flashes.

The policeman thumped on the rear doors again.

"I've told you already, you scumbag, stop kicking the van and stop playing with the bloody interior lights!"

Mr Black did not hear him. The orang-utan had started Round Four and he passed out for good this time.

Outgunned and out-smarted, the rest of Bishop's henchmen willingly sat handcuffed in the back of police cars giving full confessions, in exchange for the relative safety of a cell in Okehampton Police Station.

Peter joined Brian who was taking great delight in showing one of the interrogating police officers how the pager/calculator device worked while Rachel assured another officer that yes, *she really was* Poppy Purnell.

PC Burrows was using one of the forklift trucks to lift up the bowed and dented roller shutter door. More RSPCA officers came through, along with a special team trained in the protective welfare of larger animals. These specialists fanned out into the depths of the factory, luring in the exotic animals into purpose-made humane cages. On the other side of the shutter doors, Max saw Bishop's dejected face peering out of the back windows of a police patrol car. For him it was undoubtedly a long prison sentence. For MegaCorp, there would be exposure of X-Ingredient and ultimate financial ruin.

The crush-and-grind area was now a hive of activity with police officers and RSPCA animal welfare officers running to and fro. In the confusion, Max picked up a padded thermal jacket from the hooks beside the coldstore and slipped unnoticed though the automatic thermal doors. Max felt the chill of the cold air hit the back of his throat and his breath turned to a cloud of mist in front of him. Less than an hour earlier, he had faced Bishop in here, he had defiantly stood his ground and the bears had stood beside him, protecting him.

Max walked further into the huge deep-freeze, he was still not completely sure if it was safe but he trusted the polar bears. He took a few careful steps and the cold damp air swirled around him into a misty fog. Through the semi-darkness, he saw the place where Bishop's missed shot had punctured the coolant pipe and a steady shower of frosty snow now sprayed out of the bullet hole. He stepped a few paces further forward and as the mist parted, he saw a deep snowdrift of fresh soft white snow that filled the far end of the coldstore. Inside, two polar bear brothers had made themselves a new den.

Max crouched down at the entrance and listened to the deep gentle breathing of two contented polar bears. He remained there for a while, with the cold, frosty air swirling around him, enjoying a final, perfect moment in their presence.

He finally managed to tear himself away and returned to the busy crush-and-grind area where PC Martin and one of the RSPCA officers had found the manual override for the door sensors.

"No one else is in there, are they?"

Max shook his head and the police officer locked the doors shut.

Max found the most senior RSPCA officer and asked what was planned for the bears.

"You're the lad that was kidnapped, aren't you?"

"Yeah."

"So you must be Max?"

"That's right, but *what* about the bears?"

"It's ok, they will be fine," said the RSPCA Area Manager, "We're in contact with Churchill in Canada and they'll be released back where they belong in the Arctic."

"Churchill?" Max asked.

"That's right, polar bears that stray into Churchill are rounded up, placed in a holding pen and then they're released back to the wild."

The Area Manager pointed to an RSPCA Animal Welfare Officer who was talking on a mobile phone beside the dented bonnet of the patrol car. The AWO gave the Area Manager a thumbs-up sign.

"It seems as though the arrangements have been made, we'll keep the bears secure in the coldstore for the time being."

"And they'll be safe?"

"Don't worry, they will be in very safe hands."

Eight Weeks after the Power Crisis:

Sunday 00:30Hrs

A full moon in a clear night sky bathed the fields surrounding the factory in a gentle blue glow. A fresh breeze blew over the sweetcorn which rippled gently to and fro in rhythm with the warm summer wind. It would have been a perfect midsummer's night had it not been for the chaotic events that were unfolding at the factory's loading bay doors.

Standing in the sweetcorn field, hidden amongst the swaying stalks, was the hooded figure of Nina Glover and she was dressed completely in black, from head to toe. She had slipped unnoticed into the sweetcorn field earlier in the evening and had watched the arrest of Bishop and his team through a pair of high-tech night vision binoculars.

Nina had seen enough. She reached into her jacket pocket and took out her mobile phone, dialling a number she had on speed-dial.

A man answered with a short hello. There was no time wasted in exchanging pleasantries, Nina got straight to the point.

"I will be accepting your offer," she said.

"Do you have the laboratory data from X?" the man asked.

"Yes," confirmed Nina.

"I take it all backups of the original data have been erased and yours is now the only copy?"

"That's correct."

"Excellent," said the man, "Welcome aboard."

ABOUT THE AUTHOR

A M Hankins spent his formative years at a strict all boys' school run by Roman Catholic priests. His close friends are quick to point out that this explains a great deal.

His first literary work was a piece entitled Acorns, a one thousand word punishment essay issued by an overzealous school prefect. Upon reading the essay, it was discovered that the contents bore no relevance at all to the reproductive process of oak trees and the author was immediately despatched to the Headmaster for a solid thrashing. Undeterred, the author persevered and his second piece, Max and the Revenge of the Polar Bears, has been published for a much wider audience, safe in the knowledge that literary critics no longer wear cassocks and wield whip-like bamboo canes.

Despite the predictions of many, the author has avoided a life of petty crime. Instead, he has achieved notable success in several sales roles within the energy conservation and IT industries. When he grows up, he plans to devote his life to the conservation of sharks but for the time being, he lives as a semi-recluse, hidden away in the countryside, with a surprisingly tolerant wife and a lager-drinking, chilled-out Labrador, named Brains.

Lightning Source UK Ltd.
Milton Keynes UK
04 February 2011
166932UK00001B/2/P